SEYYED HOSSEIN NASR

A YOUNG MUSLIM'S GUIDE TO THE MODERN WORLD

Richard G. Ammerman M.D.

KAZI PUBLICATIONS, INC
CHICAGO, IL 60618

Library of Congress Cataloging in Publication Data

Nasr, Seyyed Hossein
A Young Muslim's Guide to the Modern World
1. Religion 2. Juvenile I. Nasr, Seyyed Hossein
II. Title
297'.122'0922 BP 134.P745

ISBN: 1-56744-476-8

Published in North America by:
The Library of Islam
P. O. Box 1923
Des Plaines IL 60017

North American Distributor:
KAZI Publications, Inc.
3023 W. Belmont Avenue
Chicago, IL 60618
Tel: (312) 267-7001; FAX: (312) 267-7002

For **S. Amir Ali**
soon to face the challenge of
being a young Muslim

This work was commissioned by
Mr. Sahl Kabbani
who has dedicated much of his life
to the presentation and propagation of Islam
in the West and especially to the
establishment of Dar al-Islam in
Abiquiu, New Mexico

Other Works by Seyyed Hossein Nasr in English

Three Muslim Sages
Introduction to Islamic Cosmological Doctrines
Science and Civilization in Islam
Ideals and Realities of Islam
Man and Nature
Sufi Essays
Al-Biruni: An Annotated Bibliography
Islam and the Plight of Modern Man
An Annotated Bibliography of Islamic Science (3 vols.)
Islamic Science: An Illustrated Study
Persia: Bridge of Turquoise
The Transcendent Theosophy of Sadr al-Din Shirazi
Islamic Life and Thought
Knowledge and the Sacred
Muhammad: Man of Allah
Islamic Art and Spirituality
Traditional Islam in the Modern World
The Need for a Sacred Science
Isma'ili Contributions to Islamic Culture (ed.)
Philosophy, Literature and Fine Arts: Islamic Eduction Series (ed.)
Shi'ism: Doctrines, Thought, Spirituality (ed.)
Expectation of the Millennium (ed.)
Islamic Spirituality: Volume I, Foundations (ed.)
Islamic Spirituality: Volume II, Manifestations (ed.)
The Essential Writings of Frithjof Schuon (ed.)

CONTENTS

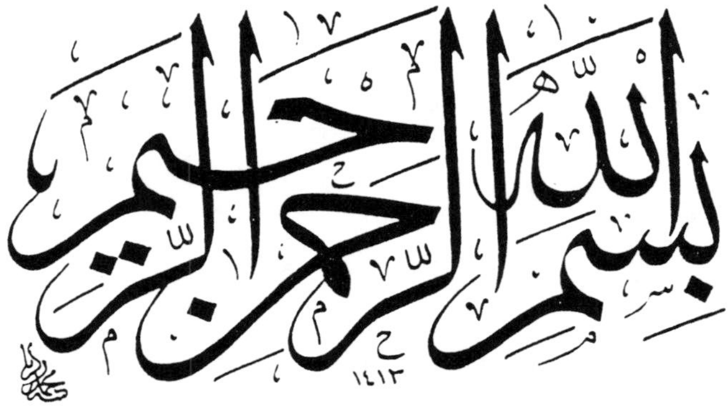
بسم الله الرحمن الرحيم
١٤١٣

INTRODUCTION

For some two centuries the world of Islam has confronted the assault of an alien civilization and worldview which have challenged the very tenets of Islam itself. This assault has also destroyed much of the civilization created by Islam over the centuries. Although during the past few decades nearly the whole of the Islamic world has gained its political independence, the philosophical, cultural, artistic, political, economic, and social impact of the domination of the modern West continues in one way or another through the width and breadth of *dār al-islām*, threatening not only the traditional institutions of Islamic society, but the Islamic religion itself. From the family to the state, from economics to mosque architecture, from poetry to medicine, all are affected by the alien worldview which the modern world, as its ethos was first incubated and nurtured in the West and then spread to other continents, has imposed upon the Islamic world and its peoples.

Numerous Muslims, especially the young, journey to the West in quest of modern education. Many others confront the challenge of the modern world within the geographic confines of the Islamic world itself and within educational institutions and certain social circles which, although in Muslim lands, are in reality outposts of the West. Many are alienated from Islam as a result of the crushing influence of alien ideologies, while others react mostly with emotional outbursts and occasional violence. But few gain a deep enough knowledge of the modern world to be able to preserve Islam in the light of the challenges of that world and to succeed in providing the necessary Islamic response to the problems posed by current ideologies. There are very few Muslim maps of the modern "intellectual" landscape which would allow Muslims to travel through this landscape without becoming lost and without losing their faith (*al-īmān*), that most precious of all divine gifts, in the process.

The task of providing such a guide is made difficult not only by the complexity and chaos that characterizes the modern world, but also by the fact that parallel with the domination of the Muslim world by the West, Muslims have come to forget many aspects of their own religious teachings. The result of this conjunction of conditions is that many aspects of the Islamic tradition which are crucial for an in-depth understanding of the modern world and for providing Islamic answers to present day issues have come to be eclipsed and forgotten. The Muslims of earlier generations not only did not suffer from many of the problems faced today, but were also more fully aware of many dimensions of the teachings of Islam which provided for them a complete worldview and satisfied their need for causality, for the explanation of the nature of things, and for the meaning of life.

What is needed, therefore, is first of all the reassertion of the eternal truths of Islam as revealed in the Noble Quran, explained and elucidated in the *Ḥadīth* and *Sunnah* of the Blessed Prophet and commented upon by centuries of Muslim scholars and thinkers. This reassertion must present the heart of the Islamic message beyond all sectarian biases and divisions, and emphasize that unity which is the very heart of the Islamic message. But such a presentation requires a contemporary language which can be understood by Muslim youth, the great majority of whom have not experienced the traditional *madrasah* education and are therefore not familiar with the intellectual language of the classical Islamic texts, even though they may know Arabic or other Islamic languages well.

Moreover, the guide for the Muslim to the modern world must be based on a thorough and in-depth knowledge of both the Western religious and intellectual tradition and the modern West. It is not enough to make certain generalizations about Westerners being materialistic or dynamic, hedonistic or hardworking. The West must be understood in its core so that the development of modernism and the historical roots of ideologies and forces which are at play can be understood. The West has produced many orientalists who have studied Islam from their own point of view, but the Islamic world has produced very few occidentalists who can study the various aspects of Western civilization from its science to art, from religion to social behavior, from the Islamic point of view.

Finally, on the basis of the truth of Islam and the nature of the modern world, a "map" can be drawn which can guide Muslims, especially the young, through this bewildering world of contending and opposing forces and anti-religious elements which make up the modern scene. With the criteria of truth provided by Islam at hand, one can be discerning when confronted with the various components of the present day world. One can understand the challenges posed by different forces and ideologies to the Islamic worldview and seek to provide an Islamic answer to them. One can, moreover, obtain the necessary intellectual and moral armor to survive and function in the modern world without losing one's faith and even to have the possibility of presenting the challenge of Islam itself as a living faith capable of providing meaning for human life to a world which has lost its direction and orientation.

The chapters which follow seek to carry out this program in a language which is fairly simple rather than being excessively scholarly. This book addresses primarily Muslim youth who are confronting various facets of the modern world through their educational and social experience and not the established scholars of Islam or those who have not been affected by the advent of modernism. We hope that this humble effort will help those to whom it is addressed to understand better the world in which Allah has placed them and to be able to carry the torch of Islam in that world as our ancestors did in the many centuries which separate us from the advent of the Quranic revelation. The task may seem more difficult today than ever before, but with the aid of Allah even what is difficult can be achieved.

In conclusion we wish to thank Mr. Sahl Kabbani whose generous support has made this book possible. May his efforts be rewarded by Him Who is the Source of all blessings.

Wa mā tawfīqī illā bi'Llāh

Seyyed Hossein Nasr
Washington, D.C.

Part I
The Message of Islam

Chapter 1
Islam, the Noble Quran and Ḥadīth—Revelation and the Meaning of Religion

Islam is a religion based upon surrender (*taslīm*) to the Will of the One God or Allah and upon knowledge of His Unity.[1] It is the religion of subservience to Allah, the Supreme Reality, from whom all orders of reality issue forth, and to whom everything returns, for Allah is the Origin, Creator, Ruler, Sustainer and End of the universe. Islam is also gaining peace (*salām*) by virtue of this very act of surrender or *taslīm*. Islam is nothing other than living according to the Will of Allah in order to gain peace in this world and felicity in the world to come. Islam envisages religion as not just a part of life but as the whole of it. In fact, *al-islām* or *al-dīn* as Islam sees itself, is life itself and it incorporates what we do, what we make, what we think and what we feel as well as addresses the question of where we come from and where we are going. That is why the Islamic religion always uses the term *al-dīn* as embracing all the facets of human life, leaving nothing outside its dominion. In the traditional Islamic perspective there is nothing secular, nothing outside the realm that is governed by the religion ordained by Allah.

At the same time Islam places extreme emphasis upon the one eternal truth which had been there from the very beginning, that is the truth of *tawḥīd* or unity. According to the Quran, man testified to the unity of Allah and His Lordship even before the creation of the world. Therefore, Islam is not based upon a transient message or particular aspect of the reality of Allah Who is the Absolute God, but upon that Absolute Reality Itself, that Reality which is characterized more than anything else by its uniqueness and oneness. Islam emphasizes the fact that Allah is al-Aḥad, the One, that He neither begets nor is begotten according to the text of the Quran, and that He is transcendent *vis-à-vis* everything. That is why the central truth of Islam is contained in the *shahādah* or testimony of Islam, *Lā ilāha illa'Llāh*, which among many other things means that there is only one Allah; there cannot be a like or partner unto Him. This doctrine is so central to Islam that it is said that Allah will forgive all sins except the sin of *shirk*, or of taking a partner unto Him.

This unitary conception of the religious message as presented by Islam entails also the whole history of humanity. In a sense Islam was there from the beginning. Adam was a Muslim by the fact that he was the first prophet and that he testified to the oneness of Allah. This oneness was gradually forgotten as it is in the nature of man to forget. But always Allah sent other messengers to renew the message of unity, to bring man back to the awareness of the One. Hence we have a series of prophets who, although they established religions by different names, were in the profoundest sense Muslim. That is why the Quran refers to Abraham as *musliman ḥanīfan*, that is, Muslim and follower of the primordial religion, although he lived millennia before the Prophet of Islam and the advent of the Quranic revelation. He is called Muslim by the Quran itself to affirm that the idea of a religion based upon unity is not new but is synonymous with the religious history of mankind. There has never been a time when the religion of God which calls man to the One has not existed in some place or other. But we have a multiplicity of religions precisely because of the gradual loss of this message and the necessity for its being reconfirmed again and again by successive revelations.

In a sense, therefore, Islam is the religion which came to bring nothing new but to reassert the truth of *tawḥīd* which always was. It is a universal religion, a primordial religion. It is a return to the basic and primordial pact or *mīthāq* made between man and Allah through which man has been given not only the function of being Allah's servant, *al-'abd*, but also His vicegerent on earth, *khalīfat Allāh fi'l-arḍ*, bestowed with many gifts and blessings for which he must always remain thankful. One does this by being aware of Allah's Oneness, by bearing testimony to that oneness, and by drawing all the consequences of that Oneness.

From another point of view, Islam is the final religion. The Prophet of Islam is the *khātam al-anbiyā'*, the seal of prophets, and fourteen centuries of human history have proven the validity of Islam's claim to this finality. Since the death of the Prophet,[2] no major religion has appeared upon the surface of the earth, nothing to compare to the religions which preceded Islam such as Christianity, Judaism or Zoroastrianism and the like. There have been religious movements here and there occasionally, or offshoots of two religions meeting each other as they have done in India but there has not appeared a prophet such as the Prophet of Islam and no universal message from heaven such as Islam since the first/seventh century and none will appear until the end of the world. Therefore, Islam is the final religion of the present cycle of human history; it is the last major world religion. By expressing in the most complete, total and perfect manner the doctrine of unity and by applying it to all facets of human life, Islam is in a sense the very perfection of the message of unity. That is why in the last verse of the Quran to be revealed, a verse which the Prophet iterated during his farewell address it is said, " *This day have I perfected your religion for you and completed My favor unto you, and have chosen for you as religion al-islām*"(V:4).

Therefore, Islam is on the one hand the primordial religion, the religion that always is, the religion that is in the nature of things, the religion of unity which all prophets came to assert throughout history, and on the other hand it is the final religion, the final seal and link of this long prophetic chain, of what is traditionally said to be the chain of 124,000 prophets all of whom came to bear testimony to the oneness of God. This conception of religion in Islam is extremely important for the understanding of the Islamic religion itself both in itself and in its historical unfolding because most other religions base themselves upon the founder, the messenger, a particular historical event as in Christianity or a particular historic people as in Judaism, whereas Islam bases itself neither on a particular event nor even on a particular messenger nor on a particular people. It bases itself upon the Oneness of the Absolute, Allah, the Absolute Reality, and the primordial nature of man, of all humanity and not a particular people such as the Arabs or Persians or Turks, nor upon a particular event. The basis of Islam is the nature of reality and Islam appeals to what is in the nature of things. It just happens that Allah Willed that the last assertion of the truth concerning the nature of reality should come with the advent of the Quran. But there had been other affirmations of the unity of Allah before. The supreme reality of Islam contained in the *shahādah, Lā ilāha illa'Llāh* was not invented as a result of the Quranic revelation which descended upon the Prophet in Arabia in the first/sevenh century; rather it is an assertion of the truth which has always been, is and will be.

That is why Muslims have a kind of non-historical perspective upon the reality of religion. The religion does not depend upon a historical event such as, for example, the life of Christ as seen in Christianity. It does not depend upon a particular fact, be it historical or otherwise, but upon a reality which is what it is and which is inscribed upon the heart of man as Allah's vicegerent, as a creature created to reflect Allah's Names and Qualities. Man is brought into this world to affirm Allah as the Absolute, the One whom man is in fact brought into this world to obey. The Muslim must live according to the Will of the One Who has created him. That is why throughout the Islamic tradition, the Muslims have always spoken about not only Islam as their own religion but also about religion as such and have affirmed the reality of the *dīn al-ḥanīf*, the primordial and perennial religion which has always existed at the heart of all the messages brought by the *anbiyā'* or the prophets of Allah throughout the history of mankind. And that is why also Muslims have been called upon by the Prophet and by the text of the Quran to protect the people of other religions as long as they confirm the unity of God and do not fall into one form or another of polytheism.

From the Islamic point of view religion is, therefore, in the nature of man and is not something added to it by accident. It is not a luxury but the very *raison d'être* for human existence. And it is religion alone which bestows upon human life its dignity, which allows man to live to the fullness of the reality or nature which Allah has bestowed upon him, and which alone provides ultimate meaning for human life. Religion is seen by Islam as a necessity for human existence. Without it man lives below himself and he is only accidentally human. It is only by having faith in a religion, by accepting the original covenant made between man and Allah, that man can be fully himself. It is very difficult for the Muslim mentality to even understand atheism, to understand how people could live without religion, to conceive how people could go through the whole of life without being aware of the presence of the transcendent Reality which is Allah. And that is why also it is very difficult for Muslims to see even modern people in the West not in categories of Christians or Jews or non-religious followers of other religions, but as people who do not follow any religion at all. The vast majority of Muslims continue to see religion as part and parcel of human life.

Moreover, there is no particularism in the Islamic perspective concerning religion considered in its ultimate sense. The only particularity which Islam imposes upon its conception of religion is the fact that it considers Islam to be the last expression of the long chain of prophetic utterances based upon expressing the unity of Allah and His Message for various peoples in different climes, geographical settings and epochs of human history.

Islām—īmān—iḥsān

The religion revealed in the Quran through the Prophet Muḥammad may peace and blessings be upon him—is usually called Islam, but the Quran often refers to those who accept this message as *mu'minūn*, literally those who have *īmān* or faith. Also the word *iḥsān* or virtue as well as *muḥsin*, he who possess *iḥsān*, are used in both the Quran and *Ḥadīth*. In order to understand totally the meaning of religion in its Islamic context, it is necessary to understand the traditional definition of all the three Arabic terms: *al-islām, al-īmān* and *al-iḥsān*. As for *al-islām*, every Muslim who has received the most rudimentary education in his religion knows full well that there are certain *arkān* or fundamentals which define *al-islām*,: these being the *shahādatayn*, that is, bearing testimony to the unity of Allah, *Lā ilāha illa'Llāh*, and the messengership of His Prophet, *Muḥammadun rasūl Allāh*; the performance of the daily prayers; fasting during the month of Ramaḍān; the pilgrimage or *ḥajj* if the conditions set by the *Sharī'ah* are fulfilled; and paying of *zakāh* or religious tax. Some have added *jihād* or effort for the realization of Allah's Will as expressed through his religion as the sixth *rukn* or fundamental element, although in a sense *jihād* is contained in all of the others because to accomplish any of these rites one must exert oneself in the path of Allah. To be a good Muslim one must exert one's effort (*jahd*); one must perform *jihād* in the deepest sense of the word.

As for *al-īmān*, its definition like *al-islām* and *al-iḥsān* is contained in the famous *ḥadīth* in which Jibra'īl (Gabriel), upon whom be peace, appears to the Prophet.[3] There, *īmān* is defined as having faith in Allah, His messengers, books, angels and the Day of Judgment. It is important to realize that according to this *ḥadīth*, not only must a person of *īmān* or faith, a *mu'min*, have faith in Allah and the Prophet of Islam but also in the prophets in the plural, not only in the Quran, the supreme *kitāb* or book which is the sacred scripture of Islam, but in all revealed books, *kutub*, not only in this world but also of course in the world to come, in eschatology or *ma'ād* and not only in the forces which are visible to man but also in Allah's angels who play such an important role in the Quranic description of the governance of the universe and of man's relationship with the Divine.

As for *iḥsān*, it too is defined in the famous *ḥadīth*, as seen above. *Iḥsān* is the worship of Allah with such a presence and concentration as if one were to see Him or as if being unable to see Him, then knowing that Allah nevertheless sees man. Therefore, it means that intensity and perfection of living according to the most inward meaning of the tenets of the religion which can only come when man has realized fully what it means to be human. In a sense religion (*al-dīn*) or Islam, as we usually use the term, comprises not only the first element or *al-islām* which consists of the acceptance of the *shahādatayn* and the fundamental practices of the Divine Law, but also *īmān*, faith. Furthermore, on the highest level it also includes *iḥsān*, that is, that virtue or beauty of soul which enables man to live in perfect conformity to the Will of Allah, to worship Him in perfection, to remember His Will at all times and at the highest level to remember Him at every moment for as the Quran has said, "*Remember Me, I will remember you*"(II:152). The Quran also asserts, "*Verily, through the remembrance of God the hearts find rest*" (XIII:28).

The Noble Quran

The Noble Quran, *al-qur'ān al-majīd*, is the central, sacred reality of Islam. Its meaning, words, sounds, the letters with which its words are written and the physical book in which these letters are contained, all of these are considered by Muslims to be sacred. The Quran is not simply the human transcription of the Word of God. It is the verbatim Word of Allah revealed to the Prophet of Islam in the Arabic language which Allah chose for His last revelation, for as the Quran says, "*We have sent it down as an Arabic Quran in order that ye may learn wisdom*" (XII:2).

In contrast to many other sacred books which are very ancient and the history of whose compilation is not known to us, the Quran was revealed in the full light of history so that we know exactly when the revelation began and when it terminated. During the twenty-three year period of the prophetic mission of Muḥammad ibn 'Abd Allāh—may God's blessing and peace be upon him—the Quran was revealed through him for mankind, the first revelation comprising the opening verses of the chapter Blood-Clot revealed through the archangel Gabriel on the Mountain of Light (Jabal al-Nūr) to the Prophet when he was forty years old and the last part when he was sixty-three, shortly before his death. During this twenty-three year period, the Quran was revealed to the Prophet on different occasions, sometimes when he was talking with people, sometimes when he was walking and sometimes even when he was riding. In each instance the Prophet would utter the Word of God and his Companions would memorize it and remember it with the remarkable power of memory which the ancient Arabs, as nomadic people with a very rich poetic tradition, possessed. Gradually the verses were assembled, sometimes written on the bones of camels, sometimes on papyri but most of all upon the tablets of the hearts and breasts of the Companions who heard the utterances from the mouth of the Prophet. Gradually also a larger circle of Muslims beyond the immediate group of the Companions came to memorize the Quran.

After the death of the Blessed Prophet, as the number of memorizers of the Quran, or *ḥuffāẓ*, diminished through wars and natural causes, the Islamic community felt that the Noble Quran had finally to be recorded and disseminated. And so, what had been written down by the early *kuttāb* or people who had recorded the Quran, especially 'Alī and Zayd, from the period of the life of the Prophet and the caliphate of Abū Bakr on, was assembled. Finally at the time of the caliphate of 'Uthmān, the complete text of the Quran was put together and systematized according to the instructions of the Prophet himself resulting in the order of the 114 chapters which we have today. Copies were then made of the definitive version and sent to the four corners of the newly established Islamic world.

It is on the basis of this Quran that all other copies of the Quran have been written. There are no variants to the text of the Quran, nor have there been any revisions. There is only one text accepted by all Muslims, Sunnis and Shi'ites and other branches of Islam alike, and it is this definitive book which stands as the central source of truth, guidance and of inspiration for all Muslims.

It must also to be remembered that although we now think of the Noble Quran as a written book, originally it was a sonorous revelation, a revealed word of sound. The Prophet heard the words of the Sacred Text and the words surrounded him and embraced him. This power of the Noble Quran as the spoken word remains to this day as a central reality of the Sacred Text. That is why many Muslims who are not Arabs and who know no Arabic are moved to the depth of their being by simply hearing the chanting of the Quran. There resides a Divine Power in the very sounds of the Word of Allah which moves the soul of the Muslim to its depth even if he does not understand the meaning of the words in Arabic.

There are, of course, many sciences connected with the Quran such as the science of *iḥṣā'*, that is of counting or enumerating the verses of the various chapters or *sūrahs*, and the sciences of *tartīl, qirā'ah* and *tajwīd*, all dealing with reading, chanting and pronouncing the sounds of the Quran and of course the sciences of commentary (*tafsīr* and *ta'wīl*) which developed very extensively from the early centuries of Islamic history. In fact, there was from the very beginning an oral tradition of commentary upon the Quran which had been taught by the Blessed Prophet to his Companions and which continued from generation to generation. It was on the basis of this oral tradition and, of course, the *Ḥadīth* itself, which is the first commentary upon the Quran, that the commentators began to write all kinds of commentaries ranging from those dealing with its grammar and syntax to those which deal with its social ideas to those which concern spiritual and ethical principles. These commentaries range from the earliest ones which really go back to the Companions and then Ḥasan al-Baṣrī and Imam Ja'far al-Ṣādiq to such well known later works as those of Ṭabarī and Zamakhsharī. The writing of Quranic commentaries has continued throughout the centuries. Every generation of Muslims has written commentaries upon the Noble Quran to try to draw from its wisdom that which is necessary for the life of that generation of Muslims in the circumstances in which they find themselves. In fact, the understanding in depth of the Sacred Text has always depended upon the commentaries, the sapiential commentaries which have been composed over the centuries and which constitute an extremely precious heritage for all Muslims who wish to understand the meaning of the Word of Allah.

The Noble Quran is at once a recitation, *al-qur'ān*, discernment, *al-furqān*, the mother of all books, *umm al-kitāb*, guidance, *al-hudā*, and wisdom, *al-ḥikmah*. It is the source and origin of all knowledge, of all wisdom and of all guidance for Muslims. Everything about the Quran is related to Allah from Whom it issues. There is first of all in the Quran an incredible eloquence which is the central miracle of Islam, the *balāghah* or eloquence of the Quran having never been matched even by the most eloquent of human beings because of the impossibility of comparing human language with divine language. There is a Divine Presence in the Noble Quran which has transformed Arabic from a human to a sacred language possessing Divine Power so that no human language can ever equate it. As a result of this Divine Presence every verse recited confronts man in a sense face to face with Allah and brings him back to his Maker. There is a kind of mysterious Presence which emanates from the whole of the Sacred Text, even verses which seem to be dealing with everyday "mundane" affairs. There is a Sacred Presence in the Noble Quran which draws man to Allah no matter what part of the Quran one reads and no matter what message is conveyed by that particular verse.

The whole of the Quran calls man back to Allah. Not only does it provide guidance for life in this world but it also constantly calls man back to the Origin, to the Beginning. That is why often one or several verses dealing with particular ideas of a human or social order are interrupted by a call back to Allah and by a mention of His Name through which in fact the whole of the created order receives His blessings, His sustenance, and His laws.

The Noble Quran contains at once a science of reality or metaphysics, or what one might call knowledge of the ultimate nature of things, an ethical code which is the basis of Islamic Law and a sacred history. The Quran contains metaphysical teachings in the sense that it expounds teachings concerning the nature of Reality. In fact, most of the verses in the Quran deal not with laws or ethics but with the nature of Reality, most of all with the nature of Allah, the transcendent Truth, the One Reality which is above and beyond all that we can conceive and imagine and yet is the source of all that exists. The Quran also deals with the nature of the world, not only the physical world but first of all the angelic world, the world created by Allah above the world that surrounds us, above the visible world. And finally it concerns itself with the visible world.

There are constant references in the Noble Quran to the world of nature, to Allah's creation which in a sense the Quran embraces as part and parcel of the world to which it addresses itself. Many verses of the Quran in fact begin by Allah bringing to witness His own creation such as the sun and the moon or other realities which He has created. Only then is the message of the rest of the verse announced. There is a participation of the created order, of the world of nature, in the Quranic revelation and it seems that the Quran, although addressing itself to man, also includes the non-human domains of Allah's creation.

The Noble Quran contains the deepest doctrine concerning the nature of Ultimate Reality by unveiling in a most dazzling manner the Oneness, the Majesty, the Transcendence and at the same time the Love, Compassion, Mercy, and Nearness of Allah. On the one hand, the Quran reasserts that there is none like unto Him, that He is the Transcendent, the Beyond, the Majestic. On the other hand, it asserts that Allah is closer to man than his jugular vein. There is at once, therefore, the doctrine of the transcendence of Allah and the doctrine of His immanence, the doctrine that He is close to man and that He directs our lives in the most intimate way, being even closer to us than ourselves.

Then there is the whole doctrine of the intermediate world between Allah and man, the vast order of angels to which the Quran refers over and over in different contexts. The angels are the instruments through which Allah rules the universe and constitute the intermediate levels of reality between man and Allah. There is also included among the intermediate worlds the world of the *jinn* which refers in reality to the psychic forces, whereas the angels are purely spiritual beings. Finally, the world of nature, the world which surrounds man, is taken into account seriously not only as a background for human life but also as a participant which shares in the life which Allah has meant for all of his creation. The Quranic revelation has in a sense Islamicized a part of the cosmos, the part in which the Muslim lives and dies, and the natural order participates in the Quranic revelation for the Muslim as does the human world to which the Quran addresses itself most directly.

The second important message of the Quran is ethical. It has to do with the moral principles according to which man should live, along with the application of these principles. Man is reminded again and again of the ultimate consequences of his acts, that in fact our human actions not only affect us in this world but also in the world to come and that Allah expects of us to do good, to be just, merciful and pious. Not only are specific sins mentioned such as stealing, murder or adultery and the like but also the general principles of good and evil and the need to live according to Allah's Will and the consequences of turning against it are asserted throughout the Quran. Perhaps the most powerful word in the Quran in this domain is the term *taqwā*, which one can translate approximately as the reverential fear of Allah manifested in human life and action. Allah orders man constantly to live according to *taqwā*, to live in the reverential fear of Allah, knowing that if he does evil there is always retribution. The Quran adds, however, that Allah is merciful and His Justice and Retribution are always balanced by His Mercy and Forgiveness. In fact, according to a famous *ḥadīth* there is written upon the throne of Allah (*al-'arsh*) "Verily My Mercy precedes My Anger." And of course all of the chapters of the Noble Quran except for one begin with the sentence with which all Islamic activities begin, namely, *Bismi'Llāh al-raḥmān al-raḥīm*, that is, in the Name of Allah, Most Merciful, Most Compassionate. Hence the emphasis upon Divine Mercy.

It is through the Name of Divine Mercy that the world is created and with which the Noble Quran begins, and not with the Names which have to do with Divine Anger or Divine Majesty such as al-Muntaqim, He who takes revenge upon those who commit evil, or other Names of this kind. Therefore, although the Noble Quran mentions emphatically the aspect of Divine Justice, the importance of doing good and man's responsibility for his actions, it also emphasizes that it is always possible to ask Allah's forgiveness and that Divine Mercy is present through every moment of human life as mentioned in the famous verse, "*Despair not of the Mercy of Allah*" (XXXIX:53).

The ethical norms mentioned in the Noble Quran are the foundations of the laws of Islam, that is, the *Sharī'ah*. Some of the elements of *Sharī'ah* are mentioned explicitly in the Sacred Text, such as laws of inheritance. But many injunctions have their roots in the Quran where they are mentioned only implicitly but have been made explicit through the *Sunnah* of the Blessed Prophet along with the views of the Islamic community and the exercise of reason on the basis of the above sources.

Finally, the Noble Quran contains within its chapters a sacred history, that is, it gives an account of the lives of the prophets from Adam onward along with the history of various peoples and events. Many of the great prophets of the Semitic world, who are mentioned in the Bible, are also mentioned in the Quran, although the account is not necessarily the same. Several of the main figures, however, like Abraham, Moses and Christ—upon all of whom be peace—who are central to Judaism and Christianity, are also emphasized a great deal in Islam. There are, moreover, certain other prophets such as Luqmān and other ancient Semitic Arab prophets who are not mentioned in the Bible but cited in the Quran. There is a sacred history associated with these and other figures which the Quran unfolds on many different occasions. Certain of these accounts such as the sacrifice of Abraham, the story of Joseph, and the history of the life of Christ and Mary constitute very important elements in the religious consciousness of the Islamic people precisely because of their centrality in the Quran. Moses also plays a very significant role and many verses of the Quran are devoted to episodes of his life.

The sacred history mentioned in the Quran, however, is not meant to inform man of the ordinary history of mankind so much as to teach moral and spiritual principles. There are always moral and spiritual lessons to be drawn from sacred history which, in the deepest sense, involves the battle fought within souls of human beings between the forces of good and evil, between the various tendencies of the soul, although it is of course also the external history of the peoples who preceded Islam seen from the point of view of Allah's providence. There are, therefore, spiritual lessons to be learned from such Quranic accounts as well as lessons concerning the history of mankind preceding the advent of the Quran itself.

Altogether then the Quran constitutes the alpha and omega of the Islamic religion in the sense that all that is Islamic, whether it be its laws, its thought, its spiritual and ethical teachings and even its artistic manifestations, have their roots in the explicit or implicit teachings of the Sacred Text. The Muslim is born with the sound of the Quran in his ear, for usually the *shahādah* which is contained in the Quran is invoked into the ear of a child when it is born. He lives throughout his life surrounded by the sound of the Quran which permeates the traditional Islamic city and the countryside and to some extent even the modern Islamic city. Finally, he dies with the sound of the Quran resounding around him. The Muslim, whether male or female, is in a sense enwrapped in the psalmody of the Quran, from the cradle to the grave. The love of the Noble Quran and devotion to its teachings have remained central to every generation of Muslims, remain so today and will always remain so as long as Islam survives as a religion on the surface of the earth.

The *Sunnah* and *Ḥadīth*

The Prophet of Islam is considered by Muslims to have been the most perfect of men, in fact the most noble and perfect of all of Allah's creation, *ashraf al-makhlūqāt*. Allah bestowed upon him all the virtues and all the perfection which the human state is capable of possessing. As the Noble Quran states, he did not acquire the state of prophethood by himself but was chosen by Allah; furthermore, all of the virtues became perfectly actualized in him. Therefore, he is seen by Muslims as the perfect model for human life to imitate. He is the perfect or universal man, *al-insān al-kāmil* and the Quran itself refers to him as the example to be emulated in the verse, "*Verily in the Messenger of Allah ye have a good example*" (XXXIII:21).

Consequently, the life of the Prophet, especially during the twenty-three years of his prophetic mission, has always been seen by Muslims as the exemplary model for human life. His life, from its very beginning to end, has been studied over and over again by all the generations of Muslims from his own lifetime to our own, precisely because all those who were devout tried to find in that life guidance for their own life and keys for the understanding of the Will of Allah and the meaning of His Word which was revealed in its totality through the Prophet during his prophetic mission.

Most Muslims have some knowledge about the life of the Prophet. They know that he was born into a noble Arab family in Makkah, that he became an orphan early in life, that he was brought up by his grandfather and uncle, that early in life he already displayed a great deal of moral virtue to the extent that he was called the trusted one, al-Amīn, by even those among the Quraysh who later on were to turn against him, that he was loved by all human beings around him, that he displayed to a remarkable degree the virtues of magnanimity, love and compassion. They know that he earned his living from an early age through conducting the business of a wealthy woman from Makkah, Khadījah who was to become his wife and who was to bear for him his first children. From the age of twenty-five when he married her until he was fifty when she died, she was his only wife, and during this period she provided a great deal of support and succor for him.

It is also known that the Prophet received his mission at the age of forty while meditating one day in the cave al-Ḥirā' on top of the mountain of light, Jabal al-nūr, just outside of Makkah. It was then that the archangel Gabriel first appeared to him and for the next twelve years he spent his life in Makkah trying to propagate the Word of Allah to those who did not believe the Word which, in emphasizing the doctrine of the Unity of Allah, threatened the very existence of idol worship in the mercantile community which surrounded the Prophet. During those years which were the greatest years of hardship for him, the Prophet had to bear all kinds of insults and pressures, all kinds of opposition from not only those who were members of other tribes or those who lived far away but most of all from some of his own kinsmen, people who were close to him and who yet were the most adamant in refusing to accept the prophetic message.

Finally, as the number of his disciples, which constituted the first community of Muslims, grew, so did the danger that the community would gradually become a powerful force in Makkah. After the Prophet was offered bribes and cajoled by the powerful figures among the Quraysh, who even offered to make him their ruler and he refused, his life was finally threatened. Then the Prophet, under the command of

Allah, migrated from Makkah to Madinah. On that momentous night while 'Alī slept in his bed, the Prophet, accompanied by Abū Bakr, set out in the direction of Madinah. They spent the next three nights in a cave whose mouth, through the Will of Allah, was rapidly covered by a cobweb, an acacia tree and the nest of a bird. Thus when in the morning the Quraysh, following the footsteps of the camels, came to the mouth of the cave, they did not think of entering the cave and were not able to find him. From there, he made his way to Yathrib which was to become the city of the Blessed Prophet, Madīnat al-nabī. In this "City of Light" he was to build the first mosque at the site where a mosque stands to this very day and there he was to create the first Islamic society after many battles and tribulations which threatened its very existence.

During the next twelve years, it was from Madinah that the Prophet not only consolidated the city into the first Islamic community, but also spread Islam beyond its confines to the rest of Arabia until finally almost a year before his death, he finally reentered Makkah triumphantly. He broke the idols at the Ka'bah, reestablished peace, and unified Arabia under the banner of Islam before his death which took place in Madinah.

This twenty-three year period of the life of the Prophet in its grand outlines has always been at the forefront of the mind, thought and imagination of every generation of Muslims. Countless biographies have been written about him from the early *Sīrah* of Ibn Hishām and Ibn Isḥāq to the contemporary biographies which dot the whole of the Islamic world, written in Arabic, Persian, Urdu, Malay, Turkish and practically all the other Islamic languages. There are of course especially important events in the life of the Prophet. One of the most significant is his journey to heaven, *al-mi'rāj,* which is mentioned explicitly in the Noble Quran, and which occurred when the Prophet was taken from Makkah to Jerusalem and there in a miraculous fashion was made to ascend, stage by stage, to the Presence of Allah, to the station of nearness as mentioned in the Sacred Book. Others include his migration from Makkah to Madinah, and the important battles which took place, each of which was absolutely crucial for the survival of the newly founded community. His family life, marriages, trials, tribulations, triumphs, victorious return to Makkah and his final oration before his death, all of these events are known to the community of Muslims and provide the model for a life led perfectly by Allah's most perfect creature.

On the basis of this life there has been created a whole literature, a whole poetry about the Prophet. There is no Islamic language whether it be Arabic, Persian, Turkish or otherwise, which does not have some of its most beautiful literary works related to the episodes of the life of the Prophet, to his family, to his Companions, to the various trials and tribulations as well as to the qualities of the inner life and the spiritual perfections of the Prophet.

The Prophet also has a large number of traditional names such as Aḥmad, Ḥamīd, Maḥmūd, Waḥīd, 'Āqib, Ṭa Ha, Ṭāhir, Ya Sīn, Sayyid, Rasūl, 'Abd Allāh, Ḥabīb Allāh, Nāṣir, Manṣūr, Muṣṭafā and Abu'l-Qāsim. Each of these names alludes to a different aspect of the personality of the Prophet and the names together enable the devout Muslim to understand better his significance. A sign of piety in Islam is the love of the Prophet. No one can love Allah without loving His Prophet who himself was called the Beloved of Allah, Ḥabīb Allāh. Also the devout Muslim always remembers the verse of the Quran according to which Allah and the angels bless the Prophet: "*God and His angels shower blessings upon the Prophet: O ye who believe! Ask blessings on him and salute him with a worthy salutation*" (XXXIII:56). In asking blessings upon the Prophet man shares in the act of God and the angels.

Muslims have tried to emulate the actions and understand the word and sayings of the Prophet throughout their history with devotion, attachment and love for the person who was chosen by Allah to spread His Message and who was the first interpreter of His Word which is the Noble Quran. The wonts or doings of the Prophet are called *Sunnah* whereas his sayings are called *Ḥadīth*, meaning sayings or traditions. After the Quran, the *Sunnah* and *Ḥadīth*, comprise the second basic foundation or principle of Islam. The *Sunnah* of the Prophet ranges all the way from the manner of performing external acts such as walking into a house or a mosque, greeting a neighbor, cutting one's beard or washing one's face to the most profound religious, moral and spiritual actions and attitudes such as dealing with one's friends in times of calamity or with one's enemies, praying with concentration, having compassion toward other Muslims and more generally other human beings and other matters of such nature.

The *Sunnah* is of two parts: one is a kind of Islamization of the prevalent customs and habits of the Arab society to which Islam was revealed, those habits, of course, which were in conformity with the spirit of Islam and not just any customs and habits which happened to exist. These were Islamicized and became part and parcel of the *Sunnah*. The second part of the *Sunnah* constitutes its most essential aspects, dealing with the Islamic attitude towards Allah and His creation. It concerns therefore the most essential elements of the Islamic religion itself.

As for the *Ḥadīth*, it consists of a vast body of sayings of the Blessed Prophet assembled during the first three centuries of Islamic history by generations of devout scholars who are called *muḥaddithūn*. It is important to note here that in this field women also played a very important role, and together with men assembled the sayings of the Prophet, examined the chain of transmission and studied step by step how from the Prophet himself a particular saying was transmitted by different human beings from one generation to another until the time when they were recorded. The reliability of each transmitter was thoroughly examined and well established *ḥadīth*s were sifted out from those which had weak lines of transmission. A whole science was developed through which the completely authentic *ḥadīth*s, the partly authentic, the weak *ḥadīth*s and those without any authenticity were classified and compiled. After two to three centuries of extensive research and work, the main body or collections of *Ḥadīth*, were finalized and made available to the whole of the Islamic world.

The first group of these writings are those which were assembled by the authors of the so called "Correct Books," the *Ṣiḥāḥ al-sittah*, or the six canonical collections of *Ḥadīth* which have been accepted through the history of Islam by Sunnis as containing authentic *ḥadīth*s, whereas a century later the four Shi'ite collections of *Ḥadīth* called *al-Kutub al-arba'ah* or the "Four Books" were compiled. In this field, therefore, Sunni collections preceded the Shi'ite. But the content of most of the *ḥadīth*s in the two collections, Sunni and Shi'ite, are basically the same. It is the chain of transmission which differs in many cases, but the content of the *ḥadīth*s is nearly the same.

The *Ḥadīth* literature ranges all the way from discussions of the creation of the world, the hierarchy of angels and of light, the questions of the Will of Allah and of how He rules over the universe, and how both freedom and determinism are intertwined in human life, to human, political, economic and social questions, and practical problems of everyday life dealing with one's family, neighbors and friends. The *Ḥadīth* deals also directly and indirectly with questions relating to the ambience in which the Muslim should live, hence with cleanliness, beauty and propriety. There are *ḥadīth*s which, along with the Noble Quran, have had a very important role to play in the formation of Islamic art, architecture, city-planning and in fact the whole physical ambience which should reflect the meaning, spirit, and genius of the Islamic revelation.

The *Ḥadīth* is also of course the source, along with the Noble Quran, of the *Sharī'ah*. It is itself the first commentary upon the Quran and as a source of the *Sharī'ah*, along with the Quran, has been studied thoroughly from the point of view of its juridical content. Over the centuries, different schools of law have, therefore, developed methods of complementing the Quran with the study of the *Ḥadīth*. The *ḥadīth* is also the source of Islamic thought and nearly all aspects of this thought such as theology, the sciences, philosophy and even the grammatical sciences and sciences of language have their roots in the *Ḥadīth* as well as the Quran. There is no field of Islamic thought in which the *Ḥadīth* has not played an important role as the complement or the explanation of the Word of Allah contained in the Quran.

When the Blessed Prophet was about to die, he was asked how he should be remembered after his death. He said, "Read the Quran," for there is something of the soul of the Prophet contained in the very recitation of the sacred Word of Allah. Moreover, the sayings of the Prophet complement the meaning of the Noble Quran and without them many of the verses would not be fully comprehensible. Even the fundamental Muslim rites such as the daily prayers (*al-ṣalāh*) would not be possible had it not been in fact for the *Sunnah* and the *Ḥadīth* which have explained to Muslims how it should be performed. The Noble Quran orders us to pray but how we pray is based upon the model provided by the Prophet and the same holds true for the details of the *ḥajj* or pilgrimage and other rites of Islam as well as various daily actions. Also, many of the verses of the Quran which do not deal so much with law as with the sciences or the nature of reality are clarified by *ḥadīth*s which make very important commentaries upon them. The Noble Quran and *Ḥadīth* are therefore the great treasury which Allah has provided for Muslims.

Moreover, the first, that is, the Quran cannot be fully appreciated and understood without the help of the second, that is, the *Ḥadīth* and the *Sunnah*, which provide for all generations of later Muslims the commentary of the man who was most capable of understanding the Word of Allah and whom Allah chose as His messenger and as His friend to whom He revealed His exalted Word.

CONCLUSION

One can say that to define Islam, to try to depict what it means in essence, one must assert the central doctrine of unity. Allah is One and his Oneness is of such a nature that ultimately only He fully understands and bears testimony to it. For as the Quran says, " *Allah bears witness that there is no divinity but He* " (III:18). But we as human beings, as witnesses to Him and as His *khalīfah* or vicegerent on earth must also seek to understand this oneness, this *tawḥīd*. Not only must man understand that Allah is One but he must also understand that there is an interrelation between all things. There is a unity which runs through the whole of Allah's created order and through human society if that society is to be Islamic. There must be unity in human life; there must be unity in the relationship between man and the world of nature; there must be unity in human thought; there must be unity in what man makes, in the art, the architecture and the cities which he creates. All of these forms of unity reflect the Wisdom and Will of Allah in our world, the Will which is embodied most concretely in the Divine Law or the *Sharī'ah* and which should also be expressed in every authentic facet of the Muslim's life.

As for how this unity displays itself in human life, one must turn to the truths revealed to us by the Noble Quran which contains at its heart the doctrine of unity to which it returns over and over again and to the *Ḥadīth* and the *Sunnah* of the Prophet which are the first commentary upon the Quran and display and bring to us knowledge of the life of His Chosen Messenger. The Prophet lived according to the Will of the One and he displayed in every facet of his life, in all the different activities he performed, from being a judge to a military leader to the father of a family to a spiritual being who heard the Word of Allah directly and who transmitted it to mankind, to being Allah's last prophet, that unity which Muslims seek throughout their whole lives. To be a good Muslim is to live according to the Will of Allah, to live in virtue according to the ethical principles delineated in the Noble Quran and *Ḥadīth* and to live in the awareness of the Oneness of Allah which is reflected in His creation as well as within man and his society, to the extent that society reflects His teachings as contained in His Sacred Book and as lived and practiced by His last Prophet.

NOTES

1. The English word God is perfectly adequate as a translation for the Arabic word Allah, if the full meaning of the term God is accepted and the term is used without any of the limitations placed upon it by particular theological or philosophical formulations. In this book, written primarily for young Muslims, however, the term Allah will be usually used to avoid any misunderstanding for a group of readers who may not be fully aware of the various dimensions of Western thought and the full amplitude and depth of meaning associated with the term God. In our other writings in English which are addressed primarily to the English speaking reader, however, we always used the term God for Allah to avoid religious misunderstanding.

2. In this book wherever the word Prophet appears capitalized, it means the Prophet of Islam, Muḥammad ibn 'Abd Allāh, may peace and blessings be upon him.

3. The text of the *ḥadīth* which appears in *Muslim*, I, 1, is as follows: 'Umar said: "One day when we were sitting with the Messenger of God there came unto us a man whose clothes were of exceeding whiteness and whose hair was of exceeding blackness, nor were there any signs of travel upon him, although none of us knew him. He sat down knee unto knee opposite the Prophet, upon whose thighs he placed the palms of his hands, saying: 'O Muḥammad, tell me what is the surrender (*islām*)'. The Messenger of God answered him saying: 'The surrender is to testify that there is no god but God and that Muḥammad is God's Messenger, to perform the prayer, bestow the alms, fast in Ramaḍān and make, if thou canst, the pilgrimage to the Holy House.' He said: 'Thou hast spoken truly,' and we were amazed that having questioned him he should corroborate him. Then he said: 'Tell me what is faith (*īmān*).' He answered: 'To believe in God and His Angels and His Books and His Messengers and the Last Day, and to believe that no good or evil cometh but by His Providence.' 'Thou hast spoken truly,' he said, and then: 'Tell me what is excellence (*iḥsān*).' He answered: 'To worship God as if thou sawest Him, for if thou seest Him not, yet seeth He thee.' 'Thou hast spoken truly,' he said, and then: 'Tell me of the Hour.' He answered: 'The questioned thereof knoweth no better than the questioner.' He said: 'Then tell me of its signs.' He answered: 'That the slave-girl shall give birth to her mistress; and that those who were but barefoot naked needy herdsmen shall build buildings ever higher and higher.' Then the stranger went away, and I stayed a while after he had gone; and the Prophet said to me: 'O 'Umar, knowest thou the questioner, who he was?' I said: 'God and His Messenger know best.' He said: 'It was Gabriel. He came unto you to teach you your religion.'" Trans. by M. Lings, *Muhammad: His Life Based on the Earliest Sources*, Islamic Texts Society, Cambridge, 1992, pp. 330-331.

Chapter 2
God, Man and the Universe—Questions of Eschatology

Allah

The very reason for the revelation of Islam might be said to be the unveiling of the complete and total doctrine of the nature of God, in Arabic, Allah. Every authentic religion has sought to reveal God's unity and different aspects of His infinite Reality, some emphasizing one element, some another. Islam seeks to present and to depict to the extent that is possible for human language to sustain, the total doctrine of the Divine Nature. Allah, the Supreme Reality, is at once God and Godhead, at once transcendent and immanent, infinitely beyond and infinitely close to man, majestic and merciful. He is Absolute, Infinite and the Source of all goodness. He is the Origin and End of all things. He is the Creator, Sustainer and also the Destroyer of the universe, in the sense that He gives both life and death. All things return unto Him. All positive qualities which we observe in the universe such as beauty, goodness and power come from Him and He is the source not only of the being of the universe but also of all of its qualities.

The Islamic doctrine of God emphasizes beyond everything and above everything His Oneness. "*Say Allah is One*," (CXII:1) the One

Who "*neither begets nor is begotten,*" (CXII:3) Who cannot be brought into any relation which would in one way or another eclipse His Absoluteness, the One Who has no like "*And there is none like unto Him,*" (CXII:4) and the One Who is indivisible. This oneness of God which is emphasized so much in the Noble Quran refers to God's Essence, His *Dhāt*. However, Allah also has Names and Qualities. The Quran itself not only refers to God as Allah or as He (*huwa*) but also constantly as the Source of Mercy, the Forgiver, the Sustainer, the Knower, the Hearer, the Seer and so forth. These Names which the Quran calls the Beautiful Names of Allah are the means whereby Allah reveals Himself to mankind.

Like the supreme Name of God, Allah, all of these Names contained in the Quran and the *Ḥadīth* in the Arabic language are sacred Names of Allah and it is by these Names that Muslims are invited to call upon Allah according to the famous Quranic verse, "*To Allah belong the beautiful Names; call Him by these names*" (VII:180). There is a whole science of the Divine Names which is at the base of practically all of the Islamic sciences, whether it be theology, jurisprudence or even philosophy. Muslim thinkers over the ages have written countless books on the Divine Names; among the most famous is that of al-Ghazzālī which is known throughout the Islamic world. Each Name of Allah is none other than His Essence and therefore is a path toward that Essence and yet It reveals a particular aspect of the Divine Nature.

Traditional Muslim authorities have divided these Names into two groups: Names of Beauty (*asmā' al-jamāl*) and the Names of Majesty (*asmā' al-jalāl*). Those aspects of Allah which relate to His Mercy or to His Forgiveness belong to the first category including the Name al-Raḥman which is in reality the Name of the Divine Essence as alluded to in the Quran itself. It is from this Name that, one might say, the whole of creation issues and with which in fact the Quran itself begins, for the chapters commence with the formula "In the Name of Allah, al-Raḥmān, al-Raḥīm." Both the Name al-Raḥmān and al-Raḥīm have to do with the Divine Mercy as do also such Names as al-Karīm, the Generous, al-Ghafūr, the Forgiver, and the like. Such Names represent aspects of Divine Mercy and are among the Names of Beauty. In contrast the Names having to do with justice, judgment and rigor such as al-'Adil, the Just, and Sarī' al-ḥisāb, which means Allah is quick in reckoning the accounts of man, have to do with the aspect of Divine Majesty and they are among the Names of Majesty.

Names of Majesty as well as Beauty manifest themselves in this world. That is why our life is also interwoven by rigor and mercy and the religious life in Islam at once emphasizes the importance of Allah's Justice and the importance of His Forgiveness, the importance of Allah's Wrath which must always be remembered, and the significance of His Love for His creatures. Allah sees and judges our actions and yet is Merciful when we repent and turn to Him.

As far as the difference between the Names and Qualities of Allah are concerned, it might be said that a particular Quality such as for example Generosity (*kirāmah*) when "added" to the Divine Essence (*al-Dhāt*), would result in the Name Generous, al-Karīm. There exists therefore an inextricable relationship between the Divine Essence, the Divine Qualities and the Divine Names. Qualities refer to "states of being" such as Generosity or Mercy whereas the Names of Allah reflecting these Qualities are the Merciful or the Generous.

Among the Divine Names certain ones are especially emphasized and they are sometimes referred to as the "mothers" (*ummahāt*) of the other Names from which all of the Names are derived, the *ummahāt* consisting of such Names as the Powerful (al-Qādir) and the Merciful (al-Raḥmān). These Names are all in turn contained in the Supreme Name of Allah. This Name contains all the Divine Names and is at once the Name of the Divine Essence and the synthesis of all the Divine Qualities and Names.

It is important to remember that the Islamic conception of Allah emphasizes very much His omnipotence. Allah is powerful over His Creation—as the Noble Quran asserts, "*Verily, Allah is powerful over all things*" (II:20). Furthermore, He is the Knower (al-'Alīm) "*Who has knowledge of everything*" (II:29) great and small. Allah has at once complete power over his creation and knows all of his creation. Therefore the Muslim should live in such a way as to be aware constantly of His Power dominating every moment of man's life and His Knowledge of all that man does. Allah watches over all of our actions and judges us accordingly.

This emphasis upon the Power of Allah and His Judgment is balanced by the emphasis that the Quran and *Ḥadīth* place upon His

Mercy. In contrast to what many people think, Islam emphasizes very much the Mercy of Allah. As has already been mentioned, every chapter of the Noble Quran except one begins with the Names of Mercy, al-Raḥmān and al-Raḥīm, not with the Names of Divine Wrath or Anger. Likewise, all acts in the life of a Muslim must begin with the *basmalah* (In the Name of Allah, most Merciful, most Compassionate). Therefore, this hierarchy of Names—Allah, al-Raḥmān and al-Raḥīm—in a sense present a descent from the Divine Reality, Allah, through the all-embracing Mercy which is al-Raḥmān to the individual Mercy touching a particular human being which is al-Raḥīm. Al-Raḥmān is like the sky that embraces us all and is luminous and al-Raḥīm like the particular ray of the sun which emanates from the sky to touch us individually, to enlighten us, to illuminate us and to bestow warmth upon us in the coldness of the life of this world.

The Noble Quran also refers often to the word *wajh* or Face as far as Allah is concerned. For example in the verse "*Wheresoever ye turn, there is the Face of Allah*" (II:115) or "*All things perish except His Face*" (XXVIII:88). The "Face" or *wajh*, therefore, is an important Islamic concept which must be understood. *Wajh* means in reality the sum of the Divine Names and Qualities as they concern the world of creation, that is, that aspect of the Divine Reality which has turned towards the creation. Obviously there are aspects of the Divine which are above and beyond creation and which have nothing to do with the created order. The Face of Allah is precisely that aspect of the Divinity which has turned towards and brought about creation and, therefore, embraces those Divine Names and Qualities which have to do with the creative act and the existence of the created order. "*All things perish except His Face*" means that all things of this world, the mountains, the skies and the earth and of course, we human beings, will perish one day. But the Divine Names and Qualities which are the source and origin of everything in this world abide. They endure because they are Allah's Names and Qualities whereas the things of this world considered in themselves belong to time and pass away. They are not divine; only Allah is Allah and only He is abiding and eternal in the ultimate sense.

It is very important in trying to understand the Islamic concept of Allah to remember that for the Muslim, as is emphasized so often in the Noble Quran, Allah is not only the Creator of the universe, although of course He is the Creator. This means that His relation to the universe is not limited only to the beginning of things. Rather, Allah is also the Sustainer and the end of the universe in the sense that the universe returns to Him. So the Muslim lives with the awareness not only that he comes from Allah but also that he is sustained at every moment of life by Him and that he finally returns to Him as does the whole of creation. The Quranic verse, "*Verily we come from Allah and to Him is our return,*" (II:156) summarizes this doctrine which is of extreme importance not only metaphysically but also for everyday life.

Likewise, the significance of the Quranic teaching of Allah's Wisdom combined with the dominance of His Will in affairs of man cannot be overemphasized. Of course, other religions also teach that God is omnipotent and omniscient and such a teaching is not unique to Islam. It is mentioned also in the Torah and in the Gospels. In Islam, however, this principle is particularly emphasized and integrated into the religious attitudes of everyday life through the repetition of such sentences as *inshā' Allāh*, "if Allah wills." Such formulas punctuate the everyday activities of a Muslim and remind him that the Will of Allah dominates every moment of human life. We live always according to His Will whether we like it or not in the sense that His Will dominates over the world. But also He has given us the freedom from our human point of view so as to live with our own choice according to His Will. There is, therefore, a reciprocity between the completely powerful Will of Allah and human will. To human beings He has given the freedom to use their wills to follow His Will and to surrender to Him. The whole question of determinism and free will which has occupied so many Muslim thinkers over the ages is deeply related to this question to which we shall turn later.

The important teaching, as far as the nature of Allah is concerned, is to be aware of the emphasis in the Quran and the *Ḥadīth* upon the power of Allah's Will and the domination of the whole of reality by His Will in conjunction with His Omniscience. Man must be constantly aware of the fact that He knows all things and that all things function and have their being according to His Wisdom. It is not true to say that Islam is only a religion of a Divinity who has a blind will as some people have asserted; this is totally false. There is no such thing as blind will. Islam emphasizes very much the Wisdom of Allah, His Knowledge of the universe and the importance for man to know Allah and His

Wisdom as reflected in His creation to the extent possible. At the same time it is important to realize that the emphasis upon the Will of Allah dominating over human life is one of the main features of the Quranic doctrine concerning Allah.

Finally, one must re-emphasize the balance in Islam between Allah's Mercy and His Justice. The pages of the Noble Quran are strewn on the one hand with the terrifying images of the judgment and punishment of those who have done evil and on the other with descriptions of paradise and the blessings bestowed by Allah upon those who have performed good acts. The Quran also does not cease to emphasize the Mercy of Allah and His Forgiveness. The Sacred Book continues to remind man that He is forgiving and merciful. Hence the importance of repentance (*al-tawbah*) and the request for forgiveness (*istighfār*). The *Ḥadīth* literature also emphasizes that man should always ask for Allah's forgiveness and that if he asks for His forgiveness from the depth of his heart, Allah will forgive His Servant. Therefore, there is again here an interplay of the deepest kind between the aspects of Mercy and of Justice or of Beauty and Majesty in the sense already mentioned. To gain a full understanding of the Nature of Allah as revealed in the Noble Quran and depicted in *Ḥadīth* literature one must keep both aspects in mind.

To summarize, it might be said that Islamic doctrine is based on the revealing of the total Nature of the Divinity who is the One without partner. That is the heart of the Islamic message. Islam came to the world so that man could know the Unity of Allah. The Prophet said, "Say there is no divinity but Allah and be saved." Of course, he did not mean to "say" only in the verbal and external sense of the term but rather to make a declaration of faith on the basis of understanding. The *shahādah* already contains the complete doctrine of Allah because it takes away from the Divinity all relativity, all otherness, all duality and presents the knowledge of Allah as being based upon His Unity. Allah is the One, the Absolute, the Infinite, and is also Infinite Goodness and Mercy and the Source of all that is positive in the universe. He is the Source of all reality. To Him belong in fact the "hidden treasures" as the Quran asserts, the "treasury" from which all things issue forth. There is nothing in the universe, not a blade of grass, not an ant walking upon the earth, which is not known to Allah and whose life is not ordained and protected by His Will. Man lives in a world utterly dependent upon Allah and open at every moment of time and point of space towards the Transcendent which is Allah. Islam emphasizes the extreme Transcendence of Allah who is beyond all that can be said of Him. Yet He is extremely close to man as in the famous verse, "*We are nearer to him than his jugular vein,*" (L:16) attests. Allah is even closer to us than ourselves. On the one hand He is utterly beyond and infinitely above us; on the other hand, He is at the center of our very being. That is why He has said, "The heart of the believer is the throne of the Compassionate."

Man

In the same way that Islam is concerned with the Nature of Allah as He is in Himself, in His Absoluteness, Infinity and Goodness, so does it address man as he is in his primordial and ultimately immutable nature. Man in the Islamic perspective is at once the vicegerent, the khalīfah, of Allah on earth and His servant (*'abd*). The two together constitute the fundamental nature of man. As His servant, man must be subservient to His Will. He must be totally passive *vis-à-vis* the Will of Allah, to receive from Him direction for his life and commands as to how to carry out His Will in the created order. As His Vicegerent, he must be active, precisely because he is Allah's representative in this world. He is the bridge between heaven and earth, the instrument through which the Will of Allah is realized and crystallized in this world.

Islam sees man as a being possessing at once intelligence and will, but Islam addresses man most of all as an intelligent being. It does not see man as having a will which has become deformed because of original sin as is the case in the mainstream Augustinian interpretation of Christianity. Rather, it sees man in his primordial nature (*al-fiṭrah*) in which Allah gave man the intelligence to understand that Allah is the Lord, that He is One, and to testify to His Unity. That is why in the Quran, Allah addresses mankind even before the creation of the world and asks him "*Am I not your Lord*?" and mankind answers, "*Yea we testify*" (VII:172). In this 'yea' of man is to be found the primordial covenant, (*al-mithāq*), made between man and Allah through which man accepts the Lordship of Allah and which means also that he innately bears testimony to His Oneness. The affirmation of *tawḥīd*, one might say, is in the very nature of man and Islam is the religion that addresses itself to that deep, profound nature which, although covered by layers of forgetfulness and egoism, is nevertheless present in the heart of every human being. As for the will, Islam wishes man to submit his will to the Will of Allah because it is only by doing so that man is able to lead a life which will result in his happiness in this world and the hereafter.

It is important in this context to remember that Islam is not based on original sin but that nevertheless it does accept the fall of man (*al-hubūṭ*) from the primordial and original state of perfection in which he was created. According to Islam, the great sin of man is in fact forgetfulness (*al-ghaflah*) and the purpose of the message of revelation is to enable man to remember. That is why one of the names of the Quran itself is "the Remembrance of Allah" (*dhikr Allāh*) and why the ultimate end and purpose of all Islamic rites and of all Islamic conjunctions is the remembrance of Allah. That primordial nature of man cannot but confirm the Divine Unity. It cannot but bear witness to *al-tawḥīd*. But precisely because of his fall, man's will has become warped in the sense that it has become subservient to the passions rather than to Allah. Therefore, Allah has revealed the rules and injunctions of religion contained in the *Sharī'ah*.

The Divine Law has been revealed in order to curb man's passions and to enable him to subordinate his will to the functioning of the intelligence freed from the entanglement of the passions, so that in the same way that the "healthy" intelligence (*al-'aql al-salīm*) confirms the Unity of Allah, the will follows the consequences of this Unity. This results in a life lived according to the Will of the One through following His commands.

According to the teachings of the Quran and many *ḥadīths* which confirm these teachings, Allah created man from clay and then breathed into him His Spirit—"*I breathed into him from My Spirit,*" (XXXVII:72). Man does not ascend from the apes, not man as man. He *descends* from the world of the spirit. Our spirit belongs to Allah and to Him it shall return. The greatest sin in the eyes of Allah is *shirk* or taking partners unto Him. This sin itself is the result of the forgetfulness of our origin. In forgetting our origin we also forget Allah's Oneness and deny His Uniqueness. Islam does not emphasize the importance of sin any less than do Christianity and other religions. But it does not consider the sense of guilt in the same way as does Christianity and does not believe that man is sinful by nature. In Islam sin comes first of all from forgetting the Oneness of Allah and secondly from forgetting the consequences of the Oneness of Him who is the All-Powerful and the All-Knowing, which in turn results in disobeying His commands and rebelling against Him. Islam is totally opposed to the idea of rebellion and revolt against divine authority. On the contrary it is the religion of submission to that authority. Therefore, the kind of doubt and individualistic rebellion which can be seen in so many circles in ancient Greece and post-medieval Europe and which is reflected in the literature of these periods is absent from Islam.

Man is conceived in Islam not in his Titanic and Promethean nature which rebels against the Will of Heaven in a heroic manner. On the contrary, he is leveled down in a sense to being the *'abd* or servant of Allah, his grandeur coming not from himself but from his position as Allah's vicegerent and from being able to carry out the Will of the Supreme Master of the universe. It comes from his living in witness and in the remembrance of Allah and from his acting as a creature reflects Allah's Wisdom and Power in this world. That is why man is addressed in Islamic texts as the most noble of creatures. All creatures possess a nobility in the sense that they are created by Allah and reflect an aspect of Divine Wisdom. Man, however, is the most noble among them in the sense that he reflects most directly the Divine Wisdom and most completely the Divine Names and Qualities. Man is the only central being in this world and that is why only he is the *khalīfah* or vicegerent of Allah in the full sense of the term. Man has the power to dominate all other creatures, but he also bears the responsibility to care for all of them. His responsibility is greater than all other creatures because he is given the consciousness and the awareness to understand Allah's Nature and to obey His commands and also the freedom and the possibility to disobey them.

This brings up the very important question of freedom and determinism as far as the nature of man and the moral consequences of his actions are concerned. On the one hand, the Quran emphasizes that Allah has power over all things. On the other hand, the Sacred Text addresses man as a free moral agent. If we were not responsible for our actions, we would not in fact have to be judged for them on the Day of Judgment. We cannot be responsible for our actions unless we have the freedom to choose. All the major schools of Islamic thought have debated the relationship between man's freedom and the determined nature of human existence. Some have emphasized determinism (*al-jabr*) and some free will (*al-ikhtiyār*). They have sought to provide solutions to this great enigma which only veritable wisdom (*al-ḥikmah*) is able to solve.

Without getting into very complicated theological and philosophical issues which the problem of free will and determinism involves, however, it is necessary to emphasize that the Noble Quran itself, which is the central authority as *the* source of the Islamic revelation, emphasizes over and over the reality of man's freedom in the sense that it emphasizes man's responsibility before Allah and even before the rest of His creation. In Islam there is no possibility of escaping from this freedom. Allah has created us as human beings. We have made the eternal covenant with Him and, therefore, have the responsibility of carrying out our part of the covenant. Allah has given us existence. He has given us all the different powers, blessings and gifts which include not only existence, not only life, not only life as an animal but life as human beings aware of Allah as the Infinite and the Absolute with the freedom to either affirm or negate that Supreme Reality which He is. That is part of Allah's covenant which has been fulfilled by Him. But what about us human beings? The part of the covenant which relates to man is contained in that one single Arabic affirmation "*balā*" or "Yea," in the Quranic verse already cited. Through that "yea," man accepted to follow Allah by admitting and accepting His Lordship. The consequences of that acceptance is that he must bear full responsibility as Allah's vicegerent on earth with all that it implies.

There is in Islam no freedom without responsibility and, in fact, there are no human rights without obligations. We have no innate rights unless we accept our obligations towards Allah, for we have not given existence to ourselves. We are human by virtue of having been given this form of existence by Him. We must therefore first fulfill the obligations of being human. Only then do we have rights as human beings. The idea of man having innate rights independent of his acceptance of Allah, independent of his fulfillment of his function as His vicegerent on the earth is totally alien to the Islamic perspective. Certainly there are human rights in Islam. They are delineated clearly in the *Sharī'ah* but these rights are based upon responsibility. They are based upon accepting our obligations to Allah Who has created us, Who sustains us and to Whom we shall finally return.

The Male and the Female

When the Quran refers to man, the Arabic word that is usually used is *insān* or *bashar*. Both of these terms mean the human being and not the male sex. Therefore all of the injunctions in the Quran addressing "man" are really addressed to men and women alike. There are moreover certain verses of the Quran which explicitly address both sexes, male and female, such as the following verse: "*Lo! Men who surrender unto Allah, and women who surrender, and men who believe and women who believe, and men who are devout and women who are devout*" (XXXIII:35).

It is important to understand that in contrast to modern movements within the Western world and especially America, which try to equate man and woman in a quantitative way as if there were no differences between them, Islam views men and women as complementary beings. At the same time Islam sees them equal in the fundamental or ultimate sense of having an immortal soul and therefore, having the possibility of gaining paradisal felicity after death or being punished in the infernal states for having disobeyed Allah's Will. Islamic rites are the same for men and women except for the question of women's menstrual cycle during which they are not permitted to perform their prayers (*ṣalāh*), fast or perform the *ḥajj*.

Moreover, the immortality of the soul, the promises and threats of the after life, and the ultimate possibility of the human state, are the same for men and women. Wherein the sexes differ is in the external social function in which Islam sees a complementarity rather than quantitative equality. The criticism often times made against the role of women in Islam by Westerners is based first of all on reading current Western fashions into the Islamic world. The West itself has changed its views on this matter a great deal in the last fifty years not to speak of the last two hundred years and there is no reason whatsoever why the social structure of Islam should resemble let us say 1990 America which might be very different from 2090 as 1990 has been different from 1890. Secondly, it is very important to consider that Islam, like every religion, had to take into account the social structures of the societies in which it was destined to spread. The early Semitic nomadic society of Arabia in which Islam spread, in fact, had a greater dynamism as far as male-female relations were concerned than let us say, the more sedentary societies in the north whether one considers Byzantinum or Persia and that fact is reflected in the gradual changes in social relationships which were created later as these societies further north became Islamicized.

The question of political and economic participation of women and similar issues during the history of Islam should be studied not only in the light of Quranic teachings but also by considering existing social institutions. This fact is true even as far as the veil is concerned. In early Islamic society it was related to the covering of the hair as well as the body but not the face. Later on because of local practices which were integrated into Islamic practice, it came also to include in many parts of the Islamic world the whole face except for the eyes. Today in some Islamic countries as a whole and in certain of the rural areas throughout the Islamic world, the type of veil to cover the face and the body of the female differs from what one finds in the well-known sedentary centers in the Islamic heartland.

In this very complicated question, it is extremely important to pay attention to the basic Islamic teachings in relation to the social norms and necessities which Islam has had to take into account on the one hand and to the ever-changing fashions and modes of relationship between male and female which have dominated Western society during the last century on the other. Under no condition should these changing modes in the West be accepted by Muslims as criteria for judging the good or evil aspects of any particular practices of Islamic society. What is important to realize is that from the Islamic point of view men and women are equal before Allah, that they have the same opportunity for salvation, the same moral and spiritual responsibility and ultimately the same freedom and rights in the spiritual and religious sense.

That women do not have the same economic or social rights on a certain level does not mean that they have no rights whatsoever. It means that Islam envisages the role of men and women in a complementary fashion without closing the door at all on, for example, women's activities in the economic field which has always existed. The first wife of the Prophet himself, that is, the great Khadījah, was a merchant. Nor does it mean closing the door on learning among women. In this context it must be remembered that some of the early transmitters of *ḥadīth* were women. There have also been occasionally great female Muslim scholars over the centuries and the fact that there were not many more did not have anything to do with Islamic teachings. One sees the same situation in the traditional Christian, Jewish, Hindu or Buddhist worlds where in fact, no more female scholars were produced than in the Islamic world.

The most important point to understand in this question is that Islam addresses the whole of the human species not only the male and that its teachings, although they may appear to be very patriarchal and masculine, also possess a strong feminine element. This is found not only on the highest level where even the Divinity is sometimes referred to in the feminine as well as the masculine gender, not only in the Divine Names whose aspects of beauty, gentleness and mercy reflect the feminine, but also in the conception of the human state in which a positive role is given to the female as well as to the male.

The fact that over the centuries Islamic society has been able to emphasize so much the structure of the family, to preserve the religious significance of family life and to base the whole structure of Islamic society upon the family as its basic unit goes to show the great emphasis that Islam has placed upon male and female relationship and upon the significance of women in Islamic society. Moreover, within the Islamic family, the woman has always played a crucial role. The fact that during its history Islam did produce a large number of women lawyers, economists or doctors as one finds in the fourteenth/twentieth century West and even in certain parts of the East has very little to do with the supposed eclipsing of the function and role of women by Islam. As has already been mentioned, other civilizations whose dominant religion has not been Islam have not in fact produced any more female figures in the various professional fields than did Islam and the cause for this fact must be sought elsewhere than in the structure of the Islamic religion.

To conclude the question of man, it is important to remember that since Islam seeks to attain unity in all domains, it also seeks to avoid destructive competition and confrontation whether it be between the sexes or various classes of human society. Islam is opposed to class antagonisms in the thirteenth/nineteenth century Marxist sense of the term as it is opposed to sexism or the battle of the sexes as it has become prevalent in various parts of the world during this century. Islam seeks to harmonize the whole human state in both its male and female forms and human society with all the different types of human beings who populate that society. It has been and remains strongly opposed to racism and also to a completely stratified structure which one finds in certain other traditional societies.

Islam is like a society of married monks, each person being directly responsible to Allah and participating in religion not by withdrawing from the world but by participation in it through many means including the institution of marriage. Marriage has been very strongly emphasized in Islam and there is a great deal of pressure in Islamic society for men and women to marry. Islamic society is one in which celibacy has been extremely rare and in which individuals whether male or female have usually been integrated into the larger family structure through different types of marriage which have prevented an atomization of society from taking place. All of this is related to the Islamic concept of the human being which is based upon his relationship to Allah as His vicegerent and Islam also sees men and women as existing in an extensive network of relationships in a society which in its complicated and multifarious relations is nevertheless unified and reflects the Unity of Allah. Interrelatedness is itself in fact an echo and image of *tawḥīd* on the plane of multiplicity which characterizes human society.

Islam not only sanctifies the life of the individual, but also tries to sacralize social structures themselves by bestowing a religious significance upon all social institutions and functions and by constituting within society relationships and rapports which far from being based on opposition, contention and confrontation of the interests of various classes and groups, try to integrate different elements into a single people or *ummah*. It seeks, through religious principles and institutions, to create a society which, in its totality as well as within the heart of its individual members, reflects *tawḥīd* and demonstrates the working out of the Will of Allah in the life of mankind.

The Universe

As already mentioned, the Noble Quran not only addresses man but in a sense also addresses Allah's creation. In many verses Allah Himself swears by the various creatures He has created, such as the sun and the moon or different fruits and in many of its verses the Noble Quran draws the attention of man to the incredible wisdom which is reflected in His creation. In the same way that Islam addresses itself to the primordial nature of man, it also brings into the light of day the cosmic message which is written upon the leaves of trees, over the faces of mountains and in the starry heavens. That is why both the verses of the Quran and the phenomena of nature are called *āyāt* and the Quran attests to both of these *āyāt*, within the soul of man as well as within the created order as signs or portents of Allah as in the famous verse, "*We shall show them our signs upon the horizons and within themselves, until it be manifest unto them that it is the Truth*" (XLI:53).

According to the Islamic point of view, the world is created by Allah; it is sustained by Him and it returns to Him. One of the many meanings of the verse, "*Allah is the First and the Last, the Inward and the Outward,*" (LVII:3) is that Allah is the origin and end of the universe. He is also the inner meaning of all things and even the outward signs or the outward aspect of things reflect His Names and Qualities. The whole of the world which we know and are able to experience is created by Allah. It is not eternal although the act of creation of Allah has, of course, no origin in time; otherwise there would be a change in the Divine Nature which Islam does not accept. The whole cosmic order as we know it and as we see it, has an origin and an end. The origin issues from the Divine Command *kun fa-yakūn*, "*Let there be and it is,*" (XXXVI:82), and it returns back unto Him. Moreover, Allah has the power to recreate, to bring another creation into being to which the Quran refers as the new creation (*khalqun jadīd*). The Muslim must therefore be always aware of the created nature of the world about him. The universe is not an independent order of reality. It relies at every moment of its existence upon the Divine Sustenance. Moreover, its laws, harmony and order all issue from Allah. The incredible harmony of the created order is a reflection of *tawḥīd*, of the manifestation of the One in the world of multiplicity and the many.

The Muslim sees the laws of nature not as independent laws which go on their own way as if the world had an ontological independence of its own. He sees these laws as reflections of the Wisdom of Allah and also as a result of His Will. It is Allah who has willed that the sun rise every morning in the east and set in the west, that creatures fly in the air or swim in the seas. It is incredible that so many verses of the Quran refer to the most profound laws which govern the natural order. Far from opposing man's knowledge of the natural world, the Quran continuously encourages man to study the natural order while accepting that this knowledge of the world must always be subservient to the knowledge of Allah and must always be based on the awareness that the world is not totally independent by itself but that it derives its beings, laws, harmony and transformations from the source of all being which is Allah.

In a profound sense one might say that the whole of nature is *muslim*, meaning that it has surrendered itself totally to the Will of Allah. All creatures follow the nature which Allah has given to them. A pear tree always bears pears, a fish always remains true to the nature of the fish and a bird to that of the bird. It is only man who has been given the freedom of rebellion against his own primordial nature. Therefore, the created world or the world of nature is a constant reminder to man of what it means to be a perfect Muslim in the sense of being surrendered to Allah's Will.

The Quran, while giving man the power to rule over all things through the fact that Allah taught Adam the names of all things, also gives man the responsibility of custodianship over the created order. The *taskhīr* or subjugation of nature does not mean a selfish and blind conquest and domination of nature. It means living in harmony with nature, seeing in nature Allah's Wisdom and making use of natural bounties wisely in accordance with man's final end which is to live as a good Muslim and to return to the Creator. The moral laws of Islam in a sense extend beyond human society to embrace the animals, plants, minerals and in fact, the whole of the inanimate world. To live as a good Muslim in this world is to see the Wisdom of Allah everywhere and to care for His creation as He cares for us and that creation Himself. The good Muslim must always remember that it is Allah who has created, sustained and preserved the remarkable harmony, diversity and beauty of the natural order and who has bestowed rights for other creatures and placed responsibility upon man for them.

ESCHATOLOGY

The pages of the Noble Quran are replete with references to death, the after-life, Allah's judgment of human actions, the end of the world and resurrection. There are few themes in the Quran and *Ḥadīth* which are as often repeated and are as central as what is called *al-ma'ād* in Arabic, a term which must be understood as eschatology as well as resurrection. It is therefore impossible to discuss the teachings of Islam without referring to the great significance that the eschatological teachings of Islam possess not only for man's final end but also for his life in this world. Much of the eschatological teachings of Islam are contained in the last chapters of the Quran but they also appear throughout the Sacred Text. Likewise, in all of the canonical collections of *Ḥadīth* there are sections devoted to eschatology.

The Prophet—upon whom be blessings and peace—reminded his Companions at all times of the nearness of death. It was he who said, "Die before you die," and it is said that he advised Muslims to live as if they were to die tomorrow and also as if they were to live a thousand years. The Prophet also reminded his Companions of the immortality of the human soul, Allah's judgment of human actions, and of the eternal consequences of our life and actions on earth. Therefore, from the very beginning of Islamic history, Muslim thinkers have been concerned with the questions of eschatology and the life of the individual Muslim has always been lived with full awareness of the eschatological realities.

Let us first begin with the teachings of Islam concerning that aspect of eschatology which deals with the individual human being. There is, according to Islam, not only the life of this world but also the life in the world to come. All of the teachings of Islam would crumble if the afterlife or the eternal life were to be denied. The other world or *al-ākhirah* looms as a vivid, concrete and central reality in the life of every generation of faithful Muslims and the Quran reminds man that, "*Verily the hereafter will be better for thee than the present*" (XCIII:4). It is taught throughout the pages of the Quran and *Ḥadīth* that Allah observes all of our acts, that we accrue merit for good acts and must pay the consequences for the evil acts which we perform. This world is, in fact, like a field in which our actions are sown like seeds and they grow into plants which are then harvested in the next world. This image appears in many different forms in Islamic teachings including in the *ḥadīth* "this world is the growing field or the planting field for the next world."

Human life is constituted in such a way that the actions which we perform in this world here and now have consequences not only beyond that moment, not only beyond the immediate confines of this action but even beyond this world because they affect our immortal soul. Man possesses an immortal soul and does not cease to exist at the moment of death for his soul continues to survive in various states in accordance with the way he or she has lived and also of course according to the Mercy of Allah. Here again one sees an interplay between the Justice and Mercy of Allah which one cannot reduce to simple bookkeeping and accounting. A great sin performed by one of Allah's creatures may be forgiven by Him if that person seeks forgiveness and repents from the depth of his heart, whereas a small sin, if it continues to blemish the soul, could in fact leave an abiding effect upon it which could bring posthumous retribution upon the soul.

What is a great sin, what is a small sin, what Allah forgives and what He does not forgive and how the human being will live after the moment of death are extremely complicated questions which involve the mystery of Divine Mercy and Divine Justice and which therefore cannot be reduced to simple formulas. Nevertheless, the injunctions of Islam are very clear. According to them, those who live well die well and man's state of being after death is related to how he has lived in this world. He who lives according to the tenets of Islam will live in a state of happiness in various paradises which the Quran describes so beautifully in the symbolic language that characterizes so many descriptions in the Quran such as chapter 55, *Sūrat al-Raḥmān.* As for those who perform evil and do not repent, they face the pains of the infernal states, to which the Quran also refers over and over again as in the verses: "*In their heart is a disease; and Allah has increased their disease, and grievous is the punishment they incur because they lie,*" ((II:10) and "*Such men will find their abode in Hell—what an evil refuge*" (IV:97).

Therefore, the first important element to remember, as far as eschatology is concerned, is that it has a very important ethical implication. Its implication is that man must live ethically in this world not because of the fear of an external law, the police or the state, but because of the fear of Allah. The love of Allah and the knowledge of Allah are based on the fundamental fear of Him and that is why it has been said *ra's al-ḥikmah makhāfat Allāh* ("the beginning of wisdom is the fear of Allah"). This fear is related not only to the Majesty of Allah but also to the grandeur of being human, to the fact that we have been given the responsibility of being human and being bestowed with free will to either follow Allah's teachings or rebel against them. We do not have the possibility of trivializing the human state as if we were not free, as if we were not the vicegerents of Allah on earth. That is not a possibility for us. Our actions have consequences beyond the grave which we cannot avoid. And precisely because we are human, our life is not destroyed completely at the moment of death. Rather, the life of the soul and the spirit survive after the death of the body. Because of all these realities we must live our lives on earth according to moral principles. We must shun what is evil or more specifically what the Quran and *Ḥadīth* consider to be evil. We must live according to the Will of Allah as revealed in the Quran and expanded and further clarified in the *Ḥadīth* and *Sunnah*.

The eschatological realities of individual human life are described in great detail in later Islamic literature especially in Quranic commentaries and commentaries upon the *Ḥadīth*. There are many books in Arabic and other Islamic languages based on the twin sources of the Quran and *Ḥadīth* which describe the experiences of the soul after death. There are also many traditional works which treat the experiences of the human being at the moment of death, practices related to the rites of burial of the body, the appropriate prayers and the reading of the Quran to be carried out at the time of death and burial, and other practices related to the rites of purification and burial of Muslims. All of these teachings are related to the posthumous experiences of the deceased. They are there to facilitate the journey of the deceased from this world to the next.

There are very elaborate descriptions in traditional sources of the three different types of states that the human soul experiences after death: the paradisal, the purgatorial and the infernal. We experience one of these states depending who we are, what we are and how we have lived our lives in this world. In a sense we weave our "body of resurrection" through our actions and on the basis of what we have woven by our own actions we enter into one of the posthumous states to which our being corresponds. Some of these states are described majestically in the Quran and others in the *Ḥadīth*. There is altogether a very elaborate Islamic teaching concerning the various states beyond the grave to be found in both the sources of the Islamic revelation and later commentaries upon them.

There is moreover, the question of Allah's judgment of us, the question of the bridge (*ṣirāṭ*) over which souls must pass after the Day of Resurrection, the balance (*mīzān*) which weighs our good and evil acts and the other elements which, according to the Quran and *Ḥadīth*, constitute the eschatological realities as far as the individual human being is concerned. All of these teachings are based on the very thorough and clear insistence of the Quran upon the immortality of the human soul and the resurrection of the human being, resurrection not only of the soul but also of the body (*al-ma'ād al-jismānī*). Bodily resurrection is in fact the clear teaching of orthodox Islam in all of its schools. It is not only a question of the soul surviving and living after death. On the Day of the resurrection the body as well as the soul are resurrected before Allah.

As for the Day of Resurrection (*yawm al-qiyāmah*), one must distinguish here between the individual experience of eschatological realities and the eschatological events concerning the whole of humanity. Usually the Day of Resurrection or *yawm al-qiyāmah* refers in fact not to the death of the individual but to the final end of present humanity, not the eschatological experience which every individual must undergo at the moment of his or her death, but that of the world of the present humanity itself. The Islamic teachings reserve the term *al-qiyāmah* for cosmic eschatological events crowned by the resurrection of creation as well as the resurrection of the individual. More specifically, these sources distinguish between the greater resurrection, *al-qiyāmat al-kubrā* which is that of the cosmos followed by the resurrection of the whole of humanity and the individual death and resurrection *al-qiyāmat al-ṣughrā* which the soul undergoes following upon the event of death. What takes place between the death of the individual and the resurrection of the whole of humanity has been debated by various schools of Islamic thought and cannot be discussed in this work because it involves very complicated theological and philosophical issues.

The Quran also refers to eschatological events which concern the whole of humanity. As already mentioned Islam believes that this world in which we live is not eternal. It has a beginning and an end after which Allah will create other worlds, for He is always the Creator, al-Khāliq. But this present world was created with a definite beginning and will have a definite end marked by eschatological events. According to traditional sources, these events involve, first of all, the appearance of a figure whose name is Muḥammad al-Mahdī. This appearance is anticipated on the basis of the *ḥadīth* of the Prophet who said that when oppression and iniquity cover the earth "a member of my tribe shall appear whose name will be the same as mine." Therefore, throughout the centuries, Muslims, both Sunni and Shi'ite, have believed that a figure will appear one day who will be the Mahdī, the Guided One, who will destroy iniquity, reestablish the rule of Islam and bring back justice and peace to the world. His rule, however, will be fairly short and it will be followed by the return of Christ.

Islam and Christianity share the same vision concerning the second coming of Christ because Christians also believe in his return. Moreover, the Muslims also accept, as do the Christians, that Christ's return will occur in Jerusalem and that this city will be the place where final eschatological events will take place. Islam in contrast to Christianity, however, sees the function of the Mahdī and Christ as being associated with each other and their coming as part of the same major eschatological events. While the Mahdī will rule for some years on earth, the coming of Christ will coincide with the termination of the present history of mankind and of time as we ordinarily experience it. Historical time comes to an end and is followed by the Day of Resurrection, the final judgment of all human beings, the weighing of the good and evil acts, the determination of the inhabitants of heaven, purgatory and hell and the coming to end of the history of the cosmos. These very complicated events have been described in Islam in such a way that no man, no matter what claims he makes, can predict exactly when the Hour will arrive. In fact, there is a *ḥadīth* of the Prophet which says that all those who predict the time of the coming of the Hour are liars. Nevertheless, all Muslims believe that the Hour will come, that is, there is an end to human history, that Allah intervenes finally like lightning upon the stage of ordinary time/space consciousness, that there is the final death and resurrection of humanity and that there is an accounting for all that men have done in this world.

Most of the details of these teachings are usually put aside in every day life by ordinary Muslims who are not given to meditating and thinking about them. It is for theologians, philosophers and other authorities in the religious sciences to deal with their ultimate significance. But as far as their consequences are concerned, they are meant for all Muslims to think about them. First of all, we all die whether we are illiterate or great religious scholars, kings or beggars; therefore, the reality of death and what happens to the human soul after death are the concern of every human being. Not only every Muslim, but every human being whether Muslim, Christian, Jew or other thinks naturally of his or her end. The consequences of the eschatological teachings of Islam are there for the benefit of all Muslims and they have been thought about by all types of people and in very different forms ranging all the way from popular stories and old wives' tales to the most scholarly and intellectual expositions in which these realities have been presented in metaphysical and theological terms.

The important lesson, as far as the general teachings of Islam are concerned, is to keep in mind at all times the reality of death and the afterlife, the ultimate consequence of our human actions and our responsibility to Allah for what we do. The precious gift of human life, which has allowed us by the grace of Allah to possesses the freedom to act and to accept Allah's teachings on the basis of our freedom and not by coercion, must always be kept in mind. Without the eschatological realities the other teachings of religion would lose much of their compelling influence and the spiritual tension of human life in this world which is part and parcel of the reality of being human would disappear, leaving human life without any ultimate meaning. This would happen since no matter what man achieves in this world, there is always the certitude that these achievements will ultimately flounder and disappear. The greatest material achievements, not only of the individual but also of whole civilizations, can and in fact do wither away. It is only the eschatological realities which bring into focus the permanent, abiding and eternal consequences of human actions precisely because human beings are beings created for immortality and the eternal world.

The ordinary Muslim lives with the hope of entering into paradise at the moment of death. He, therefore, seeks to live according to the *Sharī'ah* to be compassionate, forgiving and generous, to avoid lying, deceit and calumny, not to speak of the great sins such as murder or taking a partner unto Allah which is considered to be the supreme sin in Islam. There exists in Islamic teachings this very delicate and beautiful harmony between the rigor of Allah's laws and the mercy which flows from Him as the Names al-Raḥmān, the Merciful, al-Raḥīm, the Compassionate, and al-Ghafūr, the Forgiver testify. Allah expects from man righteousness, morality and virtue but since He knows the weakness of His creature, He also forgives and has mercy upon him. In this remarkable economy which embraces both of these elements of justice and mercy, traditional Islamic life has continued its existence over the centuries, producing generation after generation of men and women, many of great virtue, who have lived in the fear of Allah's Retribution but also in the hope of His Forgiveness. They have brought virtue and ethics to Islamic society which must always reflect the realities beyond this world in the same way that our actions and deeds echo beyond this world of space and time in which they are performed, resonating in the world of eternity.

CHAPTER 3
THE SHARĪ'AH

The *Sharī'ah* or the Divine Law of Islam is central to the Islamic religion to the extent that one can define the Muslim as one who accepts the legitimacy of the *Sharī'ah* even if he or she is not able to practice all of its teachings. The *Sharī'ah*, according to authentic Islamic doctrines, is the concrete embodiment of the Will of Allah for human society. Allah alone is ultimately the legislator, the Shāri', He who creates laws, and only His laws are ultimately binding and permanent in human life. That does not mean that the *Sharī'ah* cannot be applied and "grow" according to different circumstances like the growth of a tree whose roots and trunk remain firm and whose nature does not change although its branches grow over the years. The *Sharī'ah* is contained in principle in the Noble Quran and in the Noble Quran alone, but this is in principle. In order for it to be manifested, there was need first of all, of course, for the *Ḥadīth* literature and the *Sunnah* of the Prophet. The Prophet through his practices and sayings made the Will of God known to the Islamic community and therefore his *Sunnah* and his *Ḥadīth* are the second fundamental source of Islamic Law along with the Quran.

The early Islamic community lived in the presence of these two realities. The Quran was ever present and the practices of the Prophet, which were copied and imitated by the Companions and the first generation after them, were so well known that the whole community was in a sense immersed in them. During the early period there were still no codified schools of law. The different interpretations of *Sharīʻah* and the *Sharīʻah* itself had not been codified and formulated in books of jurisprudence as we find later on, but the reality was present. How people lived and acted, how they were judged, what punishment or rewards were given, how transactions were carried out, not to speak of the part of the *Sharīʻah* dealing with religious practices, all of these were present in these earliest generations and served as models for later centuries of Islamic history. In fact, it was the danger of the gradual distancing of the later generations from the source of Islamic revelation and the gradual forgetting of the dazzling example of the Prophet as the perfect embodiment of Islam and the perfect practitioner and promulgator of the Divine Law that caused the great jurists or scholars of Islamic Law to codify the *Sharīʻah* according to various schools.

Now Islam, being a religion meant for a population spread over the globe and not just for one nation, had to possess the possibility of the development of different interpretations of the Divine Law within itself. Consequently, on the basis of the twin fundamental sources of the Quran and *Ḥadīth*, gradually Muslim jurists, the *fuqahā'*, began to elaborate methods of drawing various consequences from the sources and certain principles outside of these two sources, such as the consensus of the learned within the community, called *ijmāʻ*, analogical reasoning, *qiyās* or the welfare of the community, *istiṣlāḥ*, and so forth came to be used by various jurists.

The first great teacher of law was Imam Jaʻfar al-Ṣādiq, the descendant of the Prophet who was revered by Sunnis and Shiʻites alike. He was the teacher of Imam Abū Ḥanīfah, one of the founders of the four orthodox schools of Sunni law which have survived to this day, the Ḥanafī School. Imam Jaʻfar, who lived in the second Islamic century, was also himself the founder of Twelve-Imam Shiʻite Law which to this day is called Jaʻfarī Law. After him jurists began gradually to develop the *Sharīʻah* in both the Sunni and the Shiʻite worlds and especially in the Sunni world a great deal of activity took place in the following two centuries until finally the major schools of the *Sharīʻah* which have survived to this day, were established. These schools are that of Ibn Mālik known as the Mālikī School, the school of Imam Aḥmad ibn Ḥanbal, the founder of the Ḥanbalī School, the school of Imam Abū Ḥanīfah, the founder of the Ḥanafī School and finally the school of Imam Shāfiʻī who founded the Shāfiʻī School of law. Several other schools appeared in the Sunni world such as the Ẓāhirī but they gradually died out and only these four major schools of law remained.

Today in the Islamic world all of North Africa and West Africa follow the Mālikī School which is closest to the practice of Madinah. A large number of people in Syria and in Saudi Arabia follow the Ḥanbalī School which is the most strict in its adherence to the Quran and the *Sunnah* and does not rely as do the other schools of law upon the other principles and, in fact, rejects them. The Shāfiʻī School is followed by most of the Egyptians and most of the people in Southeast Asia, that is, the Malaysians and Indonesians, and the Ḥanafī School, which was the official school of the Ottoman Empire, is followed to this day by the Turks and most of the Muslims of the subcontinent of India. As for the Jaʻfarī School, it has remained the only school of law for Twelve-Imam Shiʻism and is the official school wherever Twelve-Imam Shiʻism survives to this day as for example in Iran, Iraq and Lebanon. There are, moreover, the Zaydī and the Ismāʻīlī schools of law which are followed by the Zaydīs of the Yemen and Ismāʻīlīs who are found in India, Pakistan, Iran, East Africa, and in small pockets in Syria, Egypt and also in the Western world.

Contents of the *Sharīʻah*

In the classical works on the *Sharīʻah* usually the contents of the Divine Law are divided into subjects dealing with worship called *ʻibādāt* and those dealing with transactions or *muʻāmalāt.* In analyzing the subjects treated in these categories one can see that the *Sharīʻah* encompasses not only the personal religious life or even the community religious life of Islam but also touches upon every phase of human activity including the economic, the social and the political. As far as the first part of the *Sharīʻah*, that is, the aspects of worship or *ʻibādāt* are concerned, they are based upon the most central acts of worship in Islam which are the daily prayers, fasting, pilgrimage and the religious tax to which, as has been mentioned earlier in this book, sometimes the noble effort in the path of Allah called *jihād*, usually mistranslated as holy war, has been added.

All of the schools of the *Sharī'ah* contain very detailed teachings concerning these acts of worship. There are usually chapters of books on the *Sharī'ah* or independent books devoted to the prayers. Such works deal with ablutions, personal cleanliness, the conditions of body, mind and heart required in the prayers, the actual movements and the words enunciated, different types of prayers whether they be the five canonical daily prayers, the Friday congregational prayers, or the prayers of the various Muslim festivities such as those of the end of Ramaḍān and at the end of the pilgrimage or special prayers offered at moments of fear or hope and so forth. There is also usually an elaborate section, in works on the *Sharī'ah*, devoted to the legal conditions under which prayers must be undertaken. Some of these conditions are external such as external cleanliness or praying on a site which is either one's own or which, belonging to someone else, requires permission in order for the prayers to be performed. Others of these conditions are internal, dealing with having a normal state of consciousness and therefore not being drunk, crazy or psychologically demented and also having purity of intention and the correct inward attitude towards Allah.

The same holds true for the other major rites. The section of works on the *Sharī'ah* dealing with fasting again specifies, on the one hand, the external conditions of fasting such as when to begin, when to stop, the question of fasting for the ill and travelers, what other days during the year are especially appropriate for fasting and on what days fasting is forbidden, what to do during Ramaḍān besides abstaining from eating, drinking and sexual activity, and on the other inward conditions such as the correct mental attitude towards other people, inner purification and abstention from evil thoughts, backbiting, lying and deceit. Works on fasting also deal with the social and charitable aspects of fasting such as giving alms to the poor, feeding those in the neighborhood, giving the *fiṭriyyah* or religious tax at the end of Ramaḍān etc.

As for the *ḥajj*, again there are sections, even books, devoted to the very complex and difficult rites of the *ḥajj* all the way from the economic conditions which must be fulfilled before a person can undertake the *ḥajj*, that is, having the necessary means to provide for one's family for at least a year and having no immediate neighbors who are so poor as to be in dire need and certain other conditions, to the actual specifications for the journey and the wearing of the special dress (the *iḥrām*). Instructions are also provided for all the different prayers, movements, rites to be performed such as circumabulation around the Ka'bah, the day at 'Arafāt, the casting of stones upon the devil or what symbolizes the devil, the *sa'y* or running between Ṣafā and Marwah, the sacrifice at the end of the *ḥajj*, etc. And then there are again the inward conditions since every rite has both an external and an inward aspect which in this case includes the sense of detachment from the world, asking forgiveness of Allah, feeling the total equality of all believers before Allah as it will be in the Day of Judgment and the loss of all pride and of all social distinctions based on external factors. It also includes the drawing close to Allah by visiting His House. Regaining through the circumabulation the perfect state which is the Edenic state possessed by the ancestor of mankind, Adam, the reliving and experiencing the purity of faith of the prophet Abraham, may peace be upon them, and other factors of this kind.

As for the religious tax, *zakāh*, to which certain other kinds of religious tax such as *khums* have been added in Ja'farī Law, and also as far as booty of war is concerned in certain schools of Sunni Law, these again have been treated separately often in books, which bring out the great economic and social significance of the religious tax. Such works also mention what kind of goods have to be taxed, how they should be taxed, the difference between the *zakāh*, the religious tax, and other forms of taxation including those which are incumbent upon the people of the Book who are protected by Muslims and who pay a certain amount of tax for the protection that they receive from the Islamic government under which they live.

As far as the *jihād* is concerned, not all schools of *Sharī'ah* have devoted separate sections to the institution of *jihād*, but the discussion has always been carried out extensively concerning conditions under which an external *jihād* should be declared. Most jurists believe that when the existence of the Islamic community or borders of the Islamic world are in danger, *jihād* should be declared and also that constant *jihād* should be carried out against forces of evil. Altogether the aspect of the *'ibādāt* or worship in the *Sharī'ah* make clear both the external and internal conditions necessary for worship to be carried out in such a way as to be acceptable to Allah according to the norms which He Himself has constituted for human beings through the teachings of the Noble Quran and the norm established by the Blessed Prophet.

Morality and Rights

Closely connected to this aspect of the *Sharī'ah* is the question of morality. In Islam morality is not an abstract ideal. To be good, generous or charitable are of course emphasized but these virtues are defined in a more concrete and definite sense in the *Sharī'ah* itself. All principles of ethical action and all aspects of morality are contained, in principle, in the Quran, but they are made concrete through the teachings of the *Sharī'ah* One learns through the *Sharī'ah* how a general moral principle such as justice is to be applied in concrete human actions. In Islam man does not himself decide what is just or generous but relies upon God's injunctions while there is also an important role for the conscience which Allah has placed within the being of each person. The norms are determined by the *Sharī'ah* for certain basic actions while in each type of human activity room is left for man to apply the Islamic ethical teachings according to the dictates of his conscience. There is, therefore, nothing mechanical or blindfolded in Islamic ethics as some have claimed. Islam does provide concrete directives for man to follow but also leaves a vast area of human life open for man to apply Islamic moral principles as a servant of Allah bestowed with conscience,*'aql*, and the sense of discernment.

The Muslim has duties which he must perform toward Allah, others towards himself, his family, his immediate society, the larger society embracing ultimately the *ummah* or the whole of the Islamic community, and beyond that towards even the whole of humanity and finally the whole of the created order. There are in the *Sharī'ah* clear teachings concerning these duties. What are the rights of Allah, the *ḥuqūq Allāh*? They include most of all His possession of our soul and therefore the need for us to dedicate our lives and the fruits of our actions to Him. This question is discussed in various ways either directly or indirectly in works on the *Sharī'ah* and of course also in the commentaries on the Quran from which this knowledge emanates.

Man has no rights of his own; rights are given to him by Allah when he fulfills the obligations that he has towards Him and these obligations, as mentioned before, are based on the fact that man has accepted the covenant (*mīthāq*) with Allah. By virtue of this covenant man has been given the powers, faculties and possibilities which are to be found in the human state but the duties that the man has towards Allah have also been defined for him. These duties include of course bearing witness to Allah's Oneness, carrying out the acts of worship and acting as Allah's vicegerent on earth. Likewise, man has duties towards himself. He must keep his body healthy; hence he has no right to commit suicide. He must care for his immortal soul and think constantly of his salvation. He must accept the burden of his human state, that is, that he is Allah's vicegerent on earth and must accept all the gifts that Allah has given to him as a human being.

Then man has certain duties towards his family. Islam mentions over and over again the importance of the family and respect for parents, both the father and the mother, as well as the more extended family which Islam made the central unit of society rather than the tribe or other pre-Islamic social units which had existed not only in Arabia but elsewhere. The teachings about one's duties towards one's parents, children, siblings and the larger family are of course, contained in the Quran and *Ḥadīth* but they have become formalized in legal form in the *Sharī'ah*. Parts of these duties are economic, dealing with inheritance and the like, but they also include taking care of the family, being kind to its members and protecting them.

Likewise, man has a duty towards his immediate society, starting with the neighborhood. Traditional Islamic society creates a very strong sense of neighborhood identity because a man's immediate society is what he feels and touches at all times. Personal contact with the neighborhood is the basis from which there grows an awareness of the larger society embracing the whole of the *ummah*. And then beyond Islamic society there is the responsibility of man to the whole of humanity. The *Sharī'ah* promulgates teachings concerning how to deal with other human beings although much of the non-legal aspects of the relation with followers of other religions is discussed not so much in the texts of the *Sharī'ah* but in other forms of Islamic thought to which we shall turn later.

Finally as far as the created order is concerned, there are laws in the *Sharī'ah* which deal with how human beings should deal with animals, plants, water and earth, with Allah's creation in general. Man is instructed to care for them and to accept their right to existence along with man's own. The *Sharī'ah* does not accept blind domination and use of other creatures without man thinking of their rights and the duties that he also has towards them.

Transactions

A major aspect of the *Sharī'ah* concerns social, economic and political teaching and is usually categorized as "transactions" (*mu'āmalāt*) although sometimes the political aspect of the *Sharī'ah* is not discussed explicitly in this context. Nevertheless, for our discussion in this book the social, political and economic aspects can be brought together as constituting the second part of the *Sharī'ah* as distinct from the first which deals basically with various aspects of worship.

Society

Islam envisages a society in which close relationships exist between its members based on the one hand upon servitude *vis-à-vis* Allah and, on the other hand upon a close bond of brotherhood and sisterhood among the members of that society. The concept of brotherhood or *ukhuwwah* in Arabic is so strong that in traditional Islamic society usually men address each other as *akh* or *akhī* meaning brother or my brother and likewise women use the term sister, emphasizing the idea of a family that in a sense embraces the whole of the Islamic world.

One might say, in fact, that the social reality of Islamic society, as envisaged in the Quran and *Ḥadīth* and as realized in traditional Islamic society to a great extent but not perfectly, because everything in this world is imperfect, is based on two poles or realities: the first being the Islamic peoples, the *ummah*, the vast and therefore impalpable Islamic world which no one sees in its fullness but which is experienced inwardly and spiritually, and secondly, the immediate family. One might say that these two poles, that of the *ummah* and that of the immediate family, comprise the most salient social reality of a veritable Islamic society. It is these two poles around which the social fabric is woven.

There are, of course, many other social units within Islamic society such as tribes, clans, members of townships and quarters within the city, guilds, professional groups, military associations, spiritual (Sufi) orders and the like. These are all without doubt of great importance. Some of them such as the tribal bond were opposed by the universal perspective of Islam. Others such as professional groups or spiritual orders have had a strong religious basis within the Islamic tradition itself. But from a social point of view all of these associations are secondary in comparison with the whole of the Islamic world, or the reality of the *ummah*, on the one hand and the family on the other.

Islam envisages humanity not on the basis of race, ethnic grouping or linguistic divisions but on the foundation of attachment to a religion. Therefore, from the Islamic point of view, the most important characteristic of a human collectivity is not whether its members are white, black or yellow, or are Arabs, Persians or Russians each speaking his or her own language, but whether they are Muslims, Christians, Jews, Zoroastrians etc. belonging to a particular *ummah*, such as the *ummah* of Christ the *ummah* of Moses the *ummah* of the Prophet, etc. Even in Islamic eschatology, the resurrection before Allah is seen in terms of each humanity being represented by and standing around the prophet who is the founder of the religion followed by that humanity. When we say *ummah*, in the Islamic context, we usually mean the Islamic *ummah*, but it must be remembered that there are other *ummahs* in the world if the followers of the other religions are seen from the Islamic point of view which looks upon its followers and those of other religions as members of various *ummahs*.

This concern with the *ummah* has been an overriding reality for Muslims although, except for during the early history of Islam, this reality has never been translated into a single political entity. Despite political divisions over the centuries, however, the reality of the *ummah* has remained and there is an invisible bond which unites all Islamic peoples throughout the world whether they be Arabs or Persians, Malays or Chinese, whether they be white or black, whether they live in Africa, Asia, Europe or America. It is a bond based upon the idea of brotherhood and sisterhood which is contained in the Arabic word *ukhuwwah*.

The Family

As far as the family, the other pole of Islamic social reality, is concerned, Islam has placed the greatest emphasis upon its preservation. As already mentioned, by family in this context is not meant the atomized modern family comprised of the husband, wife and their immediate children but the extended family which includes usually the grand-parents and often aunts, uncles and their children extending a kind of network around the individual with which the individual identifies himself or herself. Within this Islamic social and family pattern, respect for parents plays a most important role. The Quran calls upon Muslims to be respectful to their parents as in the verse "*Worship none but Allah: Treat with kindness your parents and kindred, and orphans and those in need*" (II:83). Also the preservation of relationships within the family or what is called the relationship of wombs, that is relation between those who are born from the same womb or related through various blood relationships (*ṣilat al-arḥām* in Arabic), has been emphasized so much that it is considered a religious duty for individual Muslim men and women to visit their family members, to be close to them, and to preserve family bonds.

Also the emphasis upon marriage and the discouragement of celibacy is related to a large extent to the integrating function that the family performs in Islamic society. One of the reasons for the existence of polygamy, which Islam permits under certain conditions, is to enable women whose husbands have died in wars or have been lost in other natural calamities or other women who cannot find a husband in a monogamous relationship, to become integrated into a family structure. The realistic perspective of Islam, basing itself upon the significance of the family, permits in certain cases polygamy where either the economic necessity or the social reality have made the integration of single women into a family structure impossible in any other way. Because of the nature of human society usually many more men die in wars and calamities and also they have a shorter life span than women. Since Islam emphasizes the religious significance of marriage to the extent that a *ḥadīth* of the prophet asserts,"marriage is half of religion," and since there is a greater number of women than men at most times, permission is given to practice polygamy under the condition that men be just and have the means of supporting their wives.

It is interesting to note in this case that in contrast to let us say traditional Catholicism where divorce is forbidden, Islam does permit divorce. A *ḥadīth* of the Prophet asserts that of all acts permitted by

Allah that which He dislikes most is divorce. The *Sharīʻah* allows divorce under conditions when union between a man and a woman is no longer possible. When men and women find themselves in a hopeless situation and there is no way for them to continue their marriage, then they can become divorced and part ways. Despite this teaching, however, the act of divorce has never been carried out in the Islamic world to the same extent as in the modern West despite its Christian background. Consequently even the fact that divorce has been permitted by Islam does not mean that family bonds are thereby weakened.

To understand fully the Islamic teachings about society, it is important to pay attention to the central role they give to the family, to the respect for parents, especially to the mother, to the extent that a *ḥadīth* says, "Heaven lies under the feet of mothers." Islam gives a central role also to the father who is at once the patriarch, the vicegerent and the imam of the family, and the religious pole around which the family rotates so that often the acts of prayer and other acts of worship are led within the family by him. It is also important to remember the responsibility to the other members of the family, the fact that the larger family must take care of those who have become incapacitated or fallen into misfortune such as widows or orphans. It is significant how much Islam emphasizes these realities and it is because of these teachings of Islam that the fabric of the family has survived to this day despite all of the transformations which have taken place in many parts of the Islamic world as a result of the advent of modernism during the last two centuries.

The teachings of Islam, socially speaking, also of course involve individuals who for one reason or another have been deprived of either the social or the economic support that is needed for a healthy individual to survive and to function in society. Islam emphasizes very much the care of orphans. The Quran asserts over and over again the great virtue of being kind to orphans and taking care of them, the Prophet himself having been an orphan brought up by his grandfather and uncle. Secondly, the great importance of feeding the poor, caring for the neighbor and being aware of the needs of all members of society are so much emphasized that according to a *ḥadīth* all human beings or children of Adam are like the limbs of a single body. This teaching has been immortalized in the Persian language in the famous poem of Saʻdī who says,

All children of Adam are members of a single body,

For at the moment of creation they were made of a single substance.
If fate were to cause pain for a single member,
All the other members would become restless because of this pain.

There are always callous individuals in every society and these teachings may not have been carried out fully everywhere in the history of Islam but they constitute very important and central teachings of Islam as far as society is concerned. In fact what is amazing is not that certain individuals have refused to follow such teachings but that so many people have followed them, that through the history of Islam there have been so many orphanages and houses for the poor which have functioned solely upon the contributions of individuals and their charity and respect for the teachings of Islam as far as the poor and the deprived are concerned.

Likewise, the care for the neighbor, and the need to heed and respect the rights of the neighbor have been so strong traditionally that a bond of belonging in the neighborhood and of considering the neighborhood as a kind of second family, developed gradually in most Islamic cities to the extent that allegiance to a town or, in bigger cities, to a particular quarter of the town became almost a religious allegiance with certain moral virtues existing in being able to defend the order, property and life of the individuals in one's quarter of the city. During the history of Islam, in fact, groups of men came forward who were of great moral virtue and who saw to it that the life and belongings of all members of the particular quarter of the city to which they belonged could be protected and that women could walk about at different times of day and night without being molested. It is amazing how the fear of Allah and respect for His Laws have been so strong in Islamic society that even to this day, despite the weakening of some of the traditional social bonds in many Islamic cities, there is a greater sense of security for people to walk around at night even in the poorest quarters of an Islamic city than in most cities in the Western world where people might be much wealthier and where there seems to be much less cause for theft and other acts of aggression.

The Islamic teachings about the ideal society are contained in the *Sharī'ah*. Injunctions have been provided for these teachings to be put into practice and the breaking of these practices have also been made punishable by law. Some of these practices are, of course, related solely to moral principles such as kindness to one's neighbor, while others such as laws forbidding theft, intrusion upon the rights of the neighbor or molesting people in the street are punishable according to the provisions of the *Sharī'ah* if broken. The most important preventive and that which has enabled these teachings concerning society to take root, however, has not been so much the presence of a physical force in the form of a police (*muḥtasib* or *shurṭah*) or other law enforcement agencies but the constant awareness of the Presence of Allah, His Might, His Power and His Judgment over all human actions.

Economics

As far as the economic teachings of Islam are concerned, they are intertwined, both in the Quran and *Ḥadīth* and in the actual practices which grew from them throughout the history of Islamic society, with the social teachings. The family itself has acted as an economic protection for its members while at the same time being a social reality for them. And the *ummah* itself has also been an extremely important economic reality in the sense that most of the bartering, trading, and economic transactions which took place throughout the history of Islam was done among various parts of the Islamic world, *dār al-islām*. Not that trade was not carried out with non-Muslims, but most trading activity was among Muslims and there has always been a great deal of virtue attached to economic practices within the *ummah*. Also certain rites, especially the *ḥajj*, which brought Muslims from all over the Islamic world to the noble city of Makkah facilitated economic exchange as well as a kind of exchange of *barakah* of various parts of the Islamic world which accompanied the exchange of goods.

Islamic economic teachings are always related to ethics and are based most of all on justice, justice in preventing excessive amassing of wealth in society to the detriment of a particular class or group of people, justice in relating the amassing of wealth to work and justice in preventing the misuse of capital and income. The complicated economic teachings of Islam are based on several basic principles which have been debated a great deal over the centuries as far as their applications are concerned, but the principles have been accepted more or less by all the major jurists throughout the history of the Islamic world. The first and foremost principle concerns property which ultimately belongs to God (*al-mulku li'Llāh*). But at the same time, man being God's vicegerent on earth, has been given by virtue of that status the right of private property. This means that although private property is a privilege given by Allah to individual human beings, at the same time it is a sacred right given by Allah which therefore, cannot be taken away by any government or social group save in exceptional cases and only on the basis of the laws drawn from the teachings of the *Sharī'ah.*

Secondly, there is the principle of the relationship between one's efforts and the amassing of wealth and the importance of participating in the risk of losing one's wealth as well as increasing it in any economic transaction. That is why *ribā'* or interest is forbidden in Islamic Law on the basis of the very clear verses of the Quran such as "*Those who devour usury will not stand except as stands one whom the Evil One by his touch hath driven to madness. That is because they say: 'Trade is like usury' but Allah hath permitted trade and forbidden usury*" (II: 275). There are also *ḥadīths* which deal with this subject. Consequently, Muslim jurists throughout the centuries have banned *ribā'*. This injunction applies not only to usury, that is, charging very high interest rates, but to interest at any rate based on receiving a sum of capital in which there is no risk of loss, whereas if one were to use capital to buy goods and sell them, it would be acceptable even if one were to make a great fortune.

Another important characteristic of Islamic economics is immediate-human relationships in economic life. Throughout the history of Islam, economic life was always related to individual and personal encounters, and based upon mutual trust in human encounters. The dehumanization of the economic life which characterizes so much of the modern world was totally absent from traditional Islamic practices. The bazaar, in which most of the economic activity of the Islamic world took place, has always been and remains to some extent even to this day a place where the sense of trust, *amānah,* of direct human relationship, of virtue, of being able to have human contacts dominate over the completely impersonal and indifferent institutions which vie with each other in the modern economic system of the modern world in which the individual and small business are more or less crushed by larger units marked by impersonalization and indifference to individual human concerns and needs.

Traditional economic activity in the Islamic world has often been based on an individual or family and the family unit and the economic unit have often gone hand in hand and enhanced each other. Also many of the family virtues which have already been mentioned have also come into play as far as the economic life of society is concerned. There has always been the human dimension and awareness of the Presence of Allah and economics has never been divorced from ethics. The Islamic economic philosophy has always emphasized the importance of effort, of making a living, of opposition to laziness, of combining trust in Allah (*tawakkul*) with *jahd* or effort, and seeing it as a religious duty to provide livelihood for oneself and one's family. Work in its economic aspect has always been considered as being related to religious duty and has never been divorced from prayer. There are many teachings based upon the *Ḥadīth* and commentaries upon the text of the Quran which have brought this truth out over the centuries. These sources have emphasized that it is as much a man's duty to perform his five daily prayers as to use his efforts to make a living. That is why a religious element has been introduced into practically all aspects of traditional Islamic economic life and this fact has given this life a moral and spiritual meaning very different from that of economic activity in the modern world. Something of this ethos survives to this day even in the modern parts of the Islamic world but of course, it has become much more dilute as the specific Islamic injunctions about economic life have become eclipsed in many regions and areas of the Islamic world.

POLITICS

Finally, as far as the political teachings of Islam are concerned, it seems that Allah saw in His Wisdom not to formulate explicitly in the Quran the injunctions for the establishment of a single political institution which would then be followed without change over the centuries. Nevertheless, certain very important principles of political rule have been established such as the principle that the real ruler of the universe is Allah and that all power ultimately belongs to Him. Secondly, the Prophet of Islam, as the founder of the first Islamic society, was also the first ruler and therefore the norm for later generations in political matters. He was in a sense a prophet-king, not only a religious leader but also the ruler over a human society. Thirdly, as a consequence, political power has never been divorced from religion in Islam and Islam in contrast to Christianity has not separated the kingdom of God and the kingdom of Caesar from each other. Political rule in Islamic society, whatever form it might take, also has an important religious dimension. Religion and politics have always been related to each other throughout Islamic history except for the modern period when many countries in the Islamic world began to emulate the Western ideas which had emanated from the French and in certain cases the Russian Revolution. Even in such cases, however, politics has never become totally divorced from religion.

The traditional Islamic teachings about politics always try to go back to the model of the Prophet and seek to relate the rule of human society to the religious teachings drawn from the Quran. That is why the majority of Muslims who came to be known as Sunnis developed the institution of the *khilāfah* or caliphate starting with Abū Bakr, the first Caliph and going through the four *khulafā' rāshidūn* or "the Rightly-Guided Caliphs," consisting of Abū Bakr, 'Umar, 'Uthmān and 'Alī. All of these men were the representatives of the Prophet within the Islamic community not as prophets or legislators nor as men who received the Word of Allah which is the Quran and His Laws, but as rulers of the Islamic community. In contrast the smaller minority Shi'ites believe that rule should belong to the Imams who were descendants of the Prophet. In either case political rule, according to the Islamic teachings, is inseparable from religion and derives its legitimacy from it.

As to how the caliphate and other political institutions took shape, after the *khulafā' rāshidūn*, the major Islamic caliphates, namely, the Umayyad, and the 'Abbāsid came into being both of which made use in one way or another of the hereditary principle. But at the same time the religious character of the institution was very strongly preserved in the sense that the ruler was always duty bound to protect the injunctions of Islam and the *Sharī'ah*. During the later history of Islam, the caliphate and the sultanate became combined, one possessing the legitimate authority relating to the vicegerency of the ruling function of the Prophet, and the other the military and actual political power which dominated over society. Therefore, throughout the history of Islam, many different forms of rule and political institutions were created, whether it was the caliphate, the sultanate or the amirate, until in the fourteenth/twentieth century when, under the impact of European ideas, various forms of republics and secular governments appeared upon the scene.

What is important from the Islamic point of view is that the institution of rule must have a religious character, that legitimacy ultimately comes from Allah Who is the ultimate Ruler; and since the Prophet is the Prophet of Allah, the principles of rule come indirectly from the Prophet and are based upon his model. There are of course, also other principles which are very important, mentioned in the Quran and the *Ḥadīth*, such as the principle of consultation, that is, the importance of consulting with the leaders, elders and scholars of Islamic society, of not being autocratic and of not forgetting of course, Allah's teachings concerning justice and mercy. The early Rightly-Guided Caliphs provided many examples of the application of these principles as can be seen in the famous letter of 'Alī to Mālik al-Ashtar who had become the governor of Egypt. In his letter 'Alī advises him as follows:

> *In the Name of Allah, the Compassionate, the Merciful*
>
> This is what Allah's servant 'Alī, Amīr al-mu'minīn, has ordered Mālik ibn al-Ḥārith al-Ashtar in his instrument (of appointment) for him when he made him Governor of Egypt for the collection of its revenues, fighting against its enemies, seeking the good of its people and making its cities prosperous.
>
> He has ordered him to fear Allah, to prefer obedience to Him, and to follow what He has commanded in His Book (Quran) out of His obligatory and elective commands, without following which one cannot achieve virtue, nor (can one) be evil save by opposing them and ignoring them, and to help Allah the Glorified, with his heart, hand and tongue, because Allah, whose name is Sublime, takes the responsibility for helping him who helps Him, and for protecting him who gives Him support. He also orders him to break his heart off from passions and to restrain it at the time of their increase, because the heart leads towards evil unless Allah has mercy.
>
> **The Qualifications of a Governor and his Responsibilities**
>
> Then, know O Mālik that I have sent you to an area where there have been governments before you, both just as well as oppressive. People will now watch your dealings as you used to watch the dealings of the rulers before you, and they (people) will criticize you as you criticized them (rulers). Surely, the virtuous are known by the reputation that Allah circulates for them through the tongues of His creatures. Therefore, the best collection with you should be the collection of good deeds. So, control your passions and check your heart from doing what is not lawful for you, because checking the heart means detaining it just half way between what it likes and dislikes.

Habituate your heart to mercy for the subjects and to affection and kindess for them. Do not stand over them like greedy beasts who feel it is enough to devour them since they are of two kinds, either your brother in religion or one like you in creation. They will commit slips and encounter mistakes. They may act wrongly, willfully or by neglect. So, extend to them your forgiveness and pardon, in the same way as you would like Allah to extend His forgiveness and pardon to you, because you are over them and your responsible Commander (Imam) is over you while Allah is over him who has appointed you. He (Allah) has sought you to manage their affairs and has tried you through them.

Do not set yourself to fight Allah because you have no power before His power and you cannot do without His pardon and mercy. Do not repent of forgiving or of being merciful in punishing. Do not act hastily during anger if you can find a way out of it. Do not say: "I have been given authority, I should be obeyed when I order," because it engenders confusion in the heart, weakens the religion and takes one near ruin. If the authority in which you are placed produces pride or vanity in you then look at the greatness of the realm of Allah over you and His might the like of which might you do not even possess over yourself. This will curb your haughtiness, cure you of your high temper and bring back to you your wisdom which had gone away from you.

Beware of comparing yourself to Allah in His greatness or likening yourself to Him in His power, for Allah humiliates every claimant of power and disgraces every one who is haughty.

Do justice for Allah and do justice towards the people, as against yourself, your near ones and those of your subjects for whom you have a liking, because if you do not do so you will be oppressive, and when a person oppresses the creatures of Allah then, instead of His creatures, Allah becomes his opponent, and when Allah is the opponent of a person He tramples his plea; and he will remain in the position of being at war with Allah until he gives it up and repents. Nothing is more inductive of the reversal of Allah's bounty or for the hastening of His retribution than continuance in oppression, because Allah hears the prayer of the oppressed and is on the look out for the oppressors. [1]

Ultimately one might say that the most important political teaching of Islam is that Islamic society should be ruled by Divine Law and by forms which issue from the teachings of the Quran and *Ḥadīth*. Islam is a nomocracy, that is a system of rule by Divine Law; consequently that form of government has been accepted over the centuries which has been able to protect the *Sharīʿah* and see to it that it is promulgated and followed and which has been able to protect society and its borders from intrusions and attacks from both without and within. Of course, there have been many wars even among Muslims, between various dynasties and states. This has been part and parcel of human history whether one is concerned with the Islamic, Christian, Jewish, Zoroastrian, Hindu or any other world. But within the Islamic world it should be noted that these local battles between this and that dynasty, tribe or other group have always remained subservient to the supremacy of the rule of the *Sharī'ah*. Until modern times neither side of any battle ever claimed to be any less an upholder of the teachings of Islam than the other. Although internecine wars took place here and there, they did not really touch upon the deeper question of rule over society which was that of Allah's Law, the major exception being the Mongol invasion which was carried out by the powerful Chengiz-Khan and his army and which destroyed a great deal of the fabric of the eastern lands of the Islamic world. The second exception is, of course, the modern invasion by the West of the Islamic world, an invasion whose effect upon the destruction of many of the traditional legal institutions and practices of Islam is even greater than that of the Mongol onslaught.

Putting those invasions and exceptional periods of Islamic history aside, one can say that all the different political forms developed in the history of Islam were Islamic in the sense that they protected the teachings of the Quran and *Ḥadīth* and promulgated the Divine Law although there were of course individual exceptions among rulers. And despite the shortcomings of many rulers, their formal protection of the Law was and remains the goal of the political teachings of Islam which is to create a nomocratic society where men and women can live according to Allah's Will as contained in the *Sharī'ah* and according to those virtues which have been manifested most fully in the exemplary life of the Prophet who is the model for both individual human life and rule over the Islamic community.

NOTE

1. *Nahj al-Balāghah* (*Peak of Eloquence*), trans. by S. A. Reza, Elmhurst, NY, 1984, pp. 534-535.

Chapter 4
Islamic Spirituality and Thought

Islam is not only a religion, but also the basis of a vast civilization spreading from the Atlantic to the Pacific and embracing the lives of many ethnic groups including Arabs, Persians, Indo-Pakistanis, Malays, Chinese, Blacks, Turks and many other peoples. This great civilization has produced numerous spiritual movements, schools of thought, theology, philosophy and the sciences; its tradition is among the richest of any of the great civilizations of the world in the domain of intellectual activity. In order to understand fully the impact of the Islamic religion upon the domain of thought and the intellectual fruit of the tree which grew from the soil of the Islamic religion and the Quranic revelation, it is important to turn briefly to these various schools. It is necessary to realize that over the centuries the great Muslim thinkers provided for each generation the means with which they could think, confront the world about them and solve, in the light of the teachings of the Noble Quran and the *Sunnah*, the problems of both a religious nature and those pertaining to this world.

Islamic Spirituality

As far as Islamic spirituality is concerned, it issues, of course, directly from the Quran and the *Sunnah* of the Blerssed Prophet. It is based on the inner meaning of the verses of the Word of God and the practices of the Prophet which pertain to the inner life. During the history of Islam, this aspect of the Islamic tradition came to be known as *al-ṭarīqah ila'Llāh*, literally the path towards God, and later on, some time in the second Islamic century, by the name of Sufism, although Islamic spirituality is also to be found in various forms outside of organized Sufism. The path to God was created from above by God Himself so that human beings who practiced the *Sharī'ah* and were devout Muslims but who at the same time wanted to cultivate inner virtues, to practice religion at its deepest level and to conform fully to the *Sunnah* of the Prophet and the inner meaning of their faith would be able to do so.

The Islamic religion has often been divided into *al-islām, al-īmān,* and *al-iḥsān. Al-iḥsān* or virtue which also means the beauty of the soul is in fact the goal of the *ṭarīqah* and throughout the centuries those who have followed this path have tried to cultivate *iḥsān*. Of course, there have been through the ages certain people who have claimed to follow Sufism but who have fallen away from the true path, from the true *Sunnah* of the Prophet and the teachings of the Quran. Their number has, however, been small in comparison with the vast number of Sufis who have remained faithful to the deepest teachings of Islam and who have played a central role in the history of Islam precisely because they have attached themselves to the very roots of the Islamic revelation.

The importance of the *ṭuruq* (plural of *ṭarīqāh*) in the history of Islam cannot be exaggerated. The revival of Islamic society from within over the centuries has usually been accomplished by the people who have followed the spiritual path, by the great Sufis such as Shaykh 'Abd al-Qādir al-Jīlānī or Abū Ḥāmid Muḥammad al-Ghazzālī or later Shaykh Aḥmad Sirhindī in India and many others. Even the Ḥanbalī jurist and reformer Ibn Taymiyyah was a member of the Qādiriyyah Order. The followers of the spiritual path have also played a very important role in the spread of Islam. Islam spread among the Persians, across North Africa and into Spain through the Arab armies. Islam did not, however, spread eastward from Persia into the vast subcontinent of India including what is today Pakistan, India and Bangladesh as well as further east into China and the Indonesian-Malay world, through Arab armies but by examples of Sufi saints, men of great piety, who brought Islam to those lands and taught it through example. Likewise, among the Blacks of Africa, we see before our very eyes during the last century and this century the spread of Islam especially into West Africa, into such a country as Senegal, mostly through the Tijāniyyah and the Qādiriyyah Orders. The same is true of the Turks who first embraced Islam through the influence of Sufism; their first great poet saints like Yunus Emre were also eminent Sufis who spread the inner teachings of Islam among Turkish speaking people. Furthermore, throughout the history of the Ottoman world the *ṭuruq* played a very important role in many walks of life.

The followers of the path also had an important share in the intellectual defense of Islam because they had access to the highest metaphysical truths of the Islamic tradition. We see many instances throughout the history of Islam in which it was the Sufis, the followers of the *ṭarīqah*, who had to defend the tenets of the faith. Even the well-known eastern Islamic philosophers such as al-Fārābī or Ibn Sīnā and also the philosophers in Spain such as Ibn Masarrah, Ibn Bājjah and Ibn Ṭufayl were all attracted to Sufism. Some of the greatest scientists of the Islamic world were likewise attracted or were members of Sufi orders, such figures as Naṣīr al-Dīn al-Ṭūsī and Ibn Bannā' al-Marrākushī.

Likewise, in the world of art the role of the followers of the path in all kinds of arts ranging from calligraphy to architecture to poetry and literature is well known. The most universal forms of literature, both Arabic and Persian, were composed by Sufi poets and the most beautiful lines of calligraphy in the history of Islam were created by calligraphers who were associated with Sufism. Finally, in Islam's confrontation with other religions, whether it was Christianity and Judaism in the Western lands of Islam or Buddhism, Hinduism and Zoroastrianism in the East, it was most of all the Sufi thinkers who provided an Islamic response to the presence of these religions and who tried to create bridges of understanding. They had a basic role to play in both the preservation of the Islamic tradition and the spread of Islam in lands beyond its original borders.

Until the second Islamic century, the followers of the path who were slowly beginning to become known as Sufis would gather around individual figures, usually men of great eminence who were spiritual teachers and who would try to live simply and ascetically to avoid the luxury which had engulfed the Islamic community during the late Umayyad and early 'Abbāsid periods. Gradually these circles of teaching became more organized and by the third Islamic century, in the city of Baghdad under the tutelage of al-Junayd, the famous Sufi of that period, Sufi circles became more formalized. It was not until two centuries later that these circles became transformed into Sufi orders or *ṭuruq*, usually named after their founders like 'Abd al-Qādir al-Jīlānī who gave his name to the Qādiriyyah Order whose followers exist today all the way from the southern Philippines to Morocco or Shaykh Aḥmad al-Rifā'ī, the founder of the Rifā'iyyah Order. Some of these orders remained local while others like the Qādiriyyah spread very widely throughout the length and breadth of the Islamic world.

During later centuries many important Sufi orders arose throughout the Islamic world. Among the most famous are the Shādhiliyyah Order founded by Shaykh Abu'l-Ḥasan al-Shādhilī which has had especially great influence in the Arab world all the way from Morocco to Syria and Egypt; the Naqshbandiyyah Order, of Persian origin, which had its center in Afghanistan and what is today called Central Asia and which spread rapidly into India (the Order survives to this day as a powerful religious and even political element and is most responsible for the preservation of Islam in those Muslim lands which were until recently part of the Soviet Union); and the Mawlawiyyah Order named after Mawlānā Jalāl al-Dīn Rūmī, the famous Persian poet. This Order, having been especially important in the Ottoman empire, still survives in Turkey despite its ban by Kamal Ataturk after the destruction of the Ottomans. Other major orders include the Tijāniyyah Order in North Africa which started from Morocco and spread south among the Blacks and is responsible to a large extent for the spread of Islam in West Africa; the Ni'matullāhī Order which is the most popular order in Iran, with important offshoots in India and many other orders which have survived over the centuries and are still prominent today. Other orders had a greater following in earlier centuries but today have become limited in number, for example the Kubrawiyyah Order which was once widespread in Khurasan, Central Asia, Pakistan and certain areas of India but which now has become more limited in number but is still important from the point of view of its historical influence.

Be that as it may, the Sufi orders have been able over the centuries to preserve the original instructions of the Prophet concerning inner purity, the following of the *Sunnah*, the cultivation of the virtues within the human soul, the embellishment of man's being with honesty, sincerity and humility and the attempt to understand the inner meaning of the faith and of the teachings of Islam, and to realize *al-tawḥīd* in its ultimate sense. Many of the Sufis have also been great teachers of the *Sharī'ah* over the centuries. Others have been great theologians and yet others even men of action. During the last century when Muslims were subjugated by the colonial powers, in many parts of the Islamic world such as North Africa, the Northwestern provinces of India and Caucasia the resistance against the French, British and Russians came from various Sufi figures such as the Algerian Amīr 'Abd al-Qādir al-Jazā'irī, the famous Moroccan fighter 'Abd al-Karīm or in the case of Caucasia Ishmael who fought so valiantly against the Czarist armies. These men were all followers of Sufism who were at the same time great *mujāhids* and warriors in the cause of Islam. Now, there is no doubt that some spurious practices also entered into certain Sufi orders which became decadent especially during the last two hundred years, but the living Sufi orders have always been able to revive themselves and to this day they continue to play a central role in the intellectual and spiritual life of Islam.

Islamic Theology (*Kalām*)

Besides the very diverse and rich spiritual tradition associated with Sufism within Islam, Islam has also produced extensive and variegated forms of theology which came to be known in Islamic thought as *kalām*. It is said that this term refers to the understanding of the Word of God (*kalām Allāh*) or the Quran and that the founder of this form of Islamic thought was 'Alī ibn Abī Ṭālib who was thus considered as the first *mutakallim* or scholar of *kalām*. There is no doubt that the discussions of *kalām* go back to the very early Islamic community.

After the death of the Prophet of Islam, the early community was faced with certain questions which the inquiring human mind obviously poses when confronted with the verities of religion. For example, who is saved? Is it the man who does good works or is it the man who has faith? Or, what kind of sin one must commit before one is no longer considered to be a Muslim? Another set of questions which faced the Islamic community concerned the nature of the Quran. Is the Quran created or uncreated? Since the Quran is the Word of God, if one believes that it is created, then one must accept that the Word of God changes, therefore, His Attributes change. Or is it permanent and eternal in which case how is it that we have the actual Quran which is heard and read and which came into the world at a particular time? Another set of questions concern the Names and Attributes of God. It is said in the Quran "*the Hand of God is above their hand*" (XLVIII:10) or "*God is the Hearer and the Seer*" (XXXI:28). Now how does God see, how does God hear? How can God have a hand since the Quran also asserts that He is above everything, that "there is nothing like unto Him?" And yet another set of questions involved the knowledge of God. Do we know God through seeing Him? Is it possible to have a vision of God? Is that vision inward or outward? Are we able to see God on the Day of Judgment, and if so, does God have a form?

All of these questions, some of which were directly theological and others also had important political implications, continued to engage the early Islamic community during the first century of Islamic history. These debates were accentuated by the presence of other religions in the midst of Muslims, religions whose followers had debated similar issues for many centuries, these religious communities consisting of Christians, Jews, Zoroastrians, Manichaeans and even Sabaeans. Among these groups the Christians were especially important from this point of view because they had already developed over the centuries an elaborate theology of their own. They had all kinds of arguments drawn from Greek philosophy and logic to defend their doctrine of Divinity or to try to explain their belief in incarnation and many other important aspects of Christianity. The Muslims had no choice but to try to formulate their own theology both as a result of the challenge of Christian, Jewish, Zoroastrian and Manichaean thinkers, philosophers and theologians, and also because of the internal need of the Islamic community. Consequently, there developed what we call formal *kalām*.

The Mu'tazilites

The great figure from whose teachings early *kalām* developed is Ḥasan al-Baṣrī, one of the outstanding scholars of *Ḥadīth* who lived from the first generation of Islam, that is, the year 21 when he was born, until nearly the end of the Umayyad period, that is, the year 110 when he died. During his long life, he taught *Ḥadīth* and *tafsīr* of the Quran to several generations of Muslims. He is one of the early pillars of the science of *Ḥadīth*, and one of the great patriarchs of early Sufism. Ḥasan al-Baṣrī also taught what came to be known later as *kalām*, that is, doctrines pertaining to such questions as those which have been mentioned above. In fact, it was one of his students, Wāṣil ibn 'Aṭā', who "separated" (*i'tazala*) himself from the teachings of Ḥasan and established a school that is called Mu'tazilite, from *al-mu'tazilah* in Arabic. This school became known for five principles which its various adherents held: First of all, Divine Unity (*al-tawḥīd*); secondly, Divine Justice (*al-'adl*); thirdly, reward and retribution (*al-wa'd wa'l-wa'īd*); fourthly, station between two stations (*al-manzil bayn manzilatayn*); and fifthly, commanding the good and forbidding the iniquitous (*al-amr bi'l-ma'ruf wa'l-nahy 'an al-munkar*).

These five principles unite several diverse schools of the Mu'tazilites connected with Basra and Baghdad. But despite this diversity, the Mu'tazilites came to be distinguished by their attachments to these five points, by the fact that they relied upon the use of reason in the interpretation of religion and by their emphasis upon free will and the responsibility of man in carrying out his actions.

Some of the great Mu'tazilite thinkers of early centuries were al-Naẓẓām, Abu'l-Hudhayl al-'Allāf, al-Jāḥiẓ, the famous literary figure, and al-Bishr. These men wrote the first works of speculative theology in Islam. Some of them even turned to the study of nature and began to develop the doctrine of atomism (*juz' lā yatajazzā*) which was to become part and parcel of *kalām* thought in later centuries.

During the caliphate of al-Ma'mūn, the Mu'tazilites were at the height of their power in Baghdad. The caliphate supported them openly and the great Imam Aḥmad ibn Ḥanbal, who was opposed to the Mu'tazilites, was even imprisoned for a while because of his opposition to them. Gradually, however, the power of the Mu'tazilites began to wane. They lost their support from the caliphs and by the year three hundred of the *hijrah* one of their members named Abu'l-Ḥasan al-Ash'arī rose against them and founded a new school of *kalām* called the Ash'arite (*al-ash'ariyyah*).

Abu'l-Ḥasan al-Ash'arī is one of the most important of the early religious thinkers of Islam. According to his own testament, in a dream the Prophet appeared to him and ordered him to change his ways, to leave the school of the Mu'tazilites and to begin to teach the doctrine of the eternity of the Quran against the Mu'tazilite thesis of its createdness and the doctrine of the all powerful Will of Allah which dominates over all things and which eclipses *ikhtiyār* or free will which the Mu'tazilites had emphasized so much. He differed from the Mu'tazilites in many ways. Of course, he accepted the doctrine of unity but he did not accept the reduction of Divine Unity to an abstraction. He considered the Divine Names and Qualities to be real, to be understood through a method which was neither *tashbīh* nor *tanzīh*, neither pure anthropomorphism nor pure abstraction, but in between. He accepted the doctrine of atomism which became the cornerstone of his thought but he rejected the excessive use of reason in discussions of religious faith. He tried to strike a balance between the Mu'tazilites and the people of *Ḥadīth* and *Sunnah* such as the Ḥanbalīs who were opposed to all use of reason in religious matters.

Abu'l-Ḥasan al-Ash'arī was Shāfi'ī and soon he gained a great deal of following among the Shāfi'īs. He wrote a number of important books which became the foundation of Ash'arite *kalām* like the *Kitāb al-ibānah* ("The Book of Elucidations") and also wrote an extensive work on the views of various Islamic schools and sects called *Maqālāt al-islāmiyyin* ("Doctrines of the Muslims"). He was a prolific writer and a powerful figure who changed the theological scene and established Ash'arism as the central theological school which replaced the Mu'tazilite school in the Sunni world.

Al-Ash'arī was followed by his student, Abū Bakr al-Bāqillānī, who further expanded his teachings in Baghdad and like his master was also very much interested in Islamic political thought and the relationship between the caliph and the *Sharī'ah, al-dīn wa'l-dawlah* or religion and the state. However, until the fifth Islamic century, the influence of the Ash'arites remained confined to the Shāfi'īs. At this time there arose in Khurasan what is known as the new school of *kalām* (*kalām al-muta'akhkhirīn*) founded by Imam al-Ḥaramayn al-Juwaynī, the author of the *Kitāb al-irshād* ("The Book of Guidance"), and especially by his student, the great theologian and Sufi figure, Abū Ḥamid Muḥammad al-Ghazzālī. In his *al-Iqtiṣād fi'l-i'tiqād* and several other works, al-Ghazzālī universalized the teachings of Ash'arism while giving them a greater philosophical dimension and spreading them beyond the confines of the Shāfi'ī world.

After him, the *kalām al-muta'akhkhirīn* or new *kalām* developed elaborately up to the eighth Islamic century by such figures as Fakhr al-Dīn al-Rāzī, 'Aḍud al-Dīn al-Ījī, Mīr Sayyid Sharīf al-Jurjānī and Sa'd al-Dīn al-Taftāzānī. These men created a philosophical *kalām* of vast proportions which continues to be taught in such major universities as al-Azhar in Cairo, the Zaytūniyyah in Tunis or other great seats of classical Islamic learning to this day. Ash'arism, in fact, remained the most dominant form of *kalām* in the Sunni world until modern times and many treatises and summaries of the theological works of the early centuries have continued to be written and read by religious students.

Despite the dominance of Ash'arism, however, there developed also certain Ḥanafī forms of *kalām* associated with the names of al-Māturīdī and al-Ṭaḥāwī which continued to remain popular in certain circles especially in Khurasan and Egypt. But it was Ash'arism which dominated in the Sunni world far outweighing both Māturīdism and Ṭaḥāwism in its influence. Of course, the influence of Ash'arism was not total in the sense that certain Islamic thinkers, especially the Ḥanbalīs, opposed all forms of *kalām* and remained critical of Ash'arism as well. But to the extent that *kalām* was taught and spread in the Sunni part of the Islamic world, it was the works of al-Ash'arī that dominated the scene.

In the thirteenth Islamic century in Egypt, a number of religious thinkers appeared, the most important among them being Jamāl al-Dīn al-Afghānī and Muḥammad 'Abduh, who tried to revive *kalām* and bring it out of its old mold by presenting certain new theses and trying to solve some of the problems posed by modern civilization for Islam. In this task the works of 'Abduh are especially important, particularly his *Risālat al-tawḥīd* ("The Treatise of Unity") in which he tried to take a new step in reviving *kalām* by giving a great deal more emphasis to the use of reason, by espousing Western science and by reviving certain of the theses of the Mu'tazilites which had in a sense remained dormant for a long time. Also, like most of the modern scholars of *kalām*, he was not very much attracted to the natural philosophy of Ash'arism and emphasized mostly elements of a religious and moral nature contained in Ash'arite teachings. Furthermore, during the last hundred years, a number of other Muslim theologians and thinkers have tried to contribute to what one might call new *kalām*, chief among them Muḥammad Iqbāl of what was India and later Pakistan (of which he was in a sense the founder) whose book *Reconstruction of Religious Thought in Islam* represents an attempt to formulate a contemporary Islamic theology.

Shi'ite *Kalām*

As for Shi'ite *kalām*, the Ismā'īlī form of Shi'ism developed its *kalām* early in the history of Islam and in the third and fourth Islamic centuries one already sees the appearance of important texts of Ismā'īlī *kalām* which then continued over the centuries. This form of *kalām* developed its own very distinct doctrines concerning the relationship between the Prophet and the Imam, the outward and inward meanings of revelation, the cycles of prophecy and of the imamate and other distinctly Ismā'īlī doctrines. After the establishment of the Fāṭimids in Egypt, Cairo became the center of Ismā'īlī theological activity while Khurasan in Persia was the other great center. Most of the Ismā'īlī theologians were also philosophers. The major figures among them such as Abū Ḥātim al-Rāzī, Ḥamīd al-Dīn al-Kirmānī and Nāṣir-i Khusraw must be considered at once theologians and philosophers. After the resurrection of Alamut in Persia and the destruction of the Fāṭimid caliphate, two different schools of Ismā'īlī thought developed, one in Yemen, which followed closely the older Fāṭimid school, and the other in and around Alamut, this school being of a more "revolutionary" character but one which gradually drew closer to Sufism. Both schools continued to produce important theological works and finally settled in India which became the center of Ismā'īlīsm during the last two centuries.

Twelve-Imam Shi'ism, however, devoted most of its early religious activity to the fields of *Ḥadīth* and Quranic commentary and it was not until the seventh Islamic century that a systematic Shi'ite *kalām* developed in the hands of Naṣīr al-Dīn al-Ṭūsī. This fact appears to be strange because Naṣīr al-Dīn was one of the greatest astronomers and mathematicians who ever lived and this is perhaps the only instance in the history of the religions of the world where a great mathematician was also a theologian of such stature. After Naṣīr al-Dīn, who wrote the *Kitāb al-tajrīd* ("Catharsis of Doctrines") which is the most important text of Twelve-Imam Shi'ite theology, many scholars followed in his wake, especially his immediate student 'Allāmah al-Ḥillī. Moreover, this activity continued into the Ṣafavid period in Persia when such figures as 'Abd al-Razzāq Lāhījī wrote a number of important theological texts. There existed also a great deal of exchange through the centuries between *kalām* in the Sunni world and in the Shi'ite world. There were even certain figures such as Jalāl al-Dīn al-Dawānī who wrote *kalām* treatises belonging to the school of later Ash'arism as well as Shi'ism. In fact not only was there a great deal of exchange of views, but also occasionally direct debates between the theologians of the two major groups within the Islamic community.

To this day, the tradition of *kalām* remains an important aspect of the Islamic intellectual tradition. Although many Muslim thinkers of this century have turned their attention to Islamic political thought, the *Sharī'ah*, questions of jurisprudence, the science and the challenges which the West poses for the Islamic world, there is no doubt that the *kalām* tradition in Islam remains one of the important aspects of the intellectual heritage of Islamic civilization from which many religious thinkers continue to draw. Moreover, in order to come to know the rich tradition of religious thought which has existed in Islamic civilization, one must take cognizance of the presence of over thirteen hundred years of theological thought beginning from the second Islamic century and continuing to our own day.

PHILOSOPHY

The Prophet advised Muslims to seek knowledge wherever they could find it even as far as China as cited in the well known *ḥadīth*, "Seek knowledge even if it be in China." There is also a saying attributed to 'Alī ibn Abī Ṭālib according to which one should look at what is said and not who has said it. With the emphasis placed upon the attainment of knowledge in the Quran and the *Ḥadīth* and the examples set by the early Companions, the Muslims tried to understand every form of knowledge which they encountered. Precisely because of the providential spread of Islam outside of Arabia into the Persian empire, certain eastern provinces of Byzantinum, and North Africa, the knowledge with which the Muslims were confronted included the whole heritage of Athenian Greek philosophy and science, the philosophy and science of Alexandria as well as the learning of Persia and to some extent India and even China. In the ancient world, philosophy and science were not separated. Many of the greatest scientists like Aristotle were also among the greatest philosophers. And so, the Muslims tried to understand, to make their own and to accept the challenge of all the different forms of knowledge including both philosophy and science which confronted them, without separating one from the other.

The Muslims did not have an external reason for translating works of foreign origin into Arabic. The reason was neither political nor economic nor military. Nor was there any external religious pressure upon them to translate such works. The reason came from within the structure of the Islamic religion itself, namely, the Islamic emphasis upon knowledge and the fact that Islam considered itself to be the last religion of humanity and heir to every earlier revelation and every form of knowledge which confirmed the principle of *al-tawḥīd* or Divine Unity. With these Islamic teachings before them, once the Muslims established the foundation of Islamic society they turned their attention to the translation of foreign texts concerning various forms of learning. Most of the translations were made from Greek but there were also translations from Syriac, Pahlavi and Sanskrit and in a few instances from Nabataean and Latin.

The great centers of learning of antiquity which were heir to the schools of Greece and Alexandria and before them of Egypt and Babylonia as well as Persia, all fell into Muslim hands. Such cities as Antioch, Edessa, Harran and Jundishapur became part of *dār al-islām*. Towards the end of the Umayyad and the beginning of the ʻAbbāsid period translations began to be made into Arabic from the languages of antiquity through the help of men of learning who hailed from these and other centers. The translation process took nearly 150 to 200 years during which most of the philosophy and science of antiquity was translated into Arabic and Arabic became for the next 700 years the most important scientific language in the world. Even today it remains one of the richest languages in the world, most of all, of course, because of the Quranic revelation and secondly as a result of what Muslim thinkers wrote in it but its richness is also due to the numerous translations of the heritage of antiquity into Arabic.

The height of the period of translation was in Baghdad during the rule of al-Ma'mūn. At that time the famous House of Wisdom (*bayt al-ḥikmah*) was established and the best translators were invited from near and far to translate works into Arabic for which they were paid handsomely. The most famous and competent of these translators was Ḥunayn ibn Isḥāq, the Christian Arab physician and philosopher, helped by a number of other members of his school which included his nephew and a number of other members of his family. But there were also important translators who translated from Pahlavi, chief among them Ibn al-Muqaffa' who rendered the famous *al-Kalīlah wa'l-Dimnah* from Pahlavi into Arabic. The result of the efforts of these translators was that the science and philosophy of antiquity became available to Muslims and presented a challenge to which the Muslims had to provide a response. This response led to the foundation of both Islamic philosophy and the various sciences within Islamic civilization.

The Early Peripatetics (*mashshā' ūn*)

In this climate of intellectual activity in Baghdad certain Muslim thinkers began to think of the relationship between revelation and reason and tried to harmonize the teachings of Islam with the philosophical ideas which had been translated into Arabic. The first and foremost among these was Abū Ya'qūb al-Kindī, so-called "Philosopher of the Arabs," who must be considered the founder of early Peripatetic (*mashshā'ī*) philosophy. He spent his lifetime trying to write as a devout Muslim concerned with issues of a philosophical and religious nature about such matters as the relationship between the unity of God and the creation of the world or the world of multiplicity, the rapport between reason and revelation, the meaning of the intellect, the relationship between philosophy and science and many other key issues. He was at once a philosopher and scientist as were most of the early great philosophers. Al-Kindī is also the father of Islamic philosophy in the sense that it is he who for the first time thought and wrote of philosophical subjects in the framework of Islam and in the Arabic language and had a great deal to do with the development of Arabic as an important language for philosophical and scientific discourse.

Al-Kindī lived in the third Islamic century and after the fall of the Mu'tazilites from favor in Baghdad withdrew from public life and died in obscurity. We, therefore, have no knowledge about the last period of his life. He was succeeded by a number of immediate students who were mostly scientists but also indirectly by Abū Naṣr al-Fārābī, the second of the great early philosophers of Islam, who in contrast to al-Kindī came not from Baghdad or Iraq but from Khurasan and Transoxiana. Al-Fārābī, one of the greatest geniuses produced by Islamic civilization, was at once a philosopher, logician, political philosopher, mathematician and great authority on traditional music and many other sciences. He spent the first half of his life in his homeland near Farab, then came to Baghdad for a short period and spent the last part of his life in Damascus where he died at the age of eighty in the year 339 A.H. He continued the work of al-Kindī in trying to mold the Arabic language as a suitable vehicle for philosophical, logical and scientific discourse. He wrote a large number of treatises on logic, commenting upon all the logical works of Aristotle. He was the father of Islamic political philosophy, writing the famous book *Ārā' ahl al-madīnat al-fāḍilah* ("Opinions of the Citizens of the Virtuous City"). He tried to harmonize the philosophies of Plato and Aristotle in the context of the Islamic unitarian worldview. He also wrote the *Kitāb al-mūsīqa'l-kabīr* which is one of the fundamental sources of music theory in the early centuries of Islamic history and is used to this day as a major reference.

Al-Fārābī has often times been called the "Second Teacher." The very title teacher (*mu'allim*) given to him means in this context not a person who taught various disciplines but one who delineated the sciences, classified them, set limits to them and clarified their relationship. The Muslims used this title in this way and therefore called Aristotle rather than Plato the "First Teacher" because that is what Aristotle did for Greek learning. They also called al-Fārābī the "Second Teacher" because through his famous book, *Fī iḥṣā' al-'ulūm* ("On the Enumeration of the Sciences") which was a very influential work, he classified the various sciences and showed their relationship to each other. This book also had a great deal of influence in the educational system of the West and must be considered as a major work in the history of Islamic thought.

Baghdad continued as an important philosophical center during the fourth Islamic century and such figures as Abū Sulaymān al-Sijistānī, the great logician and man of letters, continued to teach philosophy in Baghdad, but the center of activity of Islamic philosophy shifted more and more to Khurasan. It was here that such men as Abu'l-Ḥasan al-'Āmirī tried to continue the work of al-Fārābī and al-Kindī in developing the early school of Islamic philosophy which has come to be known as Peripatetic Islamic philosophy. Al-'Āmirī is known for having written the most powerful defense of Islam by a Peripatetic philosopher called *al-I'lām bi-manāqib al-islām* ("Declaration of the Virtues of Islam") and also to have written one of the first Islamic books on ethics, *al-Sa'ādah wa'l-is'ād* ("On Happiness and Making Happy").

The work of al-'Āmirī and all other intermediate philosophers following al-Fārābī were, however, overshadowed by the appearance of Abū 'Alī ibn Sīnā who is without doubt the most outstanding philosopher-scientist of Islam and one of the greatest universal geniuses any civilization has produced. Ibn Sīnā was a giant who has cast his stamp upon all later Islamic thought and to this day the intellectual life of Islam shows the influence of his multifaceted genius. Like al-Fārābī, he came from the region of Khurasan. His mother tongue was Persian although most of his works were written in Arabic. He never traveled to Baghdad, having spent his whole life in Persia traveling from one city to another. He only lived 57 years, shorter than either al-Kindī or al-Fārābī, during a tumultuous period of the history of Persia. But his remarkable powers of concentration allowed him to write some of the most important works in the field of philosophy and medicine. He was already a famous physician at the age of sixteen and many considered him to be the greatest physician who ever lived. It was the Western people who gave him the title "Prince of Physicians" and his book *al-Qānūn fi'l-ṭibb* ("The Canon of Medicine") is not only the most famous medical book ever written, but it is also very important for the philosophy of medicine.

In the field of philosophy proper Ibn Sīnā created the final synthesis of early Islamic Peripatetic philosophy. Peripatetic or *mashshā'ī* philosophy is not only *mashshā'ī* in the sense of being Aristotelian. Rather, it is a combination of the principles of Islam and Aristotelian and Neoplatonic philosophy, the synthesis between the perspective of Islam based on the unity of God, the reality of prophecy, the use of the intellect and man's final return to God, with philosophical principles which issued from the schools of Plotinus and Aristotle. Ibn Sīnā created a vast synthesis of these various strands following the works of al-Kindī and al-Fārābī and wrote the most voluminous and definitive encyclopedia of philosophy in Islam, the *Kitāb al-shifā'* ("The Book of Healing"), which is the largest philosophical encyclopedia ever written in human history by a single human being. The book includes not only philosophy but also logic, the natural sciences and mathematics. He also wrote other philosophical masterpieces including his last work, *al-Ishārāt wa'l-tanbīhāt* ("Directives and Remarks"), in which he points to the tenets of his "Oriental philosophy," that is, a new school of philosophy developed at the end of his life and based more upon intuition than the use of reason alone.

The Attack against Peripatetic Philosophy

After Ibn Sīnā, Islamic philosophy in the Eastern lands of Islam was eclipsed for some time by the attack of *kalām* against it. At this time, because of the support given by the Seljuqs to the 'Abbāsid caliphate, the Ash'arite school of *kalām* was officially supported against *falsafah* or Islamic philosophy and Islamic philosophy became gradually eclipsed, the main attack against Islamic philosophy coming from al-Ghazzālī who thought that the Islamic philosophers held views against those of Islam on three points. These were the creation of the world from nothing, God's knowledge of particulars and bodily resurrection. He, therefore, attacked the Islamic philosophers for their views and to achieve this end first of all summarized their views in his *al-Maqāṣid al-falāsifah* ("Purposes of the Philosophers"). He then criticized them in his famous book *Tahāfut al-falāsifah*. After him Abu'l-Fatḥ al-Shahrastānī and Fakhr al-Dīn al-Rāzī followed with attacks of their own against Ibn Sīnā and other early Peripatetic philosophers. As a result, between the fifth and seventh Islamic centuries Islamic philosophy in the Eastern lands of Islam became more or less eclipsed, the only important figures appearing at this time being Abu'l-Barakāt al-Baghdādī who was originally a Jewish philosopher who converted to Islam, and the famous 'Umar Khayyām who was not only a poet and mathematician but also a philosopher very close to the school of Ibn Sīnā.

Islamic Philosophy in the Maghrib

During this period, however, Islamic philosophy had an important period of extensive activity in the Western lands of Islam, in Spain and Morocco. During this time, there appeared a number of philosophers who are important not only in the history of Islamic philosophy but also for their impact upon the West. These figures include Ibn Bājjah who wrote the famous book *Tadbīr al-mutawaḥḥid* ("Regimen of the Solitary") where he spoke about the perfect society resulting from the inner perfection of individuals within that society. The work was influenced by and in a sense continued the political philosophy of al-Fārābī. Ibn Bājjah was followed by Ibn Ṭufayl who wrote the *Ḥayy ibn*

Yaqẓān ("Living Son of the Awake") and who was influenced more by Ibn Sīnā. Ibn Ṭufayl was also at once a physician and philosopher and was in turn succeeded by Ibn Rushd who is the most famous of the Peripatetic philosophers of the Maghrib.

Ibn Rushd, who was the *qāḍī* of Cordova, was an eminent jurist and interpreter of the *Sharī'ah* but at the same time a great philosopher who was interested in the relationship between religion and philosophy; he wrote several works such as *Faṣl al-maqāl* ("The Decisive Treatise") on this subject. He was also the outstanding commentator of Aristotle to the extent that in the West he was called "The Commentator" during the whole of the Western Middle Ages and the Renaissance. Ibn Rushd also set out to answer the critique of al-Ghazzālī and wrote the *Tahāfut al-tahāfut* ("Incoherence of the Incoherence") to that end. But the influence of Ibn Rushd was much greater upon the history of the West than within the Islamic world. Without him, one cannot conceive of Medieval and Renaissance European philosophy, whereas the influence of Ibn Sīnā, also to be seen in the West, was much greater in the Islamic world itself.

After Ibn Rushd, a few other important philosophical figures appeared in the Western lands of Islam such as Ibn Khaldūn, the great philosopher of history, and Ibn Sab'īn who like many other philosophers of Spain was also interested in Sufism and the mystical life. He originated from Spain but migrated to the East and died in Makkah. After these figures, Islamic philosophy in the Western lands of Islam and in fact most of the Arab world became intermingled with *kalām* on the one hand and theoretical gnosis or Sufism of the school of Ibn 'Arabī on the other hand and thus ceased to survive as a distinct school.

The Revival of Islamic Philosophy in the East

In the Eastern lands of Islam especially Persia the situation was, however, quite different. Here in the sixth Islamic century, a generation before Ibn Rushd, a new philosophical school was established by Shaykh al-ishrāq Shihāb al-Dīn al-Suhrawardī, the name of the school being *al-ishrāq* or Illumination. This remarkable philosophical genius who was put to death at the young age of 38, came originally from Persia but died in Aleppo. During his short lifetime, he made a critique of Peripatetic philosophy and tried to introduce into philosophy the element of illumination or sapience and the importance of inner purification in addition to the training of the mind. Suhrawardī wrote a number of important works of which the most famous is *Ḥikmat al-ishrāq*, ("The Theosophy of the Orient of Light"), a book with immense influence upon the later history of Islamic thought. But he also considered the teachings of Ibn Sīnā to be a necessary prerequisite for the understanding of the School of Illumination. He wrote in a highly symbolic language and left behind a number of exquisite works from a literary point of view in both Arabic and Persian.

A generation after him, in the early seventh century, Naṣīr al-Dīn al-Ṭūsī, the famous mathematician, astronomer and theologian who was also a great philosopher, revived the School of Ibn Sīnā. From that time on, this School flourished once again in the Eastern lands of Islam and especially in Persia. During the centuries which followed and lasting until the tenth Islamic century, the Peripatetic school revived by Naṣīr al-Dīn al-Ṭūsī, the School of Illumination founded by Suhrawardī, the schools of *kalām*, both Ash'arite and Shi'ite, and theoretical Sufism of the School of Ibn 'Arabī all flourished and began to intermingle more and more with each other. Important philosophers such as Quṭb al-Dīn al-Shīrāzī, Ṣadr al-Dīn al-Dashtakī, Ibn Turkah and others began to integrate gradually these schools with each other until in the tenth Islamic century a new phase of Islamic philosophy began in Persia with the foundation of the School of Isfahan.

The School of Isfahan

The School of Isfahan was established by Mīr Dāmād, at once a poet, theologian and philosopher, who tried to combine the teachings of Ibn Sīnā and Suhrawardī. Mīr Dāmād was known especially for his concern with the meaning of time and tried to solve the difficult problem of the relationship between God's eternal being and the creation of the world in a way that would be at once satisfactory from the point of view of the Quranic teaching, "*God said be and there was*!" and the fact that since God is the Creator and nothing can change in His Nature, He must always create; otherwise the Divine Name al-Khāliq or Creator would cease to be attributable to God. His most famous work is *al-Qabasāt* ("Firebrands") in which his teachings concerning the notion of time and the creation of the world are discussed extensively.

The most important and influential member of the School of Isfahan was, however, Mīr Dāmād's student, Ṣadr al-Dīn Shīrāzī or Mullā Ṣadrā as he is usually known to his students. He represents in a sense the sum of nine hundred years of Islamic philosophical thought and the final synthesis of various schools of Islamic philosophy and theology. Drawing from both the Quran and *Ḥadīth* and the sayings of early religious authorities of Islam as well as from Peripatetic philosophy, the School of Illumination, both Sunni and Shi'ite *kalām* and the School of *al-ma'rifah* or gnosis, Ṣadr al-Dīn Shīrāzī created a vast synthesis which came to be known as transcendent theosophy (*al-ḥikmat al-muta'āliyah*). Mullā Ṣadrā believed that there are three paths open to man for the attainment of knowledge: revelation (*waḥy*), reason and intellect (*'aql*), and inner vision or illumination (*kashf*), and he sought to formulate a "wisdom" which harmonized what man was able to learn from each of these three sources. He created a synthesis which is based upon centuries of speculation of various Islamic thinkers who tried to harmonize religion and philosophy as well as the tenets of faith on the one hand with the knowledge received through the heart or inner illumination and, on the other hand, with the fruits of the use of reason which God has also given to man as an instrument of knowledge. Mullā Ṣadrā wrote a number of important Quranic commentaries but his most important work is *al-Asfār al-arba'ah fi'l-ḥikmat al-muta'āliyah* ("The Four Journeys"), which is like the "final work" of Islamic philosophy and is studied to this day by the most advanced students in the field. He also wrote shorter works mostly in Arabic including his final masterpiece, *al-Shawāhid al-rubūbiyyah* ("Divine Witnesses"), which summarizes his teachings in a shorter form. He brought about a major transformation within Islamic thought and is the founder of the last important intellectual school which was to have a deep influence not only in Persia but also in Muslim India as well as in Iraq and which survives to this very day.

Mullā Ṣadrā's teachings and those of his predecessors influenced a whole line of famous Islamic thinkers of India like Shaykh Aḥmad Sirhindī and Shāh Walī Allāh of Delhi, the great religious reformer who belongs directly to the line of the school of Mullā Ṣadrā. Within Persia itself, this school was revived during the last century by such figures as Mullā 'Alī Nūrī, Mullā 'Alī Zunūzī and Ḥajjī Mullā Hādī Sabziwārī and continues to this day as a very important intellectual tradition. As for the Arab world, it was the teachings of this school that Jamāl al-Dīn al-Afghānī brought to Egypt in the thirteenth/nineteenth century to rekindle the lamp of Islamic philosophy in that land and other

Arab countries which were intellectually influenced by currents of thought emanating from Egypt.

Conclusion

It is important for young Muslims who have not as yet had a chance to study their own intellectual tradition fully to realize that various schools of Islamic thought, whether it be theology, gnosis, philosophy or *fiqh*, all created and cultivated by men of great piety and devotion seeking to understand God's wisdom and basing themselves upon the Quran and the *Sunnah*, have created a vast treasury of thought which is able to answer the challenges that Western thought poses for Muslims today. Whether it be a question of philosophy of science, epistemology, ethics, philosophy of language or the relationship between man and God, free will and determinism, causality or other philosophical questions with which various European and American philosophers have been struggling during the last few centuries, the vast intellectual tradition of Islam has provided answers of enduring validity.

It is of the utmost importance to realize that Islam is a religion with not only a Divine Law according to which man should live, but also a vast intellectual tradition which guides man in his thinking. It is also essential to know that during fourteen centuries, Islam created one of the richest intellectual traditions of any civilization in the world. Moreover, all of these schools of thought, although oftentimes vying with each other and sometimes attacking each other, were always rooted in the teachings of the Quran and the *Ḥadīth*, in the doctrine of Unity, and were all aware of the reality of revelation and the significance of the *Sharī'ah*. Therefore, they provide the very precious means which young Muslims, faced with the unparalleled challenges of modern civilization with its secularism, humanism and philosophical and scientific claims to truth outside of revelation, can employ in their confrontation with these challenges. With the help of this intellectual tradition, they can preserve not only the religious but also intellectual integrity of Islam as both a religion and a total way of life which embraces the domain of thought, a domain which is a necessary dimension of human existence and which is particularly emphasized by Islam.

CHAPTER 5
ISLAMIC SCIENCE

Islamic science, that is, the sciences developed by Muslims from the second Islamic century onward, is certainly one of the great achievements of Islamic civilization. Without it, not only would there not have been medieval, Renaissance and later Western science but neither would one of the most important studies of nature in relation to a religious universe which the Islamic sciences represent have ever been achieved. For some seven hundred years, from the second to the ninth Islamic centuries, Islamic civilization was perhaps the most productive of all civilizations in the domain of science and Islamic science was at the forefront of activity in many fields ranging from medicine to astronomy. Gradually from about the ninth Islamic century, activity in the Islamic sciences diminished in the Islamic world but it did not by any means die out. Especially in the fields of medicine and pharmacology, a great deal of important activity took place in the eastern lands of Islam during the later period of Islamic history. Also within the Ottoman world, there was a living interaction with certain aspects of Western science in the eleventh and twelfth Islamic centuries before the advent of the penetration of the modern sciences into the Islamic world some two hundred years ago.

The significance of the Islamic sciences for Islamic civilization and also their role in the cultivation of the sciences in the West is a vast subject which needs separate treatment. Here, it is sufficient first of all to understand that the Islamic sciences were not simply the continuation of Greek science and the predecessor of Western science, being no more than a link between the sciences of antiquity, of Greece and Alexandria, and Western science which has dominated the scientific scene for the past few centuries. Secondly, although they influenced Western science a great deal, the Islamic sciences are an independent way of studying the nature of phenomena, causality, the relationship between various forms of objects from minerals to plants to animals, the meaning of change and development in the world of nature and the final end and goal of nature. All these subjects were studied by the Islamic sciences in the light of the teachings of the Quran and the *Hadīth* and a body of science developed which, although of very great importance in many specific fields of the exact and quantitative sciences such as mathematics and astronomy, must not simply be conceived as only an early phase in the development of Western science. The point of view of the Islamic sciences, which is independent of and distinct from the philosophical framework of Western science, must always be kept in mind in order to appreciate fully the significance of Islamic science for Islam as a religion and for Islamic civilization.

Translations

The same process through which philosophical texts were translated into Arabic is also found in the case of scientific texts. In fact most of the translators were the same figures and most of the centers of translation were involved with scientific as well as philosophical texts. Therefore, there is no need to repeat what has already been mentioned in the previous chapter concerning the significance and reason for the translation of the texts of antiquity into Arabic. Suffice it to say that with the emphasis placed in Islam upon knowledge, from the very first Islamic century Muslims became interested in the various sciences which they found around themselves, especially medicine and astronomy. By the second Islamic century, translations had already begun from the four major languages to which Islam became heir in the domain of the sciences, namely Greek, Syriac, Pahlavi and Sanskrit. By the third century, especially with the establishment of the *bayt al-ḥikmah* by al-Ma'mūn, Arabic had already become a scientific language and many of the most important works in the fields of mathematics, physics, astronomy, medicine, pharmacology, natural history, alchemy and other sciences were rendered into Arabic making Arabic once and for all one of the most important scientific languages in the world, a distinction which this language has not lost to this day.

Of the specific texts translated in the fields of mathematics, perhaps the most important are those of Euclid and Ptolemy, but also works of the Pythagorean School concerning the nature and meaning of numbers and works of Menelaos, Theon and many other later Greek mathematicians must be mentioned. In the field of medicine, many of the important works of both Hippocrates and Galen, belonging to the beginning and end of the great medical tradition of antiquity, were rendered into Arabic. Galen was considered to be of special importance because he believed in monotheism. Consequently, his philosophical views attracted many Muslims to the study of his medical and scientific works as well. Also the works of many other important physicians from Alexandria and the schools adjacent to it were rendered into Arabic. In the field of astronomy, besides the works of Ptolemy, the writings of Hipparchus, Eudoxus and many of the later Greek astronomers were known to Muslims either in whole or in part. In the field of natural history, the classical works of Pliny and before him of Aristotle were well known to Muslims. The biological works of Aristotle and the botanical works of his student, Theophrastus, were especially carefully studied by Muslim authors as were pharmacopoeias, particularly the writings of Dioscorides which formed the foundation of Islamic works in the field of pharmacology.

As for the field of physics, this science did not, of course, cover exactly the same subject in antiquity as it does today. On the one hand, physics was the same as natural philosophy as one realizes if one turns to the classification of Aristotle and his book *Physica* which was rendered into Arabic as were many of the commentaries upon it. On the other hand, what we call physics today includes such fields as optics which was dealt with as a branch of mathematics by Muslims. In this field the *Optics* of Euclid and several other works of Greek authorities in optics were rendered into Arabic and were known to Muslims.

There are many other sciences in which works were translated from Greek including such subjects as geography and alchemy. Works of alchemy which were especially important for Muslims were all translated from the School of Alexandria. They included the *Hermetic Corpus* and also the works of Zosimus, Democritos and many of the other classical alchemists of Alexandria. In a certain sense, Arabic is richer than Greek in the number of extant works belonging to the domain of alchemy from the School of Alexandria.

Turning East, one can see that there were also translations made from the Persian and Indian scientific traditions. As far as Persia is concerned, the two fields in which the most important translations were made were astronomy and pharmacology. Here the *Zīj-i shahriyār* ("The Royal Astronomical Tables") must be singled out as being the most important work in astronomy, one which dominated the astronomical activities of the Muslims in the early period. As for India, several important Indian astronomical and astrological works were rendered into Arabic and came to be known as *Sindhind* which is an Arabization of the word *Siddhanta.* Through these works, the numerals which were of Sanskrit origin and which came to be known in the West in their modified form as Arabic reached the Islamic world. Also a number of works were translated from Sanskrit in the field of medicine whose influence can be seen in such later works as the *Firdaws al-ḥikmah* ("Paradise of Wisdom") of 'Alī ibn Rabban al-Ṭabarī in the third Islamic century.

The translation of this vast corpus of scientific works from the languages of antiquity into Arabic is one of the major events in the cultural history of mankind. Not only did these works make possible the creation of the Islamic sciences in the bosom of the newly established Islamic civilization, but they also indirectly played a role in later traditions of science which were influenced by the Islamic sciences, such traditions as the Indian and to some extent the Chinese, during and after the Mongol period, and of course the sciences of the medieval and Renaissance West.

Mathematics

The Muslims were drawn to the study of mathematics from the very beginning to a large extent because of the "abstract" nature of the Islamic revelation and the love that Islam created in the minds of its followers for the doctrine of unity and for a vision of the universe understood mathematically as mathematics is comprehended in the traditional sense of the term. That is why the Muslims made remarkable contributions to many domains of mathematics.

In the field of arithmetic, the most important achievements of Muslims were perhaps the adoption of the Sanskrit numerals and the later transformation which they brought about upon it, creating as a final product what has come to be known as Arabic numerals in Europe and the use of the decimal system. The famous Arabic numerals appear in the *Kitāb al-ḥisāb* ("Treatise on Arithmetic") by Muḥammad ibn Mūsā al-Khwārazmī, from Khwarazm, one of the Persian cities east of the Caspian Sea. This work was rendered into Latin thereby bringing the Arabic numerals to the West and causing one of the most important transformations within medieval Western civilization. In addition to the Arabic numerals, Muslim mathematicians also carried out extensive research in the field of number theory, decimal fractions and the computation of numerical series, the whole tradition in a sense culminating with Ghiyāth al-Dīn Jamshīd al-Kāshānī, the author of *Miftāḥ al-ḥisāb* ("The Key to Arithmetic") who lived in the eighth Islamic century. He is the real discoverer of decimal fractions and the maker of devices to carry out mathematical calculation.

As far as geometry is concerned, Muslim mathematicians began where the Greek mathematicians and geometers had left off. They further developed plane and solid geometry and systematized mathematical equations for the solution of many geometric problems, creating a relationship between algebra and geometry which was to be pursued later by Descartes and which became one of the most important elements in the development of modern mathematics. One of the problems which the Islamic geometers and mathematicians studied very carefully was the fifth postulate of Euclid concerning the fact that one and only one parallel line can be drawn to an existing line from a point outside of that line, a problem the proof of which was debated over the centuries. Both Khayyām and Ṭūsī wrote treatises on the subject, indicating that this fact must be taken as a postulate and cannot be proven by Euclidean geometry itself. The criticism of the subject opened the door to a path which led finally to the development of non-Euclidean geometry in the West in the nineteenth century.

One of the fields of mathematics which was especially developed by Muslims is trigonometry. It was the Muslim mathematicians who for the first time systematized the six trigonometric functions which to this day bear the mark of their Arabic origin in Western languages, the word sine being a translation of *jayb* from Arabic (*sinus* in Latin meaning literary pocket or cavity which is what *jayb* means in Arabic). The first treatise on trigonometry which deals with the subject as an independent branch of mathematics is usually attributed to Naṣīr al-Dīn al-Ṭūsī although in reality the first independent work on trigonometry as an independent field goes back to al-Bīrūnī.

The science of algebra is also one in which the Muslims not only made contributions but in a sense they created a new field by drawing from certain elements of Greek mathematics as developed by Diophantus and also from certain ideas of Indian mathematics. The very word algebra is of course of Arabic origin, going back to another famous treatise of al-Khwārazmī entitled *al-Jabr wa'l-muqābalah* which was rendered into Latin and whose title became the origin of the word algebra. The name of the author al-Khwārazmī itself left its indelible mark upon Western languages by being used in certain languages such as Spanish for arithmetic or for number while it subsists to this day in the English language in the form of algorism. The Muslims developed algebra from its humble origins in the third Islamic century to the masterpiece of 'Umar Khayyām written in the sixth Islamic century, his work *Algebra* being perhaps the most perfect treatise on algebra written before modern times. In this book Khayyām dealt with equations up to the third degree and systematized the solution of quadratic equations.

Another branch of mathematics which one no longer associates directly with mathematics as such was music. Theoretical music was considered, following the teachings of Plato and Pythagoras, as a branch of mathematics by Muslims and appears often as such in the Islamic classifications of the sciences. Many of the great Islamic philosophers such as al-Fārābī and Ibn Sīnā were interested in theoretical music and very elaborate treatises were written by them as well as by others like al-Urmawī and al-Mawṣilī dealing both with the theory of Arabic and Persian music and relating the study of music to other sciences and the study of mathematics to proportion and harmony which are the foundations of music. In the classical treatises dealing with mathematics, often a section is devoted to music as we see in the works of Ibn Sīnā and Quṭb al-Dīn al-Shīrāzī.

ASTRONOMY

Not only because of the general impetus given to acquiring knowledge in Islam, but also because of the specific role that astronomy plays in the Islamic religious rites such as finding the direction of the *qiblah* and the times of prayers, from the very beginning Muslims were avidly interested in the observation of the heavens and the study of astronomy.

Here again Islamic astronomy brought together the traditions of the Babylonians, the Greeks, the Persians and the Indians as well as the ancient Arabs and created a new synthesis which was able to establish astronomy upon a vaster foundation than ever before. Islamic astronomy was interested at once in observation and observatories, in the devising of instruments and in mathematical astronomy.

As far as observational astronomy is concerned, many Muslim astronomers carried out fresh observations, not simply imitating older tables derived from Greek and Babylonian observations, and these Muslim tables were called *zīj.* These *zījes* became more and more elaborate until in the fourth to the seventh Islamic centuries such major *zījes* as the Ḥākimite *zīj* observed in Cairo in the fourth century by Ibn Yūnus, the Il-Khānid *zīj* observed by Naṣīr al-Dīn al-Ṭūsī and his associates in Maraghah in the seventh Islamic century and the Ulugh Beg *zīj* observed in Samarqand by Ulugh Beg and a number of other astronomers in the ninth century were composed. These works became the most important documents for observational astronomy during the whole period which the West calls the Middle Ages.

As for observatories, the Greeks did not create observatories as institutions. The observatory as a scientific institution was in fact an invention of Muslims. In the early Islamic period, observatories were associated with individuals. Oftentimes individual astronomers would observe the stars from the minarets of mosques. For example, we know that the Giralda Tower in Seville was used not only as a minaret but also as an observatory. But later, the first observatory as an institution, in which a number of scientists who observed and calculated the movement of the heavens were brought together, was established by Naṣīr al-Dīn al-Ṭusī in Maraghah. This is the first observatory in the history of mankind possessing such a feature and is the forefather of the observatory as we have known it in the following centuries. Two other major observatories were built by Muslims after Maraghah, one by Ulugh Beg in Samarqand and the other the short lived observatory in Istanbul. These observatories became in turn the immediate predecessors for the famous observatories in the West during the Renaissance and the seventeenth century such as the observatory in which Tycho Brahe carried out his famous observations.

Muslims also showed an avid interest in the development of observational instruments. Of these the most famous is the astrolabe. Although the name is Greek, the instrument is Islamic and in fact there are no extant Greek astrolabes. Islamic astrolabes began to be made early in the history of Islam and for over the last thousand years the art of astrolabe making has brought together often exquisite art with great scientific precision to create very useful and beautiful instruments which before modern times were absolutely essential for navigators and astronomers alike. One could not conceive a Magellan or Columbus sailing on the high seas without the help of the astrolabe as well as the quadrant, the sextant, the turquem and other observational instruments invented or perfected by Muslim astronomers, mathematicians and navigators.

As far as mathematical astronomy is concerned, the Muslims began to study the Indian and Persian methods of calculation of the movement of the heavens as well as the Greek ones which soon replaced them. The major astronomers of the third and fourth Islamic centuries such as al-Battānī and al-Bīrūnī in his monumental *al-Qānūn al-mas'ūdī* ("The Mas'ūdic Canon") continued in fact with certain modifications and refinements the mathematical astronomy of Ptolemy, whose *Almagest* in its English form bears to this day in its title the imprint of the translation of this work from Arabic into Latin. These early mathematical astronomers did not propound any new theories concerning the motion of the planets. However, there continued to be an undercurrent of opposition to both the Ptolemaic and Aristotelian theories of planetary motion. This is seen clearly in Spain, in such figures as al-Biṭrūjī, but the most important criticism which was to bear fruit later on came in the School of Maraghah, in the writings of Naṣīr al-Dīn al-Ṭūsī, his collaborator Quṭb al-Dīn al-Shīrāzī and their successor Ibn al-Shāṭir.

We see in the works of Quṭb al-Dīn such as *Nihāyat al-idrāk* ("The Limit of Comprehension"), followed by Ibn al-Shāṭir's writings, new methods for the calculation of the movements of the planets and a new model which has come to be called the "Ṭūsī couple." This model consists of joining two vectors one at the end of the other to explain the various motions of the planets rather than taking recourse to the epicyclic system of Ptolemy. This criticism of Ptolemaic astronomy and the new lunar model which grew out of it must have reached Poland in one way or another because in the famous book of Copernicus written in the sixteenth century under the title *Revolution of the Orbits*, a work which is foundational for modern heliocentric astronomy, the model for the moon is the same as that found in Ibn al-Shāṭir and which goes back to the *Tadhkirah* ("Memorial of Astronomy") of al-Ṭūsī and the works of al-Shīrāzī.

This later development of astronomy was not, however, pursued in the Islamic world itself except by a few astronomers. The later Islamic astronomers remained satisfied mostly with the repetition of the calculations of their predecessors and astronomy as a living practice of the observation of the heavens and mathematical calculations based upon them gradually became stultified and remained more or less stationery after the ninth and tenth Islamic centuries. In conclusion, it is important to note that some of the Muslim scientists had devised in Maraghah and also in the other later observatories means for a group of mathematicians to calculate together a large number of figures and to check their error of calculation as they went along. This achievement itself is very important in the history of mathematics as well as in the history of mathematical astronomy.

Geology and Geography

The study of astronomy was closely allied to that of geography and to some extent geology. The Muslims knew many of the classical geographical works of the Greeks and the Greek word *geographia* (*jughrāfiyā*) was known to the Muslims and appears in Arabic, Persian and other Islamic languages although gradually the term *ṣūrat al-arḍ* became more prevalent. Muslim geographers began to write on geography from the third Islamic century and such figures as Ibn al-Ḥawqal and al-Bīrūnī wrote major geographical works which finally culminated in the works of al-Idrīsī and the magnificent maps which he drew in the seventh Islamic century at the Sicilian court of Frederick the Great. These geographical writings expanded the knowledge contained in the works of antiquity and contained a great deal more knowledge of the Indian Ocean, Africa, the southern region of the Mediterranean and many parts of Asia and even Europe than was found in Greek and Roman texts. Such major discoveries as the source of the Nile River, which is attributed to nineteenth century European explorers, are already described in these early geographical texts. And one must remember that it was with the help of Islamic geographers and navigators that Henry the Navigator, Magellan, Columbus and many other important explorers of the Renaissance were able not only to cross the Atlantic but also to go around the Cape of Good Hope and paradoxically with the help of Muslims put an end to Islamic dominion and power in the Indian Ocean.

As for geology, a number of Muslim scientists such as Ibn Sīnā and al-Bīrūnī were greatly interested in geology, in the question of rock formation, sedimentation, differences between sedimentary rocks, granites and basalt, and even the study of meteors, the creation of sedimentary basins, the transformations which take place between mountains and oceans and many other important geological problems. Al-Bīrūnī stands out among the geological writers especially for his awareness of the vast changes which have taken place on the surface of the earth between the seas and the land and also for his discovery of the plain of India as a sedimentary basin filled by the major rivers flowing south from the Himalayas and of his identification of the origin of fossils.

Physics

As mentioned earlier, the science of physics as understood today does not correspond exactly to any science in the traditional Islamic classification of the sciences. However, there are three major areas of what would be called physics today which were of great interest to Muslims and in which major achievements were made. The first of these is optics. The Muslims took special interest in the study of optics and of light phenomena. The peak of activity in the science was reached in the fourth Islamic century in Cairo with Ibn al-Haytham, the famous Latin Alhazen, who is without doubt the greatest scientist in this field between Euclid and Kepler and other major physicists of the seventeenth century who worked on optics. Alhazen is the author of *Kitāb al-manāẓir* ("Optical Thesaurus"), one of the most outstanding works of the field of optics, in which he applied the experimental method to the study of certain light phenomena and in which he carried out detailed research on refraction and reflection and the properties of various kinds of mirrors including the hyperbolic mirror. This led to the solution of the problem which is called to this day Alhazen's Problem to honor his contribution. This field was also cultivated two centuries later in Persia by Quṭb al-Dīn al-Shīrāzī and his student Kamāl al-Dīn al-Fārsī who wrote a commentary upon the *Kitāb al-manāẓir.* These men explained for the first time in the history of science the correct reason for the formation of the rainbow as being caused by both refraction and reflection.

The second field of physics in which Muslims showed great interest was the question of motion, this fundamental question which, as pursued in the thirteenth and fourteenth Christian centuries in the West, prepared the ground for the Scientific Revolution with Galileo and his criticism of Aristotle. The criticism against Aristotle's theory of motion is to be seen in the Islamic world already with Ibn Sīnā whose ideas in this domain were based upon some of the earlier writings of the Christian philosopher John Philoponos. In Ibn Sīnā's criticism is to be found the development of the new doctrine of "inclination" (*al-mayl* in Arabic) and also the idea of the significance of what later on came to be known as momentum. There was also an attempt on behalf of certain Muslim physicists including Ibn Bājjah in Spain to study projectile motion in a quantitative manner and to apply mathematical formulas to the study of motion. Although these did not come out to be correct in the light of Newtonian mechanics, they represent an important criticism of the prevalent Aristotelian theory of motion as far as the later history of science is concerned. We know that in the early 1609 *Pisan Dialogue*, Galileo refers to Ibn Bājjah's theory of projectile motion from the quotation which Ibn Rushd had made of it. This aspect of the study of physics among Muslims is one of the most important in the general history of science because without this criticism of the Aristotelian theory of motion, the later development of physics in the West up to Galileo and Newton is inconceivable.

The third field of physics in which Muslims were interested was the whole question of weights and measures and the tradition of Archimedes concerning the determination of specific weight and the measurement of the weight and volume of various objects which we see in his works. His ideas were further developed by Muslim physicists and mathematicians and a large number of treatises appeared in this field of which perhaps the most famous are those of al-Bīrūnī and al-Khāzinī.

Natural History

The Muslims were able to exchange ideas concerning the flora, fauna, minerals and geography of vast lands which were parts of the classical *dār al-islām* stretching from North Africa to East India. The exchange of these ideas took place in many ways of which one of the most important was the *ḥajj*. The annual rite of the *ḥajj* served not only as a pivotal religious rite which brought Muslims from all over the world together in Makkah, but it was also a kind of scientific conference during which Muslims were able to exchange scientific ideas with each other. It is, therefore, common to find rather exact knowledge of the flora of Khurasan in a treatise written in North Africa or of Sicily in a work written in Marw. The knowledge that Muslims had of natural history was far greater than that of even the greatest Greek natural historians because it included vaster lands and much greater detailed knowledge of many species of animals and plants which had not been known to classical Greek and Roman authors.

The Muslims divided the realm of nature into the three well-known kingdoms consisting of minerals, plants and animals and they studied them carefully. The study of minerals and metals was often combined with the study of alchemy but not necessarily so and also occasionally with the study of medicine because of the medical use that was made of various minerals. As for plants, on the one hand, they were studied again in the light of their medical properties and on the other in the light of their agricultural significance. There are many important botanists whose works were used in both agriculture and medicine, perhaps the greatest of them being al-Ghāfiqī from Spain.

As for zoology, the Muslims followed mostly the tradition of Aristotle who was the greatest zoologist of antiquity. But they also added a dimension which had to do with the moral significance of the life of animals. We see this already in the early work of al-Jāḥiẓ, the *Kitāb al-ḥayawān* ("The Book of Animals") and again in a much later work, the *Ḥayāt al-ḥayawān* ("The Life of Animals") of al-Damīrī, in which animals, especially those mentioned in the Quran, are studied in order to better understand the Wisdom of God in His created order as well as of course to provide scientific knowledge of animals, their behavior, generation, life patterns, etc.

Alchemy and Chemistry

The terms alchemy and chemistry in the English language refer today to two distinct concepts but they derive originally from a single word which entered into Latin from Arabic, the word being *al-kīmiyā'*. There has been some debate as to the origin of the word *kīmiyā'* to which the Arabic prefix *al* has been added. Most likely it is an Egyptian word related to the black soil which covered the two sides of the Nile River once the water overflowed the banks and left its very rich sediments that made cultivation so easy on the two sides of the Nile River. The word *kīmiyā'* is most likely in reference to this black soil, the science or the art of alchemy having become systematized in Alexandrian

Egypt. Alchemy was not only a prechemistry. It was at once a science of the cosmos, a science of the soul and a science of materials related also to the field of medicine. It made use of minerals and studied them but mostly in the light of the symbolic significance of minerals and their relationship to the inner states of the soul.

It was from the material aspect of alchemy that chemistry was gradually born. The first great Islamic alchemist lived very early in the history of Islam and this art reached its peak with him. This figure whose name became identified with alchemy was Jābir ibn Ḥayyān who lived in the second Islamic century. He was from Khurasan and also from Kufah for he was called al-Ṭūsī and al-Kufī. Moreover, he was a student of Imam Ja'far al-Ṣādiq. Jābir composed a large number of works dealing with many different sciences but especially alchemy and established this discipline once and for all within the world of Islam, becoming the chief authority in the subject throughout the whole of Islamic history.

It was the second major figure in the field of alchemy, Muḥammad ibn Zakariyyā' al-Rāzī, the famous physician and alchemist who lived in the third Islamic century, who on the basis of Jābir's work gradually created chemistry as distinct from alchemy. He formulated a science of substances without the inner, symbolic and spiritual significance which alchemy has always emphasized. Not that al-Rāzī achieved this overnight, but he took the first step in this direction. As a result, gradually the science of chemistry was born without alchemy having ever died.

Many of the important instruments which have been used in chemical laboratories and which continue to be used to this day go back to those developed by Muslim alchemists, some of these instruments such as the alembic still bearing Arabic names. Also the root of such basic chemical ideas as the division of substances into mineral, plant and animal or the acid and base theory corresponding to the alchemical theory of the active and passive principles, can be found in Islamic alchemical writings. The West had no alchemy before Arabic texts were translated into Latin in the eleventh Christian century and therefore the whole of Western alchemy and chemistry are based upon the Islamic tradition which developed early with Jābir and which continued down through the centuries up to practically modern times.

There are many important later alchemists such as al-'Irāqī, al-Majrīṭī and al-Jaldakī who are well known but also many later alchemists whose writings have not as yet been fully studied. In any case, Islamic alchemy is an important field for the understanding of both certain aspects of Islamic science and a certain kind of spiritual psychology or science of the soul as well as for certain schools of cosmology. Alchemy is a way of relating the world of nature to the divine creative forces which govern nature and which operate within it. It is also a way of relating man as both the observer and actor in the world of nature to the natural world on a deeper level than the purely physical and empirical.

MEDICINE

One of the most extensive fields of activity in the Islamic sciences and one which occupied the attention of numerous Muslim scientists over the centuries and is still alive today is Islamic medicine. The foundation of Islamic medicine is what is called *al-ṭibb al-nabawī* (Prophetic Medicine) that is, certain sayings and wonts or actions of the Prophet which deal with health, hygiene, the care of the body and of course the soul's relation to the body. At the same time, the Prophet himself had a physician, Ḥārith ibn Kaladah, who had studied some Greek medicine and from the early period of Islamic history there was interest in the Islamic world in Greek medicine. Later on, Persian and Indian medicine also attracted attention and soon, as in other fields of science, the Muslims created a synthesis between the major traditions preceding them, in this case the Greek, the Persian and the Indian on the basis of Islamic norms and Islamic teachings. Islamic medicine itself was in a sense born with the major work of 'Alī ibn Rabban al-Ṭabarī called *Firdaws al-ḥikmah* ("The Paradise of Wisdom") which was written in the third Islamic century. This major encyclopedia on medicine was followed by other encyclopedic works especially the *Kitāb al-ḥāwī* ("Continens") of al-Rāzī, the famous Rhazes of the Latin world, who is one of the two or three greatest Islamic physicians and who is the most outstanding clinician and observer in the field of medicine, the discoverer of many new maladies and the person who is said to have used alcohol for the first time as a medical antiseptic. Following upon the wake of his writings, one can mention the *Kitāb al-malikī* ("The Royal Book") of al-Majūsī and finally the grand encyclopedia of medicine *al-Qānūn fi'l-ṭibb* ("The Canon of Medicine") by Ibn Sīnā.

The works of Ibn Sīnā are in a sense the crowning achievement of early Islamic medicine. As already mentioned, in the West he was called "the Prince of Physicians" and his book *The Canon* is without doubt the most famous of all medical books in the history of medicine including the works of Hippocrates and Galen. It was taught for 700 years in the Western world and is still taught wherever traditional Islamic medicine survives in such countries as Pakistan, India, Bangladesh, Sri Lanka and also certain areas of Persia and the Arab world. Ibn Sīnā was the great synthesizer and systematizer of the two grand traditions of Hippocrates and Galen and all of the experiments, experiences and speculations of Islamic physicians before him as well as certain elements of Indian and Persian medicine especially in the field of pharmacology. His *Canon* deals on the one hand with the philosophical basis of health and illness of the human body, of causes for disease, of the relationship between the body and the soul and other major aspects of the philosophy of medicine, and on the other hand, with specific illnesses and with pharmacology and the development of a pharmacopoeia.

Like al-Rāzī, Ibn Sīnā is credited with the discovery and diagnosis for the first time of certain illnesses such as meningitis as al-Rāzī has been credited with the treatment and diagnosis of smallpox. But the greatest achievement of Ibn Sīnā was to synthesize in an incredible way the vast medical traditions before him. After him the tradition of Islamic medicine bifurcated into several branches, the Persian, the Ottoman, the Arabic and later on the Indian, each with its own further subdivisions. And this medical tradition continued strongly. Numerous scholars and physicians appeared who wrote commentaries upon *The Canon* such as Fakhr al-Dīn al-Rāzī and Quṭb al-Dīn al-Shīrāzī. Others developed new ideas based upon the works of Ibn Sīnā and made major new discoveries. One such figure is Ibn Nafīs who discovered the minor circulation of the blood before Michael Servetus who had been credited with it for a long time.

The Islamic medicine associated with Ibn Sīnā became part and parcel of the cultural and daily life of Muslims. The diet they used and in fact use to a large extent to this day is related to this medicine. In later centuries, as this medicine began to wane in the heartland of the Islamic world, in such places as Persia, Egypt and Syria, it began to gain a strong following in India where to this day it remains a living medical tradition with its own medical schools and practitioners. This altogether Islamic medicine, which is, in fact, sometimes called Yūnānī or Ibn Sinan medicine in Pakistan and India, is an important branch of the traditional Islamic sciences, one which has survived to this day and which is still of great significance for the everyday life of many Muslims.

In certain respects, this medicine has distinct advantages over the prevalent modern medicine. Islamic medicine is a form of medicine which is holistic, in which treatment of the body and of the soul are considered together, where psychosomatic elements important in certain diseases are recognized, where certain herbal treatments which can cure without being harmful to the body as a whole are emphasized along with many other factors to which the alternative forms of medicine that many people are seeking in the West today are beginning to pay attention. Islamic medicine is certainly one of the major achievements of Islamic civilization and to this very day its fruits have not ceased to be of benefit. Moreover, during the last few decades even greater attention has been paid in many Islamic countries to reviving and making use of this medicine in a living fashion rather than looking upon it as being of simply historical interest.

The Influence of the Islamic Sciences

The Islamic sciences had a great influence upon both the Western world and the two major civilizations east of the Islamic world with which Islam had extensive contact, namely India and China. Without the Islamic sciences, the course of the development of science in those three civilizations would have been very different. This is especially so of the West which is naturally of central interest because of the development of modern science in the West and its later impact upon the whole of the globe. Between the eleventh and the thirteenth Christian centuries many of the major works of Islamic science were translated into Latin mostly in Spain but also in Sicily and occasionally in other places in Italy, and some of the Muslim scientists such as Ibn Sīnā and al-Rāzī became household names in the Western world. Islamic medicine became the foundation for European medicine to the extent that such an iconoclastic figure as Paracelsus, when he wanted to rebel against traditional medical practices and establish a new medical science, burned *The Canon* of Ibn Sīnā in Basel as a symbol of traditional medicine.

One can see the same pattern in the field of mathematics. The major works of al-Khwārazmī and others were taught in Western universities for several centuries. The astronomical tables that were assembled in the West such as that of Alfonso the Wise in Spain were based upon Muslim *zījes*. The treatises on algebra that were written in the later Middle Ages and the Renaissance were mostly based upon the work of Khayyām. The alchemical and chemical works in Latin incorporated an extensive Arabic vocabulary precisely because there was no Latin vocabulary available in this field. One could go on practically *ad infinitum*. The full impact of Islamic science upon Western science, although studied by many scholars, has not really been as fully appreciated by the general public as it deserves to be.

It is also important to mention at this point that nearly all the treatises of Islamic science translated into Latin were in Arabic. Many of the treatises in Persian, which is the second major Islamic language in the field of the sciences and in which much of later Islamic science was written in Persia as well as in Turkey and India, did not become known to the modern world. Consequently much of the later history of the Islamic sciences remains unknown. It is for Muslim scholars to study the whole history of Islamic science completely and not only the chapters and periods which influenced Western science. It is also for Muslim scholars to present the tradition of Islamic science from the point of view of Islam itself and not from the point of view of the scientism, rationalism and positivism which have dominated the history of science in the West since the establishment of the discipline in the early part of the twentieth century in Europe and America.

Conclusion—The Significance of the Islamic Sciences for Muslims

The significance of the vast Islamic scientific tradition for Muslims and especially for young Muslims today is not only that it gives them a sense of pride in their own civilization because of the prestige that science has in the present day world. It is furthermore a testament to the way Islam was able to cultivate various sciences extensively without becoming alienated from the Islamic world view and without creating a science whose application would destroy the world of nature and the harmony that must exist between man and the natural environment. The Islamic sciences are not only important from the point of view of science understood in its current Western sense, but they also have a spiritual and intellectual significance. Their study and understanding is important in order to create a bridge in the mind of young Muslims between Western science, which many of them are studying, and the tenets of

Islam to which they must remain faithful. The great achievement of the Muslim men of science was that they had the most rigorous standards of critical thought and were scientists of integrity without at the same time losing their faith or becoming alienated from the Islamic view of the universe within which all of the Islamic sciences were cultivated.

The tradition of Islamic science of course gradually weakened but it did not decay as rapidly as some people have claimed in the West. It continued on into the tenth, eleventh and twelfth Islamic centuries especially in the fields of medicine and pharmacology. If one is going to talk about the decay of the Islamic sciences, it is only of the last two or three centuries that one should speak if one takes the whole of the Islamic world into consideration. And one should not be ashamed of that fact because no civilization in the history of science has been avidly interested in the natural sciences throughout its whole history. There have been periods of greater interest and those of lesser interest in every civilization, and there is no reason why one should equate the gradual loss of impetus in the cultivation of the sciences in the Islamic world with an automatic decadence of that civilization. This is a modern, Western view which equates civilization with science as understood in the modern sense. It is, however, an erroneous point of view which many people in the West themselves are beginning to doubt.

In any case, from the Islamic point of view, although it is true that interest in the sciences decreased after the first few centuries of Islamic history, Islamic civilization did not automatically begin to decline nor did general decadence set in. The decadence which did occur in the Islamic world belongs to a much later period of Islamic history than is usually claimed. This fact would be fully substantiated if the integral history of Islamic science and civilization were to be written one day. Unfortunately to this day such a detailed history does not exist and moreover much of the scholarly work that has been done in this field has been carried out by Western scholars who have been naturally primarily interested in those aspects of the Islamic sciences that have influenced the West. It remains the task of Muslims scholars and scientists to look upon the whole of this scientific tradition from the point of view of Islam and the inner dynamics of Islamic history itself.

Chapter 6
Literature and the Arts

Islam and Art

Islam brought into being a civilization in which the arts always held, and continue to hold to the extent that the civilization is still alive, a position of central importance. One might say that the Islamic perspective is based on the dimension of beauty in life and relates beauty and goodness to the very nature of Allah as asserted in the well known *ḥadīth*, "Allah is beautiful and He loves beauty" (*Allāhu jamīlun yuḥibbu'l-jamāl*). The emphasis upon propriety and cleanliness in one's religious and daily life as well as the direct injunctions in the Quran to appreciate the beauty of creation and of all objects created by Allah reflect the central Islamic concern for beauty. As one looks upon creations of Islamic civilization from architecture and city planning to poetry and other forms of literature, one sees the significance of art as traditionally understood in the Islamic universe. The great masterpieces of Islamic art, such as the grand mosques of Cordova in Spain, Qayrawan in Tunis and Ibn Tulun in Cairo or farther east, those of Istanbul, Isfahan and Samarqand represent directly not only the spirit of Islamic revelation but the very essence of that spirit and in a sense provide the most direct and visible answer to the question, "What is Islam?"

They crystallize in their harmony, clarity, serenity and peace some of the most important aspects of the Islamic message.

Islamic art has been able to provide over the centuries an ambience in which Muslims have been able to live and function in the state of the remembrance of Allah and with the vision and in contemplation of the beauty which ultimately can only come from Allah who is the Beautiful (al-Jamīl) in the absolute and final sense. Islamic art is related directly to both the form and the spirit of the Quran and the Islamic revelation. This art seeks to reflect Divine Unity, hence its avoidance of any iconic and representational form of the Divinity. It emphasizes the fragility of the world and the permanence of what lies beyond it. It seeks to relate art to the everyday activities of man; it does not separate art from life. In fact the most prevalent words for art in Arabic such as *ṣinā'ah* and *fann* mean not only art in the current Western sense of the term, but also the making and doing of anything correctly and well. Moreover, Islam always emphasizes the close relationship between art and knowledge as has been asserted traditionally in the Islamic world by many of the great master craftsmen and artists who have emphasized over and over again that art comes from the wedding of *fann* and *ḥikmah* or technique and wisdom.

The external form of the Quran as well as its inner beauty and meaning come from Allah. In the same way Islamic art presents a message which is at the heart of the Islamic revelation in forms which also directly reflect the spiritual and heavenly origin of Islam and which lead back to Allah. Both the spirit and forms of Islamic art are inspired by and related to the Islamic revelation. A thorough study of the Quran, its inner meaning as well as its cadences, sounds, letters, prosody and hypnotic power over the soul of Muslims, combined with the deeper study of the life of the Prophet and the beauty of his soul as reflected in his actions and sayings or *Ḥadīth*, will reveal what are the inner and ultimate sources and the basic foundations of Islamic art. Islam, of course, borrowed many techniques from various civilizations such as the Persian and Byzantine in such fields as architecture, the weaving of textiles, brass and copper works and many other types of art. But it transformed all the material that it borrowed from various civilizations in the light of the Quranic revelation and created very distinct artistic forms which can be seen in lands stretching from East to West.

Although there are local differences between various schools of art belonging to diverse regions of the Islamic world, of which Persian art represents perhaps the most productive and extensive, all of the varying types and schools of art within Islamic civilization share together certain basic principles. This art is characterized by the constant use of the arabesque, geometric patterns, and calligraphy as the symbol of the ubiquitous presence of the Divine Word. It emphasizes what is called "abstraction," which really means an opening unto the intelligible world and stylization and repetition of patterns which in a sense lead man to the contemplation of the Infinite in finite forms. All of these elements are to be seen in Islamic art whether it be that of Andalusia, Egypt, Persia or elsewhere. Of course, each of the major ethnic groups within the Islamic world has created an art that is distinctly its own, such as Persian art, Turkish art, Egyptian art, North African and Andalusian art, Indian Muslim art, Indonesian and Malaysian art etc., but the unity of Islam is reflected through all of these diverse and rich artistic traditions.

LITERATURE

Among all the arts of Islam, the chanting of the Quran is the most important and central. It is the supreme sacred art of Islam. The art of chanting of the Noble Quran is of course combined in many contexts with the art of writing the Divine Word and also with the recitation of the stories and tales which are found in so many chapters of the Sacred Text. Herein lies the reason for the supreme position which literature holds within the cultural world of Islam. The impact of the Quran upon the soul of Muslims was so great that the Islamic cultural environment turned to the word or literature as a central form of artistic expression wherever Islam spread and wherever the influence of the Quran was felt.

Obviously it was first of all the Arabic language and literature which received the imprint of the Quranic revelation as the Quranic revelation had transformed Arabic itself and made of it the appropriate vehicle for the expression of the Word of Allah. The Arabs had already produced major literary works in the form of poetry before the Islamic period during the age of ignorance (*al-jāhiliyyah*), but it was the impact of the Quran that transformed this literature into an Islamic literature. We see already during the lifetime of the companions of the Prophet such a literary masterpiece as 'Alī ibn Abī Ṭālib's *Nahj al-balāghah* ("The Peak of Eloquence") comprising some of his sermons and sayings, the work having been collected in its present form in the fourth Islamic century by Sayyid Sharīf al-Raḍī. This work, which marks one of the early masterpieces of Arabic religious literature was followed by the prayers and supplications of his grandson Zayn al-ʻĀbidīn al-Sajjād whose *al-Ṣaḥīfat al-sajjādiyyah* ("The Book of al-Sajjād") has been called by many the "Psalms of the Family of the Prophet."

During the early Umayyad period there appeared also a number of important poets writing in Arabic who began to reflect more and more the ethos of Islam in their poems. Such poets as al-Farrazdaq and later on al-Ḥallāj wrote poetry which is distinctly Islamic and not only Arabic. Likewise in prose, with the appearance of writers such as al-Jāḥiẓ, Arabic literature gained a very distinctly Islamic dimension. Even in simple stories such as *The Thousand and One Nights*, which belongs to the later ʻAbbāsid era, many of the aspects of the teachings of Islam and the life of Islamic society can be seen as reflected in literature.

Arabic is, of course, very rich in its literary tradition. There are all kinds of Arabic works of great poetic and literary merit ranging from the *qaṣīdah*s of al-Buḥturī and the moral and didactic poetry of al-Mutanabbī to the mystical poems of Ibn al-Fāriḍ and Ibn ʻArabī and from the essays of Abū Ḥayyān al-Tawḥīdī to the historical and philosophical works of great literary merit such as *Ḥayy ibn Yaqẓān* ("Living Son of the Awake") of Ibn Ṭufayl which continued to appear over the ages. Not all the literature produced by the Arabs, however, was of a distinctly Islamic character as happens among all nations, but the vast majority of works in the Arabic language reflect directly the ethos of Islam. This is true especially of the great literary works which have been popular over the centuries such *al-Burdah* ("The Mantle Song") of al-Būṣīrī in praise of the Prophet. Such a work is a clear example of an Islamic literary art of a high order which reflects both the form and the spirit of the Quran and the *Ḥadīth*.

The effect of the impact of the Quran upon Arabic literature is to be found also in the other Islamic languages. After Arabic, the most important literary language of Islam is Persian which became, like Arabic, a universal language in that it was not only spoken and read by those born in the Persian world but also by many people in the Turkish, Indian and even Chinese worlds far away from Persia. Persian developed directly under the impact of the Quran from the wedding between the earlier Iranian languages of the Sassanid period and the vocabulary of Quranic Arabic. The early Persian poets emulated the Arab poets until with Rūdakī Persian poetry came into its own. Meanwhile, some of the

Persians like al-Ḥallāj wrote in Arabic and became eminent poets of that language.

Persian itself began to develop rapidly after the fourth Islamic century both with the epic works of such man as Firdawsī whose *Shāh-nāmah* ("The Book of Kings") became the national epic of Persia, and the religious and mystical poetry that is associated with the names of Sanā'ī, 'Aṭṭār and Rūmī. These men wrote some of the most universally loved poems of any language in the world. It is not accidental that Rūmī, whose impact is immense throughout the whole of Asia and outside of Persia itself, especially among the Turkish and Indian Muslims, has been called by many the greatest mystical poet who ever lived. The Persian language continued to produce even after Rūmī, who lived around the time of the Mongol invasion, major poets. Chief among them are Ṣa'dī and Ḥāfiẓ, the first primarily a moralist and the second the greatest poet of the Persian language, the memorizer of the Quran and a great authority on the *Sharī'ah*, who is also the supreme poet of love and of the spiritual world. These poets enabled Persian to reach the very peak of its literary perfection and to act upon and influence the literature and poetry of many other languages.

Turkish was one of these literatures which underwent a deep influence as a result of its contact with Persian. For centuries in the Ottoman world, the great literary figures knew Persian and some of the earlier ones in fact wrote Turkish poetry in the form of classical Persian models. Later on, however, gradually Turkish poets turned more and more to the common language of the Turkish people and a rich literary tradition was created by such famous figures as Aḥmad Yesewī, the founder of the Yesewiyyah Order and Yūnus Emre who is perhaps the greatest of all Turkish poets, a figure whose poetry remains very popular in Turkey to this day. Turkish writers also emulated to some extent Arabic literary models but even in those cases, it was mostly models which had been adopted already in Persian literature.

One could say a great deal about other languages of the Islamic people but it is necessary to be brief. In the Indian Subcontinent, such languages as Sindhi, Punjabi, Kashmiri, Gujarati and Bengali all reflect deeply the spirit of Islam and have developed vast literatures of an Islamic character, usually deeply influenced by Persian and of course by the ever living direct presence of the Quran. There also developed in India from the eighth Islamic century onward the Urdu language which came into being from a combination of Sanskrit and Persian with the addition of a number of Turkish words and which developed more and more over the centuries as an Islamic language until in the thirteenth and fourteenth Islamic centuries it came into its own as a major Islamic language in which there began to be produced a large number of literary works in both poetry and prose. Urdu was destined to become the main language of Muslim culture in India once the Persian language was banned by the British rulers and it is this language which is spoken and understood today by more Muslims than any other language putting of course Quranic Arabic aside as an exception.

Turning to Africa, one sees the same phenomenon. In Africa, as Islam spread, the local languages began to reflect in this case the spirit and forms of Arabic and not Persian literature. In this continent, the influence of Persian was minor and the influence of Arabic central. All the way from West Africa where Berber, Hausa, Fulande and other major Western African languages developed rather extensive Islamic literatures to the east where languages such as Somali, Harrari and of course Swahili became prevalent, one sees the rise over the centuries of major literary tradition in Muslim Black Africa. Some of these literatures remained oral and were written down only very late often in the Latin script while others adopted the Arabic script and were able to develop a notable written literature. But whether oral or written, the literature of the Islamic peoples of Africa represents another major branch of Islamic literature making use again of the spirit, form and content of the Quran and Arabic literary models but at the same time reflecting the local life of Muslims of the African continent.

As for the lands of Islam in Eastern Asia, we see once again among the Malays the direct impact of both Arabic and Persian literary works from the seventh to tenth Islamic centuries with the result that a number of local figures such as Ḥamzah al-Fanṣūrī, al-Sumātrānī, al-Rānirī and others began to write Malay literary works oftentimes based upon stories of the life of the Prophet or Sufi literature by such figures as Jāmī and before him Ghazzālī while also many of the major classical works of Sufi literature from both Arabic and Persian were rendered into Malay. Even among the Chinese Muslims, an important Islamic literary tradition grew in which there was direct reference to Quranic teachings as well as to early Islamic history but which developed in a very particular manner in the ambience of China and in the Chinese language, making use also of a great deal of imagery and form of the Chinese literary tradition. There are many other forms and schools of Islamic literature in various branches of Turkic languages belonging to Central Asia or other African languages which it has not been possible to mention here. What is important to realize is that in its fourteen centuries of life in this world, Islam has been able to create a number of major literatures both in prose and poetry which reflect the ethos, the spirit and the content of the Quran and the *Ḥadīth*.

There is a special emphasis in Islamic civilization upon poetry which holds an exalted position among all Islamic peoples not only the Arabs and Persians, but also people from far away regions all the way from Africa to East Asia. Certain forms of literature such as the novel which are prevalent in the West today were, however, never developed by Muslims. The reason is that such forms of literature, especially as they developed in the nineteenth and twentieth centuries, are in reality in most cases attempts to create a subjective and fictitious world in which the reader journeys in forgetfulness of the reality of Allah, a world which Islam has always opposed in principle.

As for the theater and playwriting, because of the lack of emphasis in the Islamic perspective upon drama as understood in the original Greek sense, not much attention was paid by Muslims even to Greek drama and very little was written which really belonged to the theater and to playwriting as it is understood in the West, although the Islamic literary *genres* are not totally devoid of models or of examples which in fact have some resemblance to both plays and novels. In the case of playwriting, the passion plays connected with the tragedy of Karbala' come to mind. As for the novel, philosophical novels, especially the *Ḥayy ibn Yaqẓān* of the famous Andalusian philosopher and physician Ibn Ṭufayl, whose work many people consider to be the origin of the first European novel, can be mentioned.

Altogether, however, the place of honor in Islamic literature belongs to epic and religious poetry on the one hand and to storytelling on the other. All these types of works were impregnated with the values contained in the Quran and *Ḥadīth* and supplemented directly religious texts in the traditional Muslim's life while at the same time such literary work made and still make accessible deep moral lessons which the Muslim must learn during his journey on earth. It is amazing how much of Islamic literature is really an expansion upon certain sayings of the Prophet or commentaries upon certain stories of the Quran in such a way that the whole literature of the Islamic people became impregnated by the values and teachings of the Islamic religion.

The Plastic Arts

When we turn to the plastic or visual arts, which also occupy a very important position in Islamic civilization, we immediately detect a hierarchy as far as the religious character of these arts are concerned. If in the sonorous arts the most exalted art is that of the chanting of the Quran, in the visual arts the highest arts, which are the sacred arts par excellence of Islam are calligraphy and architecture. One is associated with the writing of the Word of Allah in the form of the Quran and the other with the creation of spaces in which the Word of Allah reverbrates, the spaces of the mosque of which in all other Islamic architecture is in a sense an extension. It is important to realize that the hierarchy of the arts in Islam, differs markedly from what finds in the West. In Western and certain other civilizations, painting and sculpture are central and of great religious importance. In contrast in Islam there is no sculpture to speak of except for the few lions here and there usually in the middle of bodies of water or incidentally in front of some palace, and painting is always associated with the art of the book in the form of miniatures and does not at all occupy the same central position as one finds in the Western world.

In Islam, it is then the twin arts of calligraphy and architecture which are central in the religious life and which reflect the Word of God in the Islamic community. Calligraphy representss directly the response of the soul of the Muslims to the descent of the Quranic revelation. Arabic poetry existed before the descent of the Quran but there was no Islamic or Arabic calligraphy before the Quranic revelation. Islamic calligraphy is specifically an Islamic art without any pre-Islamic precedence. First the *kūfī* and then other styles such as the *naskhī, thuluth, muḥaqqiq, rayḥānī* and *nasta'līq* developed over the centuries with incredible precision and beauty. An art was created which gradually moved from the writing of the text of the Noble Quran to the writing of books in general and the embellishment of the objects of every day life, of houses and of course of mosques, in such a way that the Islamic physical ambience reflected the presence of the Word of Allah and therefore reminded the Muslim of Him and of the teachings of the Islamic religion.

As for architecture, it is not only the individual buildings which are significant. The building of the mosque, which ultimately goes back to, the model of the Madinah Mosque and many later techniques of dome structure, including squinches and other techniques which the Muslims learned from Sassanid architecture in Persia and Byzantine architecture in Syria and Egypt, are naturally of great importance. But what is of as much significance is the creation of a whole urban environment, the pattern of whole cities in which there was perfect integration between the various components and functions of human life, in which the mosque as the heart of the city was closely integrated with the bazaar, the economic center, with the *madrasah* , the center of learning, with living quarters, and with carvansarais and ateliers in such a way that the religious, educational, economic, domestic and political functions of society were all integrated together.

One of the most remarkable features of the Islamic city, as traditionally understood, is its total integration into its natural habitat and its harmony with the climate and other natural conditions. The Islamic city was never built to assert man's opposition to nature. Rather, it was always constructed in harmony with the forces and elements of nature. Maximum use was made of light, wind, shade and accessible materials, and materials were used in such a way as to always go back to the bosom of nature once the city was abandoned. The Islamic urban sites, whether they be in North Africa, Yemen, Persia or elsewhere, reflect to this day some of the most successful examples of the integration of the "human habitant" into the natural environment. In this age of ecological crisis, there is much to learn from traditional Islamic urban planning as well as the architecture of individual buildings.

There are also elements of directly religious and spiritual significance connected with the traditional Islamic city. The traditional Islamic city is either white, as one finds in North Africa and even in Southern Spain which to this day reflects its Muslim past, or the color of earth, as one finds in Persia, Afghanistan and elsewhere. In both cases the result is the creation of a sense of stability and peace. There is no agitation; rather, a calm seems to cover the Islamic city almost like a sepulchral repose and peace reflected in the white color which is reminiscent of the shroud. However, within the city, and especially within the house, one finds exuberant color tiles or courtyards with plants and flowers. The whole beauty of the Muslim city is turned inward and not outward. The traditional Muslim houses, whether of the rich or the poor, are not that different from the outside. Therefore, excessive inequality in the public eye is prevented. The beauty of the house is to be found mostly within its walls. It is within the house that the joy and serenity which accompanies the worship of Allah and the enjoyment of His bounties, especially the felicity connected with family life, are reflected. The Islamic city as traditionally constructed, must be considered one of the great achievements of Islamic art. Likewise, its destruction during the past century is one of the major tragedies which has befallen the Islamic world as a result of the colonization of that world by the West since the eighteenth and nineteenth centuries, followed by the actions of nominally independent Muslim governments pursuing avidly Western models of urban development.

Turning to the other arts, it is important to remember that in Islam there is no distinction made between fine arts and the crafts or the industrial arts, a division which came into being in the West as one can see in English and French where one speaks of fine arts or *beaux arts*. Although these terms have now been translated into Arabic, Persian, Turkish and other Islamic languages and become prevalent, they have no precedence in Islamic history. In the traditional Islamic world, the hierarchy of the arts was not based on whether they were "fine" or "industrial" or "minor." It was based upon the effect of art on the soul of the human being. That is why after the sacred arts associated with calligraphy and architecture, which are directly related to the Word of Allah, the most important art is that of dress because nothing influences the soul as much as that which is closest to the body, namely the dress that we wear, dress which is far from being peripheral and unimportant. Over the centuries, Muslims, basing themselves on the teachings of the *Sharī'ah* concerning sobriety and modesty and also the direct models of the Prophet and his household as well as climatic needs and ethnic genius, developed a variety of beautiful male and female clothing. The male dress has always been very virile and patriarchal and the feminine dress very feminine and gentle.

The male dress and the female dress have also always been designed in such a way as to accentuate the nobility of the form and movements of the human body as Allah's creation and the human being as Allah's *khalīfah* or vicegerent on earth and also to bring out the remarkable beauty of the movements of the Islamic prayers which in fact become hidden when the traditional dress is no longer worn. Characteristic of the male Islamic dress is the turban about which a *ḥadīth* has said that as long as the Islamic community wears the turban it will not go astray. This saying is symbolic while bringing out the significance of the turban, one of the most beautiful headdresses in the world. The use of the turban signifies, in a sense, keeping one's head straight and also making man remember his function as Allah's vicegerent on earth.

It is difficult in the traditional Islamic dress, whether it be the *'abāyah*, the *jallabah, shalwār* or other forms of traditional Islamic dress, to be an agnostic or an atheist because such dresses bring out the spiritual function of man as the representative of Allah on earth. The loss of the Islamic dress, like the loss of traditional Islamic architecture and urban texture, represents a major catastrophe for the integral and all-embracing civilization of Islam within which Muslims have lived and breathed since the beginning of Islamic history.

After dress, the objects which influence the soul of man most intimately are the everyday objects and utensils of life such as the carpet upon which one sits, the cloth upon which one places the food that one eats, utensils with which one takes food, the bowl from which one drinks and so forth. Islamic civilization paid great attention to these so-called minor objects which in fact have a great deal more influence upon man than paintings in museums which one might visit once or twice a year or at most once a week on Sundays. That is why such objects constitute a major category of Islamic art. Let us remember the significance of the carpet, not only the Persian carpet which has remained to this day perhaps the most beautiful and rich in form of all carpets made in the world, but also Anatolian, Afghan, Berber and other carpets of the Islamic world which remain among the masterpieces of carpet weaving globally. Let us also remember other objects such as the beautiful glass made in Syria, the *batiks* of the Malay world, the brass works of Mamlūk Egypt or the woodwork of the Indian Subcontinent and of North Africa among all of which one can find peaks of Islamic art in the particular *genre* in question. Such artistic questions have had a very important role to play in creating an Islamic ambience of beauty, serenity and peace within which Muslims have lived and breathed.

Of course, the best of Persian and after it the Mogul and Turkish miniatures, which were influenced by the Persian, constitute masterpieces of art and reflect the peak of the art of painting in the Islamic world. These miniatures, especially those of the Tīmūrid and Ṣafavid periods, have been in fact appreciated universally as remarkable artistic masterpieces. Persian miniatures reached a perfection which is amazing from the point of view of the execution of details, color combination and also their spiritual and non-naturalistic treatment of figures and forms. But it must be remembered that the miniature has been always associated with the art of the book and was called the miniature because it was never very large in size. The Islamic sensibility, although it did not ban figures except in relation to Allah and the Prophet, was much more given to geometric and abstract arabesque patterns and did not place figurative art at the center of its artistic concerns. Therefore, while the miniatures are among the glories of the artistic heritage of Islam, they are not as central to it as are the arts of calligraphy, architecture and urban design. The Mamlūk and Tīmūrid Qurans represent in a sense the peak of the visual arts compared to which even the greatest paintings such as those of Bihzād are of lesser religious and spiritual significance.

The Influence of Islamic Art

The artistic tradition of Islam left a great impact not only within the Islamic world but also upon the civilizations surrounding it. In the East, while Islamic art was itself influenced to some extent by Chinese art as can be seen in Persian miniature paintings, it also influenced many kinds of Chinese art all the way from vases to carpets. Likewise in India, there was a wedding in certain places such as Fatehpur Sikri between Islamic and Hindu art while Islamic art itself created some of its greatest masterpieces such as the Taj Mahal in the land of India.

As far as the West is concerned, the different aspects of Islamic art, from poetry and music to architecture, left a deep imprint upon many facets of medieval European art ranging all the way from arches in architecture to the illuminations of Latin and Hebrew manuscripts of the thirteenth and fourteenth centuries. Specifically as far as Jewish art is concerned, not only in Spain but also in such lands as Morocco, Yemen, Persia and Egypt, this art remained closely allied to Islamic art. The arches and internal decorations of the synagogues of Cordova and Toledo reflect to this day the closeness of relationship between the decorative and ornamental art of the synagogue and the mosque.

Furthermore the illuminations of Hebrew manuscripts, whether they be from Persia or Spain reflect the proximity of the artistic world in which the Jews lived with that of the Muslims with whom they often cooperated closely through many centuries in diverse artistic fields including music.

A Note on Music

Finally a word must be said about music before concluding this discussion. There are some *'ulamā'* who have considered music to be forbidden (*ḥarām*), while others have considered it to be permitted for those whose passions are not inflamed by it. Be that as it may, this question was never answered in a categorical manner by the jurists during Islamic history while music developed extensively in the various lands of Islam, much of it in a purely religious and spiritual manner. There is of course military music and the music chanted by the peasants at the time of harvesting and the like which have more of a folk nature. But there exist also the classical traditions of music of which the major ones in Islamic civilization are the Arabic, Persian, Turkish and Indo-Muslim or Northern Indian which has now come to be known as Indian music but most of whose great performers to this day have Islamic names. These schools of music reflect to a large extent the interiorizing aspect of this art in the Islamic world. They are not arts to be used for a social purpose like the music for dancing that one hears in the West. Rather, they are related usually to mystical poetry and to religious and spiritual contemplative states. Such music was developed throughout the centuries mostly by the mystics of Islam, by such Sufis as Jalāl al-Dīn Rūmī and Amīr Khusraw. In this way, traditional music became closely wed to literature, especially poetry, creating a perfect vehicle for the praising of Allah and a powerful aid for His Remembrance.

Of course, as already mentioned, the supreme art which has to do with sound and which is the supreme "music" in Islam, although the word music is never used for it, is the chanting of the Noble Quran. The chanting of the Quran is in a sense the proto-musical experience for the Muslim soul and it is the origin of the ethos of the classical schools of music as they developed over the centuries as the text of the Quran is the origin of the literatures of the Islamic people. In the same manner, the Quran contains in a subtle way the principles, and is the origin of the spirit of the visual arts of Islam whether they be calligraphy, which was originally directly related to text of the Quran, or architecture, that creates spaces in which the Muslim throughout his life hears the celestial beauty of the Word of Allah echoing from the *miḥrāb* throughout the spaces of the mosque, and from the minaret throughout the spaces comprising the Islamic urban environment.

CHAPTER 7
THE ISLAMIC WORLD IN MODERN TIMES

The Islamic world today stretches from the Atlantic to the Pacific, from Southern India and the heart of Africa to Siberia, Albania and Bosnia and also has a notable presence in other parts of Europe and America as well as in the central and southern regions of Africa. There are today over a billion Muslims living both within *dār al-islām* and as minorities in other countries. The religion of Islam is still alive and strong but the civilization which Islam created has withered away to a great extent, having been attacked from many directions for several centuries. As a result of this onslaught by both material forces and alien ideas, much of that civilization has been destroyed although elements of it still survive. Its architecture and city planning, its sciences and philosophy, its arts and literature have been partially either destroyed or transformed as a result of the domination of modern Western civilization; yet they have not disappeared completely and continue to show signs of life to some extent.

The social structure of the Islamic world, as well as its political and economic institutions, have also faced very severe pressures during the past several centuries. As a result, tensions and dislocations have been created within the body politic and the social structure of the Islamic world leading to the present situation in which the religion of Islam continues strong among Muslims but the civilization and social order created by that religion have become weakened and are faced with challenges of incredible magnitude unprecedented in the history of Islam since its inception.

In order to understand fully the situation of Islam and its society and civilization in the modern world, it is necessary to turn back to the beginnings of these challenges by modern Western civilization and the responses of the Islamic world to them. The first challenge of the modern West to the Islamic world began in the age of exploration and what has come to be known as the Renaissance in European history, that is, in the sixteenth and seventeenth centuries. Already at that time, the Portuguese, the Spanish and the Dutch, soon followed by the British and finally the French, had tried to encroach upon the lands of Islam. The sea routes of the Indian Oocean which had been of great economic significance for the Islamic world were more or less taken over by European sea powers and gradually these powers began to penetrate into the main territories of that world.

During that period parts of southeast Asia, which remains to this day an important part of *dār al-islām*, were colonized as were parts of Africa and India, while, with the increasing strength of Russia as a nation, Muslims of the northern regions of the Islamic world such as the northern Caspian areas and Central Asia began to feel the pressure of a new European power. The Ottoman Empire, Persia and North Africa remained intact somewhat longer but by the eighteenth century even the heartland of the Islamic world began to feel the threat of the encroachment of the West although it was not actually colonized then and much of it never became directly colonized.

The event which caused the conscience of the Islamic world to become aroused by the imminent danger and challenge coming from the West was the invasion of Egypt by Napoleon in 1798. That event marks a kind of watershed which bore witness to the transformation of the Islamic world as far as its awareness of and change of attitude towards the West were concerned. It is strange that for nearly three centuries, while the West was becoming ever more powerful militarily and economically and while the Renaissance, the Scientific Revolution and other major events were taking place in the West, the heart of the Islamic world remained more or less impervious and indifferent, showing little interest in what was going on in Europe. A few embassies from the

Ottoman world, Persia or Morocco had gone to Europe and written descriptions of that continent, but the main body of the Islamic world had remained more or less uninterested in the West even while its limbs were being severed by colonial powers through their domination during that period.

After the Napoleonic conquest of Egypt, however, Muslims began to realize that a great tragedy was about to befall the Islamic world. The event of the invasion of Egypt was followed by the completion of British domination of India and the loss of power of the Ottomans as well as the Persians as a consequence of major battles such as those of the Crimea and the wars between Czarist Russia and Persia leading to the loss to the West of many territories which had belonged to the Islamic world until that time. This eclipsing of the power of the Islamic world led to much soul searching and several types of reaction. From the Islamic point of view, the success that the Muslims had had in the world during their history had been a sign and consequence of both the truth of Islam and their firm allegiance to that truth, for as Allah asserts in the Quran, "*If Allah helps you, none can overcome you*" (III:160). Consequently, it seemed to many Muslim thinkers that something very serious had gone wrong with the events of history and with the Islamic world itself, something which was not only transient and of a purely worldly nature but of a practically "cosmic dimension."

There were three possible reactions that Muslims, aware of the challenge of the West and wanting to respond to it, could show. The first was to try to go back to the "purity" of early Islamic history on the basis of the teachings of the Quran and *Ḥadīth*, asserting that the later transformations, accretions and developments of Islamic history were causes for the weakness of Muslims and that they should go back to the original teachings of the Quran and the Prophet as understood by the "ancestors" (*salaf*) in order to restrengthen Islam. This group proposed that Muslims should put aside all the philosophical and artistic development of Islamic civilization, the easy mode of life of the big cities and the luxury and heedlessness which accompanied it. This return, they claimed, would strengthen Islam once again. The second possibility was to say that Islam had to be modified or modernized in order to accommodate itself to the onslaught of the West with its own worldview, philosophy and ideology. The third possibility was to assert that according to many *ḥadīth*s a day would come when oppression would replace justice and true Islam would become eclipsed leading to the coming of the Mahdī and finally the end of the world. According to followers of this view, events taking place in the Islamic world only confirmed what had been predicted in traditional Islamic sources. As a matter of fact, in the early decades of the thirteenth/nineteenth century all of these reactions occurred in one part or another of the Islamic world.

As far as the first type of reaction is concerned, the roots of it are to be seen within the Islamic world itself, in the rise of such figures as Muḥammad ibn 'Abd al-Wahhāb in Arabia, who sought to go back to a very strict juridical interpretation of the teachings of the Quran and *Ḥadīth*. Followers of this type of interpretation of Islam are usually referred to in English as "fundamentalist reformers" although the term fundamentalist is not really appropriate in the context that it is used, especially with the new meaning that it has gained during the past two decades. Such figures and their followers became gradually stronger as the domination of the West came to be felt more intensely throughout the Islamic world. Adherents of such movements stood strongly against not only Western civilization but also science, philosophy and the arts as they had developed within the Islamic world itself. What they did emphasize was the significance of the practice of the *Sharī'ah* and the importance of going back to the tenets of Islam as interpreted by the early Islamic community especially the Ḥanbalīs and a few of the later jurists such as Ibn Taymiyyah.

The second group which has come to be known as "modernists" or "modernist reformers" covers a rather wide spectrum of thinkers some of whom sought to expand the idea of nationalism, as this idea was developing in Europe, into the Islamic world leading to the first theoreticians of not only Arab but also Turkish and Iranian nationalism in the late nineteenth and early twentieth centuries. Others tried to reunify the Islamic world following the teachings of Jamāl al-Dīn al-Afghānī who sought on the one hand to go back to the political unity of the Islamic world as it had existed during the first centuries of Islamic history and on the other hand to be the harbinger of certain modernist ideas. It is, therefore, difficult to classify him exactly as either a modernist or a fundamentalist reformer like 'Abd al-Wahhāb. Furthermore some of al-Afghānī's followers had tendencies which made of them members of the fundamentalist reformist group while others, like his most famous student Muḥammad 'Abduh of Egypt, tried to modernize Islamic theology itself by giving a more central position to reason in matters of faith. As the Shaykh al-Azhar and *muftī* of Egypt, 'Abduh had a great deal of influence in the late thirteenth/nineteenth century although he did not last very long in this position. His influence, however, continued into the fourteenth/twentieth century among a notable number of modernist Arab thinkers.

One finds this modernist trend also in other Islamic countries with such figures as Zia Gökalp of Turkey who was especially interested in the development of an Islamic sociology which would separate Islam as it was traditionally understood from the domain of public life. In India there appeared many modernists such as Sir Sayyid Aḥmad Khān who tried to establish an educational system on the model of the West in order to better the position of Muslims under British rule. He was also an avid modernist in his interpretations of the Quran and the tenets of the Islamic revelation.

In the modernist group within the Islamic world during the thirteenth/nineteenth and early fourteenth/twentieth centuries, one can distinguish between Arabs, Persians and Turks on the one hand whose knowledge of Europe was more indirect because of the lack of spread of European languages at that time in areas from which they hailed, and Muslim thinkers of India who had direct knowledge of Europe as a result of their command of the English language resulting from the type of colonialism that the British had administered in India. The Indian Muslims began to write in the English language about various Islamic subjects and produced a whole array of apologetic writings to try to defend Islam against the attack of missionaries and Westerners. One can recall in this context the English works of Amīr 'Alī, the well-known Indian Muslim writer. Perhaps the most influential figure from the world of Indian Islam, however, was Muḥammad Iqbāl who was at once a philosopher and poet, a man who tried to revive the unity of the Islamic world and to arouse the Muslims to an awareness of their own civilization and identity but who was at the same time deeply influenced by thirteenth/nineteenth century European philosophy and expounded many philosophical ideas which are not at all in conformity with traditional Islamic thought.

The third group mentioned above, that is, those who had expectations of eschatological events, also found adherents in the Islamic world with the appearance of a number of figures in the thirteenth/nineteenth century who claimed to be the Mahdī or the gate (*bāb*) to the Mahdī and who began religious movements of great consequence both politically and religiously. Some of them like the Mahdī of the Sudan, 'Uthmān dan Fadio in West Africa or the founders of the Mujāhidīn movement in the North Western province of India created new political entities and in fact had remarkable success against the much superior Western colonial military might of the day. Others like Sayyid Muḥammad Bāb in Iran opened the gate to controversy within Shi'ism which led finally through his student Bahā' Allāh to the establishment of a new religious movement that separated itself from Islam completely and claimed for itself a new dispensation and a new religious form.

In addition to these three reactions which have been studied avidly by many scholars in both the Western and the Islamic worlds, one must also remember that traditional Islam, both on the level of the *Sharī'ah* and within the Sufi orders, also continued during this time and in fact there were renovations and renewals of life of a purely traditional character which are of great importance. These include, for example, the founding of the Darqāwiyyah and Sanūsiyyah Orders in North Africa, which brought about major religions, and in the case of the latter even political transformations. The Sanūsiyyah Order was widespread in Cyranaicia and finally led to the establishment and independence of Libya. One can also mention the Tijāniyyah Order in North Africa which spread very rapidly to Western Africa and was to a large extent responsible for the Islamization of that area in the thirteenth and early fourteenth Islamic centuries. Also some of the great military figures who became folk heroes for Muslims in the resistance against Western domination, such figures as 'Abd al-Karīm and Amīr 'Abd al-Qādir in North Africa or Ismā'īl in the Caucasus, were associated with the various Sufi orders and represented the revival of these orders which became the pole around which resistance against European domination took place.

During the latter part of the thirteenth and most of the fourteenth Islamic or nineteenth and much of the twentieth Christian centuries, the pressure of the West upon the Islamic world continued and in fact only increased. The millenialist response, however, gradually died out as is in the nature of such movements, but the other two, namely movements associated with fundamentalist reform and modernism, continued in different forms up to the Second World War, mostly with the goal of trying to either gain the political independence of the Islamic world or of reestablishing Islamic norms of life based upon the *Sharī'ah.* Many of the battles fought against European domination were in fact carried out by members of groups with strong fundamentalist tendencies. One must recall here the role of such groups as the Ikhwān al-muslimīn and the Salafiyyah in Egypt or the Jamā'at-i Islāmī which was active before the partition of India and continued later in Pakistan and other movements of this kind in the earlier decades of this century.

With the end of the Second World War, gradually the whole of the Islamic world gained its political independence. One after another countries such as Syria and Lebanon in the Arab East, Morocco, Tunisia, Libya and later Algeria in North Africa, Pakistan, and Bangladesh in the Indian Subcontinent, Indonesia and Malaysia in Southeast Asia and many countries in Africa and the Persian Gulf became independent. Consequently, a great hope that with political independence would come the cultural, religious and social independence of the Islamic world flowered and reached a new level of intensity. However, this hope was not fulfilled since with political independence there came usually even greater economic dependence and also further Western cultural penetration into Islamic countries. The more a country in the Islamic world was successful in making use of modern technology, modern education and modern science, the more was it also exposed to the cultural patrimony of Western values which seem on the surface not to be related to technology and science but which in depth are very much intertwined with it. The result of this further cultural subjugation was a greater threat to the identity of both Islam and Islamic civilization, hence the new reactions which have set in during the past few decades in order to try to preserve the unity of Islam and also its identity and vitality.

These post-Second World War reactions within the Islamic world also began at a time when the West gradually lost its self-confidence and when the modernist group within the Islamic world, which had preached the simple imitation of the West could no longer find a defined and clear Western model to follow. First of all, Marxism and socialism which had come to dominate Eastern Europe and Russia also began to enter the arena of modernist thought within the Islamic world in contrast to the earlier period when modernists looked solely to the capitalistic and liberal West. Secondly, even the existing Western models of development and social change as well as the meaning of philosophy, science and technology began to be questioned and challenged within the West itself. The great calamities of the two Wars, the impasse created by the West as a result of its unilateral and materialistic point of view which is reflected in not only modern science but also in a great deal of modern thought, the ecological catastrophes brought about by the Industrial Revolution and its aftermath, the breakup of the social fabric in the big cities in the West, these and numerous other happenings caused many Muslim thinkers within the Islamic world to begin to question the value of simply imitating the West as a model. There arose in the Islamic world a number of thinkers who tried to seek ways other than simple imitation in order to preserve the identity of the Islamic world and its values while that world remained still in the position of dependence upon the West in one way or the other for military, technological and economic needs. The whole modern enterprise began to be cast in doubt by many among the Muslim intelligensia while the West continued its domination over the Islamic world in so many domains.

It is with this background in mind that we must turn to the events and reactions, some intellectual and cultural, some social and political, some moderate and some violent, which have taken place within the Islamic world during the past few decades and which have affected the understanding of the Islamic world in the world at large as well as the understanding of the Muslims of themselves. These factors have played an especially important role among the younger generation whose members have been deeply affected by both the West and the reactions which have been created in the Islamic world against the encroachment of the West during the past decades.

In this situation in which the Islamic world gradually gained political independence after the Second World War for all of its areas except those within the Soviet Union and China, while becoming ever more dominated economically and culturally by the West, a number of responses and reactions took place within the Islamic world which have continued to this day. For the sake of simplicity, these very diverse and sometimes complicated reactions and movements can again be divided into the modernist, the revivalist or what the West now calls the fundamentalist, the millenialist and finally the response of traditional Islam itself.

The modernist group has continued its effort during this period as it had done in the earlier decades of this century to try to provide a modernistic interpretation of Islam and Islamic thought so as to accommodate Western ideas and ideologies, and also until very recently even socialist and Communist ideologies among a number of people in certain circles. During the past few decades, gradually the older Western liberalism which had had many followers in the Islamic world began to wane in most countries while the fashion of socialism in the form of Arab socialism or Islamic socialism became popular for a short while.

None of these ideologies, however, were able to solve the deeper problems with which the Islamic world was confronted. As a result, on both the political and cultural fronts, the modernist interpretations have been more or less on the defensive and weakened recently in comparison with earlier decades of this century. They have not, however, by any means died out. A number of Islamic thinkers, both within the Islamic world and those living in Europe and America, have tried to give new interpretations of Islam, ranging from the reexamination of the authenticity of *Ḥadīth* to criticism of the traditional understanding of the text of the Quran in the manner of critical Biblical commentary in the West, to the reexamination of the tenets of the *Sharī'ah* in the religious realm, and also to an opening of Islamic thought to the acceptance of Western ideas in the philosophical, political, social and economic domains. Moreover, there have been and continue to be a number of Muslims who have become secularized and who represent secularist forces within the Islamic world and are therefore, strictly speaking, not Islamic thinkers with a modernist bent. Nevertheless, they must also be considered along with the modernists in reviewing the present situation in the Islamic world.

Almost all of the important ideological positions and philosophies which have been fashionable in the West during the past century, ranging from evolutionism and progressivism to egalitarianism, Marxism, socialism, existentialism, positivism and all of the other schools of thought which comprise modernism as such, have had followers or at least partial followers within the Islamic world. Some of these followers have even tried to create a synthesis between Islam as a religion and Western thought of a leftist color especially during the past few decades. During this time, many elements drawn from leftist ideologies have penetrated into the Islamic world in the garb of expressions taken from the language of the Quran and *Ḥadīth* as well as of classical Islamic thought. Some have even tried to transform Islam as a religion into a leftist ideology.

As for revivalism or what the West has now come to call the new wave of fundamentalism, although this term is really not correct when it is applied to Islam, this type of reaction has not only continued during the last few decades upon the earlier foundations established by such groups as the Muslim brotherhood, the Jamā'at-i Islāmī of Pakistan founded by Mawlānā Mawdūdī and the Salafiyyah movement, associated with such figures as Rashīd Riḍā, which has had strong following in both Egypt and Syria as well as Arabia itself, it has also manifested itself during the last fifteen years in more politically active and in some cases revolutionary movements such as those of Ayatollah Khomeini in Iran, the Shi'ites in Lebanon and the Islamic movements of Egypt and Algeria.

The whole phenomenon of revivalism or so-called fundamentalism is a very complicated one and covers a spectrum ranging from moderate forms which go back to the puritanical and revivalist movements of the thirteenth and fourteenth Islamic century reformers to types of movements which, while trying to reassert the primacy of the *Sharī'ah*, also use a great deal of the language and ideas of nineteenth century European revolutionary and ideological thought. It is not, therefore, possible here to give a general description which would cover every aspect of all of these phenomena known under the rubric of revivalism or "fundamentalism." Nevertheless, it can be asserted that most of these movements share together on the one hand a concern for the preservation and revival of the *Sharī'ah*, the political and social independence of Muslims and opposition to Western social norms, and, on the other hand, a passive attitude and indifference to the penetration of Western science and technology and various kinds of Western managerial and administrative institutions and ways of thinking which accompany the adoption of technology. Also, nearly all these movements share in the fact that they ignore the significance of Islamic art, architecture and city planning and are impervious to the need for the preservation of the artistic and aesthetic environment of Islam and for its protection from intrusion by Western norms. This attitude also holds true for the Islamic intellectual tradition which they usually neglect except for what concerns directly the faith, juridical matters and ritual practice. In fact none of these movements has led to a flowering of Islamic thought or art, philosophy or literature.

Related to these revivalist movements, but not identical with them, is a kind of millenialism or Mahdiism which, as already pointed out, also manifested itself in the 1820's and 30's or the latter part of the thirteenth Islamic century when Muslims became fully aware for the first time of their subjugation by the West. During the last two decades, different movements in parts of the Islamic world as far apart as Nigeria and Iran have demonstrated Mahdiist or millenialist elements within them. There are those who believe that the unprecedented subjugation of the Islamic world which comprises nearly a billion people by forces from the outside, against which the Muslims have not been able to do a great deal, marks the advent of events of an eschatological nature. They believe that existing problems can be solved only with the direct help of Allah and through His intervention in history.

In certain instances these usually traditional and pious sentiments and attitudes have, however, been either taken over or become combined with more revolutionary ideas and movements which have manifested themselves during the past decades. As a result, it is not always possible to draw a clear line between the revolutionary and the Mahdiist elements in a particular movement. As a matter of fact, this whole phenomenon is not very different from what happened in certain periods of European history when millenialist movements within Christianity led also to revolutionary social and sometimes political movements.

It is important to note here that the transformation of Islam from a religion and total way of life into an ideology is to be seen in many current revivalist movements as well as among certain modernist ones. Both groups forget that the word "ideology" is in fact a purely Western term which had no correspondence in classical Islamic thought and cannot even be translated easily into Arabic or other Islamic languages. In converting Islam to an ideology, therefore, even the revivalists who stand opposed to the West, at least in their open declarations, often pursue trends of thought which have very much to do with the history of the Western world where religion became converted in many quarters into ideology and finally into a secular ideology as is to be seen in the case of Marxism.

In addition to these reactions within the Islamic world during the last few decades namely, the modernist, revivalist or fundamentalist and the millenialist or Mahdiist, traditional Islam has also begun to assert itself intellectually and even socially and artistically in a way that it had not done previously except within the confines of certain limited circles within the Islamic world. During the past few decades, Muslim writers, who belong to the traditional Islamic perspective, have begun to write extensively in not only Islamic languages but also in European ones to explain the realities of Islam to the West and also to the young Muslims who have been brought up in a Western educational system either in the West itself or within the Islamic world. These thinkers have also sought to provide answers to the challenges of the West whether they be philosophical, scientific, economic, social or technological, basing their response not on emotional reactions or simply juridical opposition, but upon a veritably Islamic intellectual perspective. They have gone to the very roots of the various Western ideologies and schools of thought which stand opposed to the Islamic worldview and yet have influenced Muslims. The traditional school has also been very active in trying to bring back to life the principles of Islam as they can be applied to the condition of contemporary humanity. It has tried to rethink, on the basis of the Islamic worldview, the foundations of Western science and technology and to confront the challenges of modern thought, science and technology in depth rather than simply through emotional response. It has also sought to preserve and revive Islamic art and its principles which have been so severely eclipsed during the past few decades with the onslaught of Western technology and Western ideas concerning architecture, interior decoration, city planning, etc.

The question of the meaning and methodology and also the problems involved in the adoption of Western science and technology have been the concern of not only the traditional thinkers but the other groups as well, especially the modernists. For a long time, many in the Islamic world followed the views of Jamāl al-Dīn al-Afghānī, who thought that modern science was simply Islamic science as it had been transplanted in the West, but which the Christian West could not treat appropriately and come to terms with successfully in contrast to the Muslims who had no problems in harmonizing science and their religion. As a result, until recently many Muslims had not given much thought to problems arising from the adoption of Western science and technology. This naive misjudgment about the nature of modern science is in fact still shared by both the revivalists or fundamentalists and the modernists. Both groups espouse openly the acceptance in almost a blind fashion of all Western science and technology without examining their consequences for Islamic life and thought.

During the last few decades, however, a much more critical attitude has begun to develop in this domain. Extensive discussion is now being carried out as to the meaning of Islamic science, its relation to the Islamic revelation, the relation of that science to Western science and how Western science can be integrated into an Islamic worldview. The final answers to these basic questions have not, however, been as yet provided in such a way as to be acceptable to the whole of the Islamic world. The questions remain very burning ones and conferences are held throughout the Islamic world almost every year in order to come to an understanding of these fundamental problems.

The same holds true for technology. All Muslim countries have been trying to industrialize as rapidly as possible. It is only now that the negative consequences of industrialization for the environment as well as for the religious life and the fabric of society, resulting in cultural dislocation and psychological and personal malaise, as can be observed in the larger Islamic cities where industrialization has been successful to some extent, have become manifest. As a result, many Muslims are beginning to reformulate the Islamic attitude towards modern Western technology. A great deal of thought is now being given in certain quarters to the question of alternative technology and different ways of using energy in such a way that Muslims will not simply emulate all the mistakes that Western technology has made to this day, mistakes which now threaten the very fabric of life over the whole globe.

Another field in which there has been a great deal of activity, led by not only traditionalist Muslims but also participated in by the revivalists and the modernists, is that of Islamic education. Since the thirteenth Islamic century, numerous Muslims have been sent either to the West to study and to master Western science, medicine and technology or to modern schools and universities within the Islamic world. The latter were established either by missionaries to propagate Christianity and along with it Western humanism and later on secularism or by Muslim governments seeking to create institutions which would train their citizens in such a way as to be able to gradually hold the reins of power in their hands and run a modern society and economy. Although the goal of many of these educationists was commendable from the point of view of the immediate needs of their societies, their efforts nevertheless resulted in the creation of a major hiatus and cleavage within the Islamic world. Within most Islamic countries, two types of Islamic institutions came to vie with each other. One was an educational system based upon Western ideas, often presented very subtly in the domain of the humanities where Islamic teachings could be substituted and more openly in the social and natural sciences; and the second was traditional schools where students continued and still continue to learn Islamic subjects such as jurisprudence and, of course, Quran commentary and *Ḥadīth*.

During the last two decades, many Muslim leaders have become aware of the tragic consequences of such a situation which creates a society divided against itself. The first World Muslim Educational Conference, held in Makkah in 1977, marked a major step in trying to correct this problem within the Islamic world. Since then several major conferences have been held, curricula have been devised and institutions have been created throughout the Islamic world to try to unify the two educational systems and bring into being a system which will train students who will remain devoutly Muslim and attached to their own tradition while learning disciplines such as modern physics, chemistry, engineering or the social sciences which have come from the West. Here again, there has been as yet no final and successful solution nor the creation of a model which all Muslim countries could adopt. Nevertheless, there is a great deal of intellectual effort being spent in this domain and in what is now coming to be known as the "Islamization of knowledge" which means integrating various subjects into the Islamic worldview. The dimensions and parameters of this important undertaking are being debated within many institutions and by many of the leading thinkers in the Islamic world today.

Unfortunately, despite these activities and efforts, the number of students sent from the Islamic world, often intellectually and spiritually unprepared, to the West as well as those going to Westernized educational institutions within the Islamic world continues to increase from year to year and with it the cultural and social and even religious dislocation within Islamic society continues to be felt to an ever greater degree as time goes on. It is sad to say that there does not exist enough in-depth knowledge of the West within the Islamic world. Conditions have improved somewhat in this domain but still within the whole width and breadth of the Islamic world how many scholars do we have who know Greek and Latin, which are the basic intellectual and historic languages of the West, in comparison with the number of people in the West who know Arabic and Persian and who can study the roots of Islamic civilization and thought throughout the centuries from their own point of view? The same holds true for the number of Muslims who are experts in Christian thought or in medieval European civilization or Renaissance and seventeenth century European history, in the rise of the Scientific Revolution and the many other important transformations which have made Western civilization what it is.

Most of the Islamic world still suffers from the lack of a profound knowledge of the West while it is being deeply affected by the ideas, products, external manifestations and activities of the Western world ranging from cars to computers, from the cinema to literature, from philosophical ideas to economics. Western ideas and values continue to flood the Islamic world through the mass media and other means for the transfer of information from one side of the world to the other. What is lacking is not information about the West or Muslims who have contact with the West, but a knowledge from the Islamic point of view of the roots of the culture and ideas of the Western world, a knowledge which alone can provide Muslims with the means necessary to confront the challenges of the modern West and to provide an Islamic response to them.

It is precisely with this need in mind that we turn in the next section of this book to an analysis of Western civilization that gave rise to the modern world which in turn has left the imprint of its ideas and points of view upon the Islamic world during the last few centuries. It is hoped that the young Muslim, who must carry the responsibility and the burden for the future of the Islamic world upon his or her shoulders, will be able to carry out this responsibility more successfully by gaining a more profound knowledge of the West. Such a knowledge will not only enable that person to navigate more successfully upon the very dangerous and stormy sea of the modern world and to protect his or her faith against all of the dangers lurking at every corner, it will also help to formulate, with the help of Allah, the necessary Islamic responses which would guarantee for those young Muslims and for the Islamic world as a whole, for which young educated Muslims will of necessity become leaders, a safe future, and will also safeguard the continuation of a civilization impregnated by the message of the Quran. But more important than that, such a knowledge will help to defend the religion at the heart of that civilization, a religion which has continued to echo over the ages and is still the vehicle for the truths revealed in the Noble Quran through the Blessed Prophet of Allah who was destined to bring the final plenary message from Heaven to present day humanity.

Part II
The Nature of the Modern World

CHAPTER 8
RELIGION IN THE MODERN WEST

Despite the extensive contact that Muslims have had and continue to have with the Western world since the last century, there has been very little study carried out by them about religion in the West. As stated previously, there are very few Muslim scholars who know the classical languages well enough to study the history of the main religion in the West, namely, Christianity, and also very few who have dealt in depth with Christian theology and religious thought. This is a sad state of affairs when one sees that there is such a large number of Western scholars both Christian and Jewish, as well as those who are secularized and therefore do not accept the religious point of view, who have taken the trouble to master Arabic, Persian and other Islamic languages in order to study Islam itself. They write about Islam in all of its facets from their own point of view and some have even tried to dictate to Muslims how they should study their own religion.

In any case, there is no equivalence between the West's knowledge of Islam, however slanted its point of view may be for Muslims, and Islam's understanding of religion in the West from the Islamic point of view. The latter is very rare and much that has been written by modern Muslim scholars about religion and thought in the West is in fact for the most part based on either the Western point of view or upon shallow and limited knowledge which has prevented most such studies from penetrating in depth into the meaning of religion and its history in the Western world.

Two diametrically opposed points of view concerning religion in the West are to be seen among Muslims. Some consider all Westerners to be Christians, with the small Jewish minority being of course an exception, and often refer to Westerners as "those Christians" as if the West were the West of the Middle Ages when the Crusades were carried out and Western civilization lived in what has been called the Age of Faith. Another group of Muslims hold the opposite view that all Westerners are materialists or agnostics and skeptics and in fact there is no religion among the Westerners.

Now it is essential to insist that both of these views are false. On the one hand, the West since the seventeenth century and even before that since the Renaissance has been moving in the direction of secularization and the dilution of religion in the everyday life of men. As a result, there are numerous Westerners who are no longer technically speaking Christians or Jews although they are inheritors of Christianity and Judaism. And yet there are still a fairly large number of people who practice Christianity and also Judaism within a civilization which itself can no longer be called a Christian civilization. It is very important for Muslims to understand the exact situation as far as the role of religion in the West is concerned and to avoid the extreme views currently held by so many people in the Islamic world. A young Muslim will never be able to understand the modern world without understanding the role of religion and also its eclipse in the West during the incubation, birth, growth and spread of the modern world in Europe and America and its later spread to other lands.

The West has been of course predominantly Christian since the rise of medieval Western civilization. This civilization was not simply a continuation of the civilization of Greece and Rome. It was essentially a civilization created when Christianity spread into the Roman Empire, after the weakening and gradual decline of that empire, and also among the Germanic and Celtic people of Northern Europe. The result was the birth of a new civilization which, while inheriting important elements from Rome and also from Greece, was nevertheless thoroughly Christian. Therefore, the history of religion in the West as we know it today is related most of all to Christianity. For many centuries Christianity in the

West, in contrast to the East where it was divided into small churches easily overcome after the rise and spread of Islam, was nearly monolithic in the sense that it had a single institution and organization identified with Catholicism. The pope remained the supreme head of the Western Church. As for the Orthodox Church, which is the other major branch of traditional Christianity, it did not accept the authority of the pope and therefore remained distinct from Catholicism. Henceforth, Catholicism remained the single Western Christian institution during the long period of the birth and formation of Western civilization.

It was Christianity in its Catholic form that was responsible for what has come to be known as the Middle Ages during which some of the most important institutions of the West as well as its thought patterns were formulated and crystallized, while this period also marks the peak of Christian sacred art in the West. During the Middle Ages, the Christians in the West followed a life of great devotion to religion and dedication to Christianity as interpreted by Catholicism and therefore felt in a way akin to the Muslim despite the great enmity they displayed against Islam, for the Christians witnessed in the Islamic world the presence of a community of faithful dedicated completely to the Word of Allah and to His injunctions. However in the West, in contrast to Islam, opposition began to be created against the authority of religion and against Catholicism in particular as a result of very complicated internal factors. These factors included the gradual loss of certain aspects of the inner teachings of Christianity, the excessive use of consolations and relics, the gradual rationalization of Christian religious thought and the skepticism inherent in late medieval nominalist theology.

This opposition took several different forms during what has come to be known as the Renaissance. During this period, one can see, on the one hand, the rise of humanism and individualism which were to become later hallmarks of modern civilization and which opposed the domination of religion in general and the religious civilization of the Middle Ages in particular. On the other hand, there was a religious reaction resulting in the rise of Protestantism and the Reformation, which sought to go back to early Christianity rooted in the Bible and especially the Gospels, hence the term Evangelicalism, which became associated with this movement.

Protestantism and Catholicism must not be compared to Sunnism and Shi'ism in the Islamic context as has been done by certain scholars. Sunnism and Shi'ism both go back to the origins of Islam and the very beginning of Islamic history whereas Protestantism is a later protest against the existing Catholic Church and came into being some fifteen hundred years after the foundation of Christianity.

In contrast to Catholicism which preserved its monolithic and unified structure through the papacy and the hierarchy upon which the church was based, Protestantism soon divided into many different schools, not only the churches associated with Calvin and Luther who were the two most important early reformers, but many new religious groupings. These churches ranged all the way from the Church of England which has remained "Catholic" in a certain way but which has refused to accept the authority of the pope and therefore is considered to be a branch of Protestantism to Protestant churches which arose in the eighteenth and nineteenth centuries such as the Methodist, Presbyterian and Baptist which placed a great deal more emphasis upon individual effort based upon the authority of the Gospels, individual interpretation of the Bible and social action. The number of churches which developed and even continue to develop within Protestantism is vast. It is in fact difficult for the Muslim upon first coming to America or Europe to understand how it is possible to have so many different denominations and churches.

It is important, nevertheless, to understand the total phenomenon of Protestantism ranging all the way from those churches which emphasize ritual such as the Episcopal to those which are especially devoted to social action such as the Baptist and also to understand how it is possible for new communities to come together around a particular leader and find a new branch or new denomination of Protestantism. All of the Protestant churches, at least until recently, have shared in the belief in God and Christ, otherwise, they would not be Christian. They have also emphasized the significance of the Bible in contrast to the Catholic Church which, in addition to belief in God, Christ and the Bible, has always emphasized the historical continuity of the teachings of the Church, the apostolic succession and what is called in Latin *traditio* which corresponds to some extent to the commentaries upon the Quran and *Ḥadīth* composed over the centuries in the Islamic world.

As it happened, the Protestant Reformation and revolt against Catholicism began in Germany and what is now Switzerland and took root mostly in northern Europe. It did not have much success in the south although there was a critical period when Protestantism threatened the destruction of the whole of the Catholic world. The rise of Joan of

Arc, her burning at the stake and her sanctification within the Catholic Church, represent a crucial moment when the tide of the spread of Protestantism was finally stemmed and Catholicism in France, Spain, Italy, Portugal and certain other parts of Europe was able to survive. As it happened, southern Europe became the main home of the Catholic Church but northern Europe was converted mostly to Protestantism while Catholic minorities continued to survive in the north. Certain countries such as Germany remained in between, having both a large Protestant and a sizable Catholic population. Moreover, for diverse historical reasons certain countries such as Ireland, Poland and Austria preserved a special alliance with the Catholic Church and remained Catholic while being located in the north. Consequently, it is not possible to draw an exact geographical line as far as Catholicism and Protestantism are concerned. Nevertheless, for a young Muslim seeking to understand the religious map of Europe, one can say as a first approximation that from the sixteenth century onward, the religious culture of the northern European countries came to be ever more dominated by Protestantism while the religious life of the southern European countries remained predominantly Catholic. In fact in certain countries such as Italy, Protestantism remained and remains even to this day practically nonexistent. The same also holds true or at least held true until a decade ago for Spain and Portugal.

As for the American continent, the religious pattern was at first determined by the manner of its colonization. South and Central America and French Canada, colonized by Catholic Spain, Portugal and France, became Catholic and North America and British Canada became Protestant. But as a result of migration, North America has a large Catholic population today while the cultures of the United States and Canada remain still profoundly influenced by Protestantism. In fact some of the most devout but also literalist Protestants in the world who are deeply attached to the study of the Bible are found in the southern states of the United States in what is called the Bible Belt and are referred to as fundamentalists.

There is another major branch of Christianity which also needs to be mentioned although its adherents reside mostly in eastern Europe and not the West. This branch is the Orthodox Church with its Greek, Russian, Rumanian, Bulgarian and certain other branches. This Church which, like the Catholic Church goes back to the origin of Christianity and which was associated with the Greek speaking Byzantine Empire, is less centrally organized than the Catholic and still has its center in Istanbul, the old Constantinople which was the capital of the Byzantines. In its theology, spiritual practices, aesthetics and many other elements, the Orthodox Church is closer to Islam than are the Western churches and it has many adherents among Christian Arabs. But its presence in Europe is limited to the eastern countries and among emigrants from eastern Europe to western European countries and America.

The Catholic and Protestant churches fought for a long time against each other. In fact many of the wars in the seventeenth and eighteenth centuries were identified with Catholic and Protestant causes. Gradually, however, there has come into being a major movement especially during this century which seeks to make peace between the various churches. What is now called ecumenism in the West concerns not only peace between various religions but also within Christianity itself. This can be seen in the rapprochement between Catholicism and the various Protestant churches including the Church of England which broke away from the papacy during the rule of Henry VIII and also between Catholicism and Orthodoxy.

Nevertheless, the religious positions of the various Christian communities in the West differ on many issues. Catholicism continues to emphasize the ritual aspect of religion and has a certain dimension which is familiar to the ritual emphasis seen in Islam, while Protestantism usually places greater emphasis upon social action and also the responsibility of the individual, features which also have a certain resemblance to the social teachings of Islam and the emphasis of Islam upon the direct relation of each individual with God. It is, therefore, difficult to try to contend that one of these two branches of Christianity is more similar to Islam than the other. Each of them can be compared to Islam in a certain way or to certain Islamic schools because within Islam also there is of course diversity of interpretation of the *Sharīʿah,* although there is more unity within the structure of Islam on the basis of the Quran and the *Ḥadīth* than one can observe in the very complicated pattern of the Christian churches and denominations.

It is important also to understand in this context that within both Protestantism and Catholicism there have been important movements in the twentieth century which have sought either to revive or to modernize the churches. On the Catholic side, for a long time the Church, at least in its purely religious if not in its artistic and social aspects, resisted the pressure of modernism and secularization until in the 1960s with the

Second Vatican Council, the movement which is called *aggiornamento* gained ascendancy and many of the teachings of the Church became modernized. As a result, even Latin which had been used as the liturgical language of the Catholic Church throughout Western Europe and later the Americas and elsewhere for nearly two thousand years was changed to the vernacular and local languages. It might appear that this modernization made dialogue between Catholics and followers of other religions easier, but in fact this is quite doubtful. Moreover, this movement has diluted the religious teachings of Catholicism and has therefore made it more difficult for Catholics to preserve the traditional point of view which had been held in the Catholic Church for such a long time and which is closer in depth to the traditional teachings of Islam. For those seeking the traditional teachings of the Church, the whole movement has been in fact a catastrophe leading to a greater segmentation within the Church than ever before.

The modernizing movement within the Catholic Church spread very rapidly and yet did not become completely dominant. There is today within the Catholic Church a struggle between more orthodox and traditional elements and the modernizing movements. The struggle has taken different forms in different parts of the Catholic world. For example, in the United States there are many more modernists than in the churches which were oppressed behind the Iron Curtain in such countries as Czechoslovakia and Poland. It is, therefore, bewildering for Muslims today to see within the Catholic Church itself differences of views concerning nearly every major theological and social issue all the way from the acceptance or rejection of the theory of evolution to questions of abortion and the family. This was not the case in the nineteenth and the first part of the twentieth centuries when despite the presence of modernism in the West, Catholic doctrine represented a unity which was related to the unity of the Church itself. Only time will tell how these forces will work themselves out, but there is no doubt that the modernizing movements of the sixties did not create suitable conditions for the preservation of religious teachings within the Catholic Church and its spread as many of the modernist advocates had predicted. In any case, from the Islamic point of view, many of the changes brought about through this process of modernization represent in many ways the surrender of the religious perspective to secularization in the name of embracing the world and accommodating religion to every changing condition of a humanity which is falling away with ever greater speed from its norm.

As for Protestantism, it has been witness to two parallel phenomena: on the one hand one can see an ever greater diluting of the religious message among even many "believers" so that there are now Christians who no longer believe in the miraculous birth of Christ, the virginity of the Virgin, the bodily resurrection and many other fundamental tenets of traditional Christianity. On the other hand, there has occurred to an ever greater degree the rise of what is called Evangelical Christianity and fundamentalism in the original sense of the term before this term became applied in a mistaken fashion to Islam. Evangelicalism seeks to revive Christianity by going back to a literal interpretation of the Bible and although it has a very closed view as to the meaning of religion and excludes the understanding of Islam and other religions, not to speak of Catholicism within Christianity, it leads its followers to be fervent devotees of the Bible and followers of the religious teachings of the community especially in matters of ethics. This phenomenon needs to be understood by Muslims because within the very secularized ambience which any young Muslim experiences in the modern West and especially in America, there exists intense religious activity which is sometimes difficult to understand for a Muslim not well acquainted with the dynamics of the history of Christianity.

Besides the development and historical unfolding of Christianity in the West as far as theology, institutions and other aspects of Christianity are concerned, it is important to pay some attention to the long battle between religion and secularism in order to understand the meaning and position of religion in the West today. From the Renaissance until today, Christianity, and also to some extent Judaism in the West, have had to carry out a constant battle against ideologies, philosophies, institutions and practices which are secular in nature and which challenge the authority of religion and in fact its very validity and legitimacy. These challenges to religion have varied from political ideas which are based on secularism to the denial of the religious foundation of morality and the philosophical denial of the reality of God and of the afterlife or of revelation and sacred scripture. The history of the West has been marked during the last few centuries by a constant battle between the forces of religion and secularism and in fact the gaining of the upper hand by secularism and consequently the denial of the reality of religion and its pertinence to various domains of life.

First of all, secularism gradually separated philosophy and then science from the realm of religion and then removed the various political, economic and social ideas and institutions which had possessed a religious significance in the medieval period in the West from the universe of religious meaning. This also holds true for Western art which in earlier centuries had not only received the patronage of religion, but was also deeply imbued with religious values and meaning. In fact, the greatest pre-modern art of the West was produced by artists devoted to the teachings of the Church. The Church also commissioned countless buildings, works of music, paintings etc. which possess a most profound religious significance.

The process of secularization went a step further in the nineteenth century when even the domain of theology, which had until then remained naturally within the fold of religion, fell under the sway of secularism. At this time agnostic and atheistic ideologies began to challenge theology itself while the traditional theological perspective began to retreat from the one domain which had been left to it, namely the domain of purely religious thought. It is important here to point out that theology as understood in the Western context is central for Christianity in contrast to Islam where theology is not as important as Islamic Law. In Christianity, all serious religious thought is related to theology and therefore the retreat of Christian theology to an ever greater degree from various realms of thought meant also the retreat of religion in the West to an ever greater extent from the every day life and thought of Western man. This tendency reached such a stage in the twentieth century that much of theology itself became gradually secularized. During the last few decades, there have been such movements as "the death of God," Teilhardism, liberation theology and the like which have introduced various forms of secularism including the theory of evolution and Marxism into the very body of Christian theology

Nevertheless, one must remember that a large segment of humanity cannot simply lose its religious heritage so rapidly. To a great extent, what is positive in the Western soul, including the virtues which one sees among many Western people, is the heritage which has survived from Christianity. Although many Westerners no longer consider themselves to be Christians, the virtues of charity or humility which many people display even in non-religious contexts come from a Christian background and the Christian element is much stronger in the Western soul than many people would think by simply glancing at the surface of things. In fact, for centuries in the West religion and ethics were profoundly related as they have been in the Islamic world where there is no ethics (*akhlāq*) outside the teachings of the *Sharī'ah* and of the Quranic revelation. In the West also, until fairly recently, ethics was related to the teachings of the Christian Church although Christianity did not have a *Sharī'ah* as understood in Islam. Of course, the teachings of Christ are profoundly ethical and to this day the ethical concerns of Western people, even those who consider themselves to be agnostic, come ultimately from Christianity which molded the minds and souls of Western men and women for many centuries before the rise of secularism.

A word must also be said here about Judaism in the Western world. In the same way that Oriental and Sephardic Jews, that is, Jews of Spain who lived for centuries in peace and harmony with Muslims, became culturally integrated into Islamic society, European or Ashkenazi Jews became integrated into European civilization and from the nineteenth century onward joined the mainstream of Western culture. However, in contrast to the Islamic world where Jews followed their traditional and orthodox ways, in the West one can see three groups within Judaism: the orthodox, the conservative and the reformed. The latter represent, within Judaism, a phenomenon similar to liberal Protestantism within Christianity. Furthermore, it is important for young Muslims coming to the West to know that not all Jews in the West are religiously oriented. There has come into being, since the nineteenth century, a notable class of highly secularized "thinkers" of Jewish origin who have been culturally more or less identified with Judaism but who rebelled totally against the Jewish religion. The role of these figures such as Sigmund Freud, the father of psychoanalysis, in the secularization of Western thought and life has been great while at the other pole of Judaism, traditional Jewish rabbis and thinkers have been able to keep the flame of Judaism alive in the secularized atmosphere of the modern West and have been able to preserve Jewish Divine Law, the *Halakhah*, as well as Jewish mysticism in the forms of Hassidism and the Kabbala.

In order to understand the situation of religion in the modern West, it is also important to consider along with the modernization and secularization of religion the appearance of modern religious movements outside of the context of the traditional Christian churches. This phenomena includes not only such nineteenth century religious movements as

Mormonism, which now has a large following in the United States and elsewhere, and the establishment of rather modernized and "rationalized" forms of Christianity such as Unitarianism, but also during the last few decades newly founded modern "religions" in the West established by individuals claiming to be great spiritual teachers or what has now come to be known as *gurus*, a term which comes originally from Sanskrit and means teacher, the equivalent of the word *shaykh* in Arabic. These "new religions" have occasionally been founded by priests or ministers who have broken away from an existing traditional church and who have tried to create "religions" of their own. This type of phenomenon in the West has also drawn to a large extent from occultism and during the last few decades even such practices as magic, which were banned by the traditional Christian churches, have come to the fore again. There are people in the West who try to practice magic or go back to the old pre-Christian religions of Europe such as that of the Druids or the Celts and who create rather bizarre "new religions" or cults which become prevalent whenever and wherever the traditional religion has become weakened as one sees especially in America and northern Europe today.

Another religious phenomenon which is important to understand along with the so called "new religions" and revival of ancient religions is the turning of many people in the West to the religions of the East for guidance and help. From the beginning of the twentieth century and especially since the Second World War, many Westerners who have had the thirst for spiritual experience and religious knowledge but who have not been able to find what they have been seeking in the context of the existing religious institutions in the West have turned to Eastern religions. Some have turned to Hinduism, others to Buddhism and a number to Islam and especially to Sufi teachings within Islam. This tendency has certainly grown during the last few decades and continues to be strong. Some of the religious movements of Eastern origin, which have now sunk their roots in the soil of the West, are of an authentic nature while many are mere imitations leading to the establishment of devious cults strongly opposed by what survives of traditional religion in the West.

As far as Islam is concerned, it has also attracted a number of people in both America and Europe, people who have been lost in the maze of the confusion of the modern world and have sought a light which would save them from their state of despair and loss of direction. The spread of

Islam in the West is far from being negligible not only as a result of immigration but also as a consequence of the conversion of the number of often eminent and educated people to it. Islam also continues to appeal to Americans of African origin in a popular way and on the mass level. Consequently, there is now a notable African-American Muslim community in America which continues to grow especially in the larger urban centers.

Today the role of religion in the West is very different from its role in the Islamic world. All Western societies claim to be secular and in fact consider law to derive not from religion but from the voice of the people at least where there are democracies. Certain countries such as the United States emphasize very strongly the separation of church and state while other countries such as England, where the ruler of the country is also the head of the Church or Sweden where the official religion is Lutheran Protestantism, nevertheless do not base their laws upon religion. The same holds true for social practices which are supposed to emanate from laws established through the will of human beings choosing their elected officials to a legislature which then devises and passes laws.

The role of religion is, however, far from being negligible in the modern West. In fact, many of the tendencies of Westerners, even those who do not consider themselves to be religious, have a religious foundation. Also the role of religion has been important in the recent downfall of Communism in Eastern Europe and within the former Soviet Union. The young Muslim who first comes to the West should not at all misunderstand the role of religion as being totally negligible on the basis of the fact that he sees so much promiscuity and laxity in sexual morality or observes so many people who are against religious teachings and who display so much indifference to the practice of religion. Today in fact there is a greater interest in religion in the West than there was a few decades ago, mostly due to the breakdown of many Western ideologies and idols of the mind which had grown out of eighteenth and nineteenth century European thought and which had taken the place of religion. These ideologies have gradually fallen aside and their danger and power of destruction have become manifest as never before. Today religion in the West is attracting a large number of intelligent people to its study and also to some extent to its fold more than perhaps at any time since the secularization of the religious civilization of the West several centuries ago.

There is also a great deal of ambiguous and somewhat ambivalent interest in religion which expresses itself in the wide usage of the term "spirituality" or the seeking of "meaningful life styles" so prevalent throughout America and Europe. This search is often carried out with the most serious intention and in earnestness although it is not crystallized and clear for many of those who seek deep religious meaning in the secularized ambience which surrounds them. One must, therefore, remember that with the destruction of so much of traditional religion in the West during the last few centuries and especially the modernization of so much of what remained of traditional religion during the last few decades, one can also see the revival of interest in the rediscovery of the sacred.

It is in the matrix of these complicated forces and patterns that the role of religion in the West must be understood today. And it is also in the light of both the secularization of traditional religion and the quest for meaning and the rediscovery of religion as the foundation of human life in the West that one must understand the role of Islam in the West today. There has been a major migration of Muslims since the Second World War to Europe and America, many of them educated men and women who have therefore brought to these countries not only their faith but also a literate and conscious expression of Islamic culture and thought. As mentioned already, Islam has also spread in America among both African-Americans and Americans of European descent as well as in certain areas of Europe. The number among the white Europeans and Americans has not been as great as that among those of African descent but it has included a number of eminent writers, artists, thinkers and philosophers. Today Islam is the fastest growing religion in the West as well as in Africa and certain other areas of the world. It is already the second most numerous religion in Europe and by the year 2000 will probably match Judaism as the second religion in number of adherents in America.

The spread of Islam and its presence in the West is, however, still not totally successful in the sense that Islam has not as yet been able to create an Islamic culture and ambience for itself as it did when it spread into China, India, Africa or other cultural areas of the world during its earlier history. Nevertheless, Islam is already a part of the religious scene of the West and although it is still a small minority in comparison with Christianity, it is nevertheless a religion which must be recognized and reckoned with.

It is the Islamic community in the West that should in fact bear the primary responsibility for providing an understanding of religion in the West for Muslims, studying it in depth and making the result of this knowledge known to the rest of the Islamic world where the contact with the West has bewildered many Muslims, not only the young but also the old, and where the understanding of the role and meaning of religion in the experience of Western man remains usually shallow. There is, however, no aspect of Western civilization that is more important for Muslims to understand than religion both in its living reality and also in its long battle against secularism and anti-religious forces which have waged a war against it since the Middle Ages. Muslims can learn a great deal from this long battle because today Islam also has to wage the battle against secularization and secularist ideologies which have come from the West. Islam can learn from how Christianity, and also Judaism, have encountered such forces and can also come to know the soul of the Western people better by understanding the role that Christianity has had historically and even continues to have to some extent to this day upon the worldview, the ethical outlook and also the social and private lives of men and women in the West. The anti-religious modernism which now threatens Islam and Muslims everywhere can be fully understood only by understanding the religion of the civilization in whose bosom modernism first developed, against which it rebelled, and whose tenets it has been challenging through constant battle since the birth of the modern world in the Renaissance.

Chapter 9
Modern Western Philosophy and Schools of Thought

For a young Muslim, as in fact for a young person who has grown up in any other non-Western culture, the significance of philosophy in the West and its role in the formation of modern civilization and what is known specifically as modernism is at first difficult to understand. As we have seen earlier, in the Islamic world, as in other traditional worlds, philosophy has always been closely allied to religion. It has always meant wisdom and has never sought to oppose the truths revealed by God through sacred texts which for Muslims is above all the Quran complemented by the *Ḥadīth*. In the West for a long time the situation was more or less similar to that found in the Islamic world. While Christian civilization dominated over the West, philosophy was closely related and allied to theology and to the questions posed by the very presence of revelation. It sought to elucidate the deeper meaning of the religious message and to provide a rational understanding of a universe in which the religious reality of Christianity was very much present and where faith played a central role. It is only from the Renaissance and especially the eleventh/seventeenth century onward, that is, the beginning of the modern age, that the role of philosophy in the West begins to change considerably.

During the modern period philosophy in the West first separated itself from religion, then allied itself to the empirical and natural sciences and developed various modes of thinking which often sought to replace the truths of religion. Much of what one observes in the modern world today, whether it be in the realm of ethics or politics, the theoretical understanding of the nature of reality or epistemology, is rooted in modern philosophy which became more and more a rival and in many cases an opponent of theology, wisdom and religion. As a result, some have come to call much of modern philosophy "misosophy" (literally hatred of wisdom rather than love for it which philosophy implies by its very etymology). Furthermore, in the thirteenth/nineteenth century philosophy began to see itself as a complete replacement for religion as one can see in the rise of the very idea of ideology at that time, a term used widely today even by Muslims who rarely realize the essentially secular and anti-religious character of the very concept of ideology which has gradually come to replace traditional religion in so many circles.

It is, therefore, important to comprehend the significance of philosophy in Western civilization in order to understand the nature of modernism. Without this understanding the meaning of modern phenomena, whether they be in the fields of science or art, politics or economics, social realities or even private behavior, is difficult to grasp. It is certainly true that Christianity and also Judaism have survived to some extent in the West, but the void that has been created by the partial disappearance of religion from the scene has become filled by modes of thinking which have arisen from various Western schools of philosophy or more specifically from what is called modern philosophy by the historians of philosophy in the West.

The history of philosophy in its present day form is a modern Western discipline which developed in Germany in the thirteenth/nineteenth century and turned rapidly into almost a science of its own and even began to gain philosophical significance in itself. Historians of philosophy in the West usually classify Western philosophy into three periods: ancient, medieval and modern. This, of course, is a specifically European and Western way of looking at the history of philosophy, even if this classification has tried to incorporate Islamic philosophy unto its scheme, and it must not be confused with the traditional Islamic view of philosophy and its history which is quite different. In Islam the term medieval does not have the same chronological meaning as it does in the

West. Many a Muslim thinker of the thirteenth/nineteenth century would be classified as "medieval" from the point of view of the content of his thought while living in what Western historians call the modern period.

According to the Western scheme, the philosophies which grew in Athens, Alexandria and other centers of Hellenic and Hellenistic thought and Rome are called the philosophies of antiquity or classical philosophy. Those which began to flower with the Christianization of Europe from about the fourth and fifth centuries A.D. until the breakup of medieval civilization are called medieval in which Islamic and Jewish philosophy are also included. Yet, even in the West this type of thought known in its later forms as Scholasticism survived, especially in Catholic circles, into later centuries and in fact it has not completely died out even today. And then the philosophies which grew from the rejection of the wedding between philosophy, theology and Christian religious teachings and which are based on humanism, rationalism and other ideas of the Renaissance flowered especially in the eleventh/seventeenth century. They continue to this day and are called modern, to which some now add the modifier post-modern. Of these three periods of Western philosophy, the first was more or less shared by Islam and Christianity although before the Middle Ages the Christians knew much less of Greek philosophy than did the Muslims whereas later schools of Roman philosophy had a much more important role to play in Christian Europe than they did in Islam. As for what is called medieval Christian philosophy, it was of course, very closely allied to Islamic philosophy especially from the sixth/twelfth century onward when many of the Arabic sources became available in Latin. As a result, this period of Western philosophy may be said to be parallel with that of Islamic philosophy and there are many morphological and historical relations between the two.

Finally, modern philosophy, which grew from the rejection of the traditional worldview of medieval Christian civilization and is based on human reason and the senses independent of revelation, does not have a parallel within the Islamic world and is something unique to Western civilization. At least this was so until the last century when modernism began to encroach upon, and sink its roots, in the soil of other civilizations including certain areas of the Islamic world where various Muslim thinkers became influenced by modern European thought.

The Medieval Period

In order to understand the modern world which is the goal and purpose of this book, it is especially to the modern period that we must turn, but a few words need to be said first of all about medieval European philosophy which is not usually studied in Islamic universities with the result that Muslims have produced very few scholars who have possessed serious knowledge of it. Knowledge of Scholastic philosophy is important not only in order to make clear the relationship between Christian philosophy and Islamic philosophy, but also in order to understand the background of modern European philosophy which, despite the rejection of its medieval past, has quite naturally drawn many ideas from that tradition during different periods. Moreover, even the rejection of the Scholastic tradition is related precisely to the ideas which were rejected and which must therefore be known. So let us turn first of all briefly to the so-called medieval era before we turn our attention to the modern period of Western thought and the beginning of what is called modern philosophy properly speaking.

What we shall do in this section, as in the rest of this chapter, is to deal with some of the key figures in each period through whom the fundamental problems or at least some of the basic issues faced by the philosophers of each age can be known. In this way, despite the limited space available, something can be learned about some of the ideas as well as the key figures of Western intellectual history.

St. Augustine (354-430 A.D.)

Many consider St. Augustine to be the founder of Western Christian thought both in its philosophical and theological aspects. Born in North Africa, St. Augustine turned in his youth to the study of philosophy especially that of Cicero and the Neoplatonists. For some years he was even a Manichaean, that is, a follower of a religion based on dualism which had issued from ancient Persia and had spread into the Roman Empire at that time. It was not until 386 A.D. that he became converted to Christianity, rising very rapidly in Christian ecclesiastical circles until he became the bishop of Hippo and one of the most important fathers of the Western Christian Church now known as the Catholic Church. In the year 400 A.D. St. Augustine wrote his famous *Confessions* which is one of the great masterpieces of Western thought. In this work he expressed his belief that philosophy could lead to happiness and even blessedness and could be harmonized with Christianity. In fact, he considered Christianity itself to be a philosophy in which the scriptures were the authority and where faith was central.

One of the main concerns of St. Augustine to which he turned over and over again was the relationship between faith and understanding or faith and reason and at the same time the relationship between reason and illumination. His major work, which is called *The City of God*, also contains the Christian view of time and history as well as of the perfect and imperfect society wherein he emphasized the significance of the presence of sin and the importance of redemption through Christ. When St. Augustine died in the year 430 A.D., he had already left a body of work which was to influence all later history of Christian thought and even much of Western philosophy in circles outside of the specifically Catholic confession.

Boethius Anicius (470 circa-524 A.D.)

Boethius was a Roman philosopher and the author of one of the most widely read works of European philosophy, *The Consolation of Philosophy*, which is primarily a Platonic work. He wanted to translate the works of Plato and Aristotle into Latin and to harmonize them, but he was only able to translate a few of Aristotle's logical treatises which henceforth became famous throughout the European Middle Ages. At the end of his life he was imprisoned and finally put to death by the Roman authorities on the accusation of treason against the state. It was at this time that Boethius wrote his *Consolation* which became the main channel for the knowledge of Platonism in the European Middle Ages.

Johannes Scotus Erigena (810-877 A.D.)

Erigena, an Irish philosopher, was able to integrate Neoplatonism and Christianity in a manner that became very influential in both philosophical circles and among the Christian mystics. He translated the works of Dionysius the Areopagite into Latin making him available for the first time to the West with all the consequences that this translation had in the later history of Western philosophy and theology. Erigena's most famous work is *The Division of Nature* which deals with the issuing of all things from God and the return of all things to Him. He is without doubt one of the greatest metaphysicians of Christianity and presents many ideas which are similar to those of Islamic metaphysicians.

St. Anselm (1033-1109 A.D.)

St. Anselm was one of the major figures of Christian theology and philosophy of the Middle Ages and an Augustian in theology. He is known in the history of philosophy for his formulation of the ontological argument for the existence of God. He provided a rational analysis of the Christian faith and believed that such a rational understanding of faith was essential to the understanding of religion itself and was in fact a religious duty. This view is summarized in his famous statement *credo ut intelligam* which means I believe in order to understand by which he meant that man must have faith in God in order to be able to understand the nature of things, hence the reliance of philosophy upon revelation. He is one of the most important figures in the West as far as the question of the relationship between faith and reason is concerned and is one of the founders of what is called High Scholasticism. His books are numerous among the most famous being the *Monologion* and *Proslogion* which contain his famous proof for the existence of God. He also wrote other metaphysical and theological treatises dealing with specifically religious questions such as the nature of Christ.

St. Bonaventure (1217-1274 A.D.)

St. Bonaventure is one of the greatest theologians and philosophers of Christianity. An Italian Franciscan, he was declared one of the doctors of the Church and remains to this day as one of the most important authorities in the interpretation of Christian thought among Catholics. He entered the University of Paris where he joined the Franciscan Order and studied theology in which he soon became a notable figure. He is especially well known for his insistence that the pursuit of truth is part of divine worship. He wrote commentaries on the Bible as well as the *Sentances* of Peter Lombard and was well-versed in the philosophy of St. Augustine and Aristotle as well as Islamic philosophy. He sought to combine these various philosophical schools in his defense of Christian thought. St. Bonaventure was also a great mystic and wrote one of the most famous treatises of mysticism of the Middle Ages called *The Journey of the Mind to God*, while at the same time he defended the Christian faith against attacks of those rationalistic philosophers who even at that time wanted to show the superiority of rational modes of thought to the tenets of faith.

St. Thomas Aquinas (1224/25-1274 A.D.)

Without doubt the most famous and influential of all medieval

European thinkers, St. Thomas Aquinas, entitled the Angelic Doctor, was born in Sicily. He was educated in Paris and became a member of the other great medieval order in Christianity, namely the Dominican Order. He studied with Albertus Magnus who was himself influenced deeply by Islamic philosophy and science and was a defender of Aristotelian thought in the Latin world. St. Thomas taught in Paris for many years where he defended his position on the relationship between faith and reason. He was opposed to both the Latin Averroists, that is, those interpreters of Ibn Rushd in the West who emphasized only the rationalistic aspect of the thought of the great Islamic philosopher, and those Christian thinkers who were totally opposed to rational philosophy. St. Thomas created a vast synthesis based on the Aristotelization of Christian thought, drawing heavily from the writings of Ibn Sīnā, al-Ghazzālī and other Islamic thinkers and creating a *summa* of theology which has been influential to this day and which is still the most important source of Catholic theology and philosophy. His two best known works, the *Summa Theologica* and *Summa Contra Gentiles*, are the greatest summations of classical Catholic philosophy and theology and among the most important works of European thought.

After St. Thomas, his school of thought continued strong into the eighth/fourteenth century with such figures as Duns Scotus but it was also criticized by the nominalists and gradually began to wane until in the ninth/fifteenth and tenth/sixteenth centuries the new wave of Renaissance thought began to replace Scholasticism in most centers of learning in Europe. Scholasticism, especially in the form of Thomism, survived strongly, however, in Italy and Spain into the tenth/sixteenth and eleventh/seventeenth centuries. Moreover, through the influence of Spain it spread into South America where it continued to produce a large number of philosophers of local significance but was not well known within the mainstream of European philosophy which gradually turned away from the synthesis of faith and reason created by the great theologians of the Middle Ages such as St. Thomas Aquinas and St. Bonaventure.

The Modern Period

For a while during the Renaissance, as Scholasticism gradually lost its central position in European philosophical thought, diverse strands of philosophy of differing natures began to manifest themselves. A number of philosophers tried to revive ancient philosophies, especially the Platonic and the Hermetic, independent of the synthesis created by the living Christian tradition. Others turned to humanism and rationalism and gradually schools of philosophy came into being which were no longer part and parcel of the Christian synthesis although the individual philosophers were still too close to the age of faith to turn away completely from all of the tenets of Christianity.

It is not possible here to say anything about many of the important figures of Renaissance philosophy such as Ficino and Pico Della Mirandola, who had such an important role in making the Platonic and Hermetic texts part and parcel of the Western intellectual world, or Petrarch and Erasmus who were the fathers of the new humanism which naturally turned against the theocratic and sacred vision of the traditional Christian world. What we wish to do rather is to turn to some of the most important and key figures of modern European philosophy from the end of the Renaissance to the present day in order to bring out the most salient features of the philosophy of the last few centuries marked by humanism, rationalism, empiricism and later on ideologies of the thirteenth/nineteenth century such as Marxism and finally positivism, phenomenology and existentialism in the fourteenth/twentieth century.

Before turning to these individual figures, it is necessary to clarify further the meaning and significance of humanism so characteristic of the Renaissance and modern philosophy. European humanism began in Italy, not France or Germany, and in fact mostly in southern Italy and Sicily where Islamic influences were still very much alive. Recent scholarship has shown the clear relationship between Islamic *adab* and certain aspects of this humanism in the emphasis of the latter, like the former, upon the importance of books and scholarship, rhetoric, the propensity toward flowery speech and many other elements. But this close historical relationship must not confuse the meaning of humanism in the mind of the Muslim reader. *Adab* remained always within the world of faith and envisaged man as the servant and vicegerent of God whereas humanism in the Renaissance and modern thought in general is in essence secular and signifies the independence of man from Heaven and his "freedom" on earth outside the laws and dictates of God and revelation even if certain authors have spoken of Christian humanism. In any case, when we speak of humanism in this book, it is secular humanism which we have in mind.

Francis Bacon (1561-1626 A.D.)

Although Francis Bacon, a man of many accomplishments both philosophical and political, is not considered to be as pertinent in modern philosophy as Descartes and some of the other important figures of that age, he is of great significance for the understanding of a central aspect of the modern world, namely the reliance upon science as means to power and the philosophy that lies behind such a point of view. Bacon, who was an English aristocrat educated at Cambridge, rose to become the lord chancellor before falling from grace and had an important role to play in the political life of his day. He was in favor of a powerful central state as well as state financial support for science and is considered by many to be the father of modern British science. He sought, in fact, to create "a new science" which would give man mastery over nature and power and domination over the environment. He also emphasized the usefulness of science and is, in a sense, a utilitarian from the philosophical point of view. He wrote a large number of well-known and influential books including collections of essays on various moral themes. Perhaps his most important book is the *Novum Organum* meaning the new logic. It was meant as a response to the *Organum* of Aristotle which was the foundation of classical Scholastic thought. Bacon also wrote the *New Atlantis* where he depicted his vision of the ideal society.

Bacon had a highly anti-metaphysical bent and supported mostly the materialistic philosophers of Greece. He tried to describe what came to be known as the "scientific method," emphasizing that data should be amassed and experiments made in order to have the secrets of nature revealed through organized observation. He is in fact credited by many with the establishment of the "scientific method" and the great Sir Isaac Newton expressed his debt to him. The most important heritage of Bacon is therefore not in pure philosophy but in the philosophy and methodology of science and his support for science as a state enterprise which would gradually become central in the life of European civilization.

René Descartes (1596-1650 A.D.)

More than Bacon, René Descartes must be considered as the founder of modern philosophy. A French Catholic philosopher well versed in medieval thought, Descartes also studied mathematics. However, he gradually turned away from the classical formulations of medieval philosophy in order to seek a new foundation for certitude upon the wake of his famous method of Cartesian doubt which led him to the assertion 'I think therefore I am' (*cogito ergo sum*). This most famous dictum is, in a sense, the foundation of modern philosophy in that it posits the cognitive act of the individual ego and human reason independent of revelation as the ultimate criterion of the truth and even the foundation of existence. This is why many consider him as the father of modern rationalism. Descartes' famous works *Discourse on the Method* and *Meditations on Prime Philosophy*, as well as the *Principles of Philosophy,* which contain his cosmology, are models of French prose and have had immense influence upon modern thought.

Descartes asserted the famous dualism according to which reality consists of two dimensions or two substances, one being the world of extension or matter and the other the world of consciousness or thought. Henceforth, European philosophy has always had difficulty in understanding the relation between the two. Later philosophers have continuously asked how can one substance which is the mind know the other which is the world of matter. It is from this radical dualism that has issued the later division of much of modern philosophy into the camp of the materialists and that of the idealists, or those who consider the material substance to be real and the other unreal or on the contrary, those who believe the world of the mind or "idea" to be real and the second unreal. In any case, the role of Descartes in the foundation of modern philosophy is immense. Moreover, his mathematicization of space and the discovery of many important mathematical ideas, especially descriptive geometry, were also very influential in the rise of modern science although his physics was totally rejected by Newtonian physics which became accepted as the norm a generation after Descartes.

Thomas Hobbes (1588-1679 A.D.)

Hobbes, another major English philosopher, is considered to be the father of analytical philosophy which has become so prevalent in the Anglo-Saxon world during this century. A keen student who had studied philosophy and logic at Oxford, he later traveled to the Continent where he became deeply impressed by the science being cultivated by Kepler and Galileo. He was opposed to Aristotelian philosophy and science and shared with Bacon the view that knowledge should bestow power upon man and improve his material state. Influenced by Galileo, Hobbes tried to apply his natural philosophy to both man and society and he must be considered essentially as a philosopher of the world, of society and of human affairs rather than of pure metaphysics or epistemology.

The first philosophical work of Hobbes called *Little Treatises* was written in geometric form and tried to explain sensation in terms of the new science of motion. Hobbes tried to apply his mechanistic psychology to both ethics and politics and supported a strong central authority in the political field. Having entered into the political arena, he was exiled to France where in fact he wrote most of his philosophical works including his criticism of Descartes' *Meditations*. The most famous work of Hobbes is *Leviathan* which argues for absolute sovereignty as the foundation of political philosophy. He espoused ideas which have been very influential in the later history of political thought in the West. Hobbes was accused of atheism by his enemies but he considered himself to be an empiricist devoted to the world of commonsense and what can be perceived through the senses. Hobbes considered "primary qualities." that is, quantity to be real and everything else to be the product of matter and motion and in that sense can be considered as a materialistic philosopher.

Benedict Spinoza (1632-1677 A.D.)

A philosopher of Jewish background born in Amsterdam, Spinoza was expelled from the synagogue for his unorthodox views and lived most of his life as a recluse. He was deeply attracted to the philosophy of Descartes and wrote an account of that philosophy in order to propagate it. His most famous work, entitled *Ethics*, was published after his death and is considered to be one of the major works of modern philosophy. Spinoza was in search of the supreme good which for him meant the possession of a human nature which would be perfectly aware of its position in the universe and within the total scheme of things. He believed that the part can only be understood in reference to the whole, the first whole being what he called "God-nature." For that reason he was accused of pantheism and in fact he is, technically speaking, a pantheist for he identifies God with the totality of the universe.

He was a critic of both Cartesian dualism, which he rejected through his emphasis upon the wholeness of reality, and of Hobbsian empiricism. Spinoza is not technically speaking a Jewish philosopher. Rather, he belongs to the mainstream of modern European philosophy but at the same time there are certain elements of his thought which go back to classical Jewish philosophy which, of course, had very close relations with classical Islamic philosophy throughout the earlier centuries, some of its major figures such as Ibn Gabirol and Maimonides having even written works in Arabic.

John Locke (1632-1704 A.D.)

After Hobbes, Locke, another English philosopher, took up the task of defending the empiricist position and must be considered after Hobbes as the most important empiricist in British philosophy in the tenth/sixteenth and eleventh/seventeenth centuries. He was also a moral philosopher deeply interested in political thought which influenced greatly the founders of the American state and many of the other important political movements of the twelfth/eighteenth century. In this domain he stood opposed to the views of Hobbes and defended more the rights of the people *vis-à-vis* those of the sovereign.

Locke, who hailed from a Puritan background, studied at Oxford and later traveled to the Continent. In France he studied the thought of Descartes but he was especially at home in practical politics and political affairs. For that very reason he was exiled to Holland for some time where he began to publish his writings, the most important of which is *Essay Concerning Human Understanding* and *Two Treatises of Government*. Later he wrote the *Reasonableness of Christianity* in which he defended Christianity against criticism. At the end of his life he wrote a commentary upon the *Epistles* of St. Paul which demonstrates his interest in purely religious subjects.

Locke gave empiricism its strongest foundations within the history of British philosophy, formulating an epistemology based on the denial of the possibility of man's knowledge of the real objective existence of various substances. He emphasized the importance of the "idea" which is whatever happens to be the object of the understanding when man thinks. The Lockean "ideas" all come from experience and for him there are no such things as innate ideas. The mind is what he called the *tabula rasa*, that is, a clear tablet upon which these ideas coming from the world of the senses are impinged. The world is composed of real objects but made known to us only through experience and all ideas come either from sensation or reflection upon the data derived from sensation.

The most influential aspect of Locke's thought was his idea of the social contract by which man comes out of the state of nature to form a social body. This contract is not between the ruler and the ruled as thought by men like Hobbes but between equally free men. Therefore, the ruler cannot become a tyrant and the people have the right to remove him when he does so. It is this aspect of Locke's thinking which became very influential in the foundation of democratic ideals. It became crystallized in the American Revolution as well as within England itself and later on in many parts of the world. From the point of view of the history of modern thought, Locke must be thought of essentially as a political philosopher.

Gottfried Wilhelm Leibnitz (1646-1716 A.D.)

Leibnitz was a German philosopher and mathematician from Leipzig in whose university he studied. He is one of the foremost metaphysicians of the modern period and in many ways the one who, among the famous Western philosophers, is closest to the traditional philosophy and metaphysics which Islam, Christianity and other traditions share. He was a Protestant in a Catholic environment and therefore decided to leave his homeland, traveling to Paris where he studied for several years. He returned to Berlin in the year 1700 where he became the president of the Academy of Sciences. He was, in fact, both an eminent philosopher and mathematician and is one of the discoverers of the science of calculus.

Leibnitz sought to harmonize the traditional views of God, man and nature with new ideas which were emanating from scientific and philosophical circles. For him God's existence and final causes were necessary to provide ultimate explanations of anything. He believed the world to be a harmonious whole serving divine purposes in accordance with laws of efficient causes. He refused to separate mind and body as Descartes had done and believed in monads, that is, units whose spontaneous activity comprised the world. Leibnitz had a great deal of interest in logic and sought to create an alphabet of human thought, assembling an encyclopedia of human knowledge. The foundation of his philosophy and what underlies his logic as well as the study of the alphabet of human thought is the idea of the pre-established harmony of all the monads in the universe based on the way that God had created each thing.

Leibnitz was also very much interested in what has come to be known as the perennial philosophy and was the first famous Western philosopher to use such a term. This was based on his interest in non-Western philosophies including Islamic as well as Chinese thought. He saw a set of universal truths behind all of these expressions of traditional philosophy, truths which he saw as perennial.

The general principles of his philosophy include the principle of identity, the principle of the best, that is, God being wise chooses the best among possibilities, the principle of sufficient reason, and metaphysically necessary principles such as everything possible demands to exist. There were also the principles of order such as continuity, every action involving a reaction, the equality of cause and effect and other laws of this kind.

Most of the works of Leibnitz are expressed in letters, short essays and correspondences such as the famous exchange which he carried out with Clarke concerning his view and those of Newton on physics and nature. His one large work is *The Theodicy* which must be considered his basic opus. In any case, Leibnitz is one of the most significant philosophers of the eleventh/seventeenth century and the only one who tried to preserve at least some link with the world of traditional metaphysics and philosophy.

GEORGE BERKELEY (1685-1753 A.D.)

The Anglo-Irish philosopher and theologian, George Berkeley, is considered by many to be an empiricist although not of the same kind as Locke and Hobbes. He studied at Trinity College in Dublin where he developed the idealism with which he has become identified. Some have in fact called him the father of immaterialism, his view being that there is only the perceiver and the perceived and no ideas in between. In his *Treatise Concerning the Principles of Human Knowledge*, which is his most famous work, he states that all objects of sense are within the mind and rejects material substances completely. He also defends theism against free thinkers and deists, from those who either deny God or reduce Him to simply the first cause or architect of the universe and cut off his hands from the running of His own creation. In the *Analyst: Discourse Addressed to an Infidel Mathematician*, Berkeley defends religion strongly against the claims of certain rationalistic scientists.

At the end of his life after journeying to America, Berkeley returned to Ireland where he became a bishop and his ideas continued to be very influential, especially among those prone to idealistic philosophy and, of course, in the field of religion. In modern times, in many Islamic countries where Western philosophy has been taught in schools seriously, such as in Pakistan and Muslim India, many Muslim teachers and philosophers, who have wanted to find means of defending religion from the Western philosophical point of view, have tried to take recourse in the works of Berkeley and for that reason he is well known in that region of the Islamic world.

François-Marie Voltaire (1694-1778 A.D.)

One of the most famous of all French philosophers and essayists, Voltaire became well known by writing against tyranny and defending the rights of the individual. Although he studied at a Jesuit school, he became a free thinker and in fact is one of the archetypes of European free thinkers of the twelfth/eighteenth and thirteenth/nineteenth centuries who turned against religion. Voltaire also wrote for the theater as well as composing philosophical treatises but was criticized by both philosophical and literary opponents for his attacks against religion. In fact, he was exiled to England for some time where his philosophical interests deepened and in 1734 he wrote his *Philosophical Letters* against the established schools of both religion and philosophy. Toward the end of his life, he settled in Switzerland where he died. His most important philosophical work is without doubt *Candide* which is considered one of the literary masterpieces of the French language.

Voltaire became well known by free thinkers and rationalists as a great champion of human freedom against religious prejudice and of reason against the dictates of the church. In fact, a number of Muslim modernists were attracted to him because they thought that his attack against Christianity could also be used by them as a way of defending their rationalistic interpretations of Islam against the attacks of certain Christian writers and missionaries. Voltaire knew something about Islam and wrote about it but his knowledge was fairly shallow. He was also attracted to certain aspects of Islamic literature, especially the writings of the Persian poet Sa'dī, whom he saw mostly as a rational ethical writer rather than the devout Muslim that he was. Voltaire is remembered in history not only for his purely philosophical works but also for his impact upon the French Revolution and the ideas which emanated from it.

Jean-Jacques Rousseau (1712-1778 A.D.)

A contemporary of Voltaire, Rousseau was also a French philosopher who, however, spent much of his time in Switzerland where he wrote most of the works which were to inspire the leaders of the French Revolution. He came from a Calvinist background, but converted to Roman Catholicism. He was also interested in literature and music and wrote the article on music for Diderot's *Encyclopédie*. He also composed musical pieces though without much success. Later in life Rousseau turned back to Protestantism while living in Geneva which was then the major center of Protestant thought. His most important works are *Emile*, about education, and a treatise on social contract which caused storms politically and brought much opposition against him. In fact, he was exiled and went to England, returning *incognito* to Paris where he wrote his famous *Confessions* and where he died.

Again as in the case of Voltaire, the influence of Rousseau was great not only in the philosophical field but also in practical political movements especially the French Revolution, and he was also highly admired by a number of the founders of the United States. Likewise, Rousseau's educational ideas wielded much influence and have been discussed by many Muslim educators during the past century.

The French Encyclopedists

The twelfth/eighteenth century was witness to the triumph of rationalism especially in France where there appeared a group of philosophers of a highly rationalistic bent, devoted to modern science and with a great deal of emphasis upon humanism and deism. This group came to be known as the French Encyclopedists. Under the direction of Denis Diderot (1713-1784) and aided by such figures as the scientist D'Alembert and the philosophers Rousseau and Voltaire, the *Encyclopédie* began to be composed with the aim of amassing all of human knowledge and displaying the grandeur of human civilization in opposition to both established religion and the monarchy and with an overt anti-traditional perspective. The first edition in thirty-five volumes was simply called *Encyclopédie*. This text was one of the main works of the period that came to be known as The Age of Enlightenment, a period which asserted the primacy of human reason against all authority of both a religious or even political kind. The importance of the writings of the Encyclopedists and the ideas which they brought forth are still very much alive in the West and constitute a pillar of the modern world although from a purely philosophical point of view they were opposed and their arguments were refuted by many philosophers of the thirteenth/nineteenth century.

David Hume (1711-1776 A.D.)

One of the most influential British philosophers, the Scot, David Hume was at once historian, economist and philosopher and was known for both his skepticism and empiricism. As one of the main figures of the school of empiricism in England, Hume restricted knowledge to experience of ideas and impressions whose ultimate source cannot be verified. His early years were spent in Edinburgh, but like Locke, he journeyed later in life to France where he wrote one of his most famous works, *A Treatise on Human Nature*, expounding a full philosophical system which, however, he later repudiated as being a work of youth. He returned to England and in 1741 and 1742 wrote essays on moral and political philosophy and soon thereafter his most famous works, *An Enquiry Concerning Human Understanding* and *An Enquiry Concerning the Principle of Morals.* He also wrote a history of England and carried out disputes with Rousseau.

Hume is known in the later history of philosophy for his radical denial of the possibility of any deductive science and also of causality. He claimed, somewhat like the Ash'arite theologians in Islam, that the impression upon the mind of one event followed by another event gives rise to the idea of causality. However, in contrast to the Ash'arites who saw the Will of Allah as the bond which relates what appears to us as cause and effect, Hume did not believe in any relationship between what we call cause and what we call effect except habitual association in the mind which we identify as causality. He claimed that causality is simply based on belief and cannot be proven by either empirical observation or reason.

The influence of Hume was primarily on those who claimed that philosophy is an inductive science of human nature and that man is created of sensitive and practical sentiments rather than reason. It was this aspect of Hume's thought that would influence Immanuel Kant, Auguste Comte, John Stuart Mill as well as other British philosophers such as the utilitarian Jeremy Bentham. In the last few decades, Hume has been highly praised in Anglo-Saxon philosophy by the positivists who appreciate his anti-metaphysical position and his refutation of all deductive philosophy.

Immanuel Kant (1724-1804 A.D.)

Considered by many to be the greatest of all German philosophers, Immanuel Kant has left a very deep influence upon the field of the theory of knowledge, ethics and aesthetics. He spent his whole life in Königsberg in Germany leading a quiet and sheltered existence. He studied theology as well as Newtonian physics and mathematics before becoming attracted to philosophy. He began to attack the philosophy of Leibnitz which was popular in Germany at that time and after 1770, when he was appointed as the chair of philosophy and logic at the University of Königsberg, he began to write his major works, especially *The Critique of Pure Reason, The Critique of Practical Reason* and *The Critique of Judgement.* He is the father of what is called critical philosophy. This is a philosophy which seeks to examine the limits of reason itself, a philosophy which Kant called critical or transcendental.

Kant came to the conclusion that human reason cannot know the essence of things or anything in an ultimate sense. He sought to make philosophy a science and believed that the fact that we perceive objects in time and space is as a result of the imposition of the categories of time and space by the mind upon the world around us. Kant believed that human reason cannot reach either the knowledge or in fact the proof of the existence of God and that God can only be known through practical reason and not pure reason. He emphasized the significance of ethics, a field for which he has been particularly known in later centuries.

After his death, Kantianism became an important school of thought especially at Marburg. It was revived later in the thirteenth/nineteenth and fourteenth/twentieth centuries by such philosophers as the neo-Kantian Ernst Cassirer and influenced even Martin Heidegger. In any case, the idea of the critique of reason by use of reason itself and the founding of what was called critical philosophy by Kant marks an important point in the history of Western thought. It must be considered as a watershed after which philosophy gradually turned away from the age of rationalism to the age of ideological philosophies and also the rebellion against reason which occurred in Western thought in the thirteenth/nineteenth century.

The philosophy of Kant also attracted many Muslim thinkers. His works were translated into Arabic, Persian and Turkish, while during the past century the first encounter of Islamic philosophy with Western philosophy came in the form of the response of the Persian philosopher Mullā 'Alī Zunūzī in his *Badāyi' al-ḥikam* to some of Kant's ideas.

HEGEL AND GERMAN IDEALISM

In the thirteenth/nineteenth century a major new school of philosophy arose in Germany called Objective Idealism, associated with the names of Friedrich Schelling and Johann Fichte. The thesis of this school was that reality can be known and that this reality is ultimately ideal and not material. The most important figure of this important school was without doubt Hegel.

GEORG FREDERICK HEGEL (1770-1831 A.D.)

Hegel, the father of German Idealism, developed what is called dialectical philosophy, that is, a philosophy that is based on a dialectical movement from thesis to its antithesis and then the synthesis of the thesis and the antithesis. This dialectical flow of ideas became the foundation of Hegelianism. Although influenced by Kant, Hegel did not accept the limitation placed by Kant upon reason and wrote his own work entitled *The Phenomenology of the Mind* in order to show the possibility for the mind to know reality. His dialectical logic is developed in *Science of Logic* which is one of the fundamental works of Hegelian philosophy.

Hegel also wrote extensively on the philosophy of history, which he considered to be an important branch of philosophy itself, as well as on law and aesthetics. He believed that philosophy should deal with the whole rather than starting with parts and it should be based on the process of dialectic as a result of which higher entities grow out of the conflict of lower ones leading finally to the Absolute Idea. This process of the manifestation of the Absolute in history can be seen in the movement from tribal organizations to the fully rational state. The whole of reality in fact is rational and can be known rationally.

Hegel applied his dialectic to every realm from religion to politics, from art to history and created one of the most comprehensive philosophical systems that the West has ever known. His idea of the manifestation of the Absolute in history must not, however, be confused with the traditional ideas of either revelation or the appearance of the Universal Man associated in Islamic esoterism with the inner Reality of

Muḥammad, peace be upon him, as has been done by some modern Muslim and Western scholars and thinkers.

After Hegel, many of his followers considered him to be a Protestant Christian and supporter of the Prussian state. However, his influence is to be seen among both the so called leftist Hegelians such as Feuerbach, who gave an atheistic interpretation of Hegelianism and who was closely associated with Marxism, as well as with rightist Hegelians who were closely related to religious circles in Germany. Hegelianism was also influential in England, America and Italy where many philosophers were attracted to the holistic and idealistic aspects of Hegel, such men as J.E. Moore in England, J. Royce in America, and B. Croce in Italy. Although Hegel was eclipsed by the rise of positivism in the late thirteenth/nineteenth and early fourteenth/twentieth centuries, he has again begun to attract a great deal of attention during the last few decades in both Europe and America.

ARTHUR SCHOPENHAUER (1788-1860 A.D.)

Schopenhauer was a contemporary of Hegel and strongly opposed to his idealism. He in fact developed what he called the metaphysics of the 'will' in order to oppose Hegelian idealism directly. Although not by any means as influential as Hegel at that time in Germany, he began to attract the attention of later existentialists in the fourteenth/twentieth century. Schopenhauer began his studies as a physician and later on turned to the philosophy of both Plato and Kant. After finishing his studies, he went to Weimar where he met Goethe with whom he became good friends and was also introduced to the Vedanta and Hindu mysticism. He considered the Upanishads, the sacred scripture of Hinduism, as one of the foundations of his philosophy and he is the first major European philosopher in the modern period in whom one can see the influence of Oriental thought. He supported Goethe against Newton in their debates over the nature of color.

Schopenhauer's major work is *The World as Will and Idea* in which he turned from the centrality of reason in Hegelian philosophy to the power of intuition, creativity and even the irrational. It is this aspect of his thought that has influenced modern existentialism as well as psychology and anthropology. Schopenhauer also exercised a great deal of influence on German arts and letters and was also one of the figures who attracted a number of Muslim thinkers and writers who had studied in Europe in the early part of this century.

Soren Kierkegaard (1813-1855 A.D.)

Kierkegaard, the most famous of all Danish philosophers, was one of the major critics of Hegelian rationalism and a figure who has been considered by many as the father of existentialism. He received a rigorous Lutheran education and was always deeply involved in matters of religion. He studied both theology and philosophy and his major work *Either/Or* emphasizes the significance of choice and free will in human life. In *Fear and Trembling* and *Repetition* he deals with the question of faith and the paradoxes that it involves for the existence of man in a world in which religion is not accepted by everyone. His *Philosophical Fragments* presents Christianity as a form of existence based on free will and attacks the prevailing Hegelian philosophy based on determinism. In *The Concept of Dread* he extends the idea of freedom to psychology and this work is considered by many to be the first book in "depth psychology". Finally, in *Stages on Life's Way*, which is one of his most mature works, Kierkegaard distinguishes between aesthetic, ethical and religious fears of life. Finally, in his *Concluding Unscientific Postscript to the Philosophical Fragments*, which is his most important philosophical work, he attacks again the Hegelian attempt to create a vast synthesis of existence within a system.

Kierkegaard criticized Hegel's epistemology and praised subjectivism over objectivism which is a mark of fourteenth/twentieth century existentialist ideas. He also spent a good part of his life attacking the established church which he believed had abandoned Christ while Kierkegaard was at the same time deeply involved with matters of religion. At first his ideas were not received seriously but gradually they became better known and especially since the Second World War, he has become an influential philosophical figure on both sides of the Atlantic.

Karl Marx (1818-1883 A.D.)

The very famous German political theorist, sociologist and economist who wrote *The Communist Manifesto* with Friederich Engels and *Das Capital*, Marx is not technically speaking a philosopher but a social theorist although he has had great influence in certain political and philosophical circles. He studied both history and philosophy and was influenced by Hegel but also by socialist writers and ideas especially when he went to Paris. While in exile in Brussels, he wrote *The*

Communist Manifesto containing his whole social philosophy. He then returned to Germany for a while where, as a result of the Socialist Revolution of 1848, his ideas had become somewhat more acceptable. But soon he was forced to leave Germany again this time for England where he spent the rest of his life and where he wrote his *magnum opus*, *Das Capital*, which is the analysis of the economics of capitalism.

In this work Marx developed the idea that man's existence is based on his creativity to exert labor upon the objects of nature and to produce goods; therefore, the whole species should enjoy the fruit of this labor. According to Marx, this has not, however, been the case since the working class is oppressed by those who possess capital. There is, therefore, a constant class warfare between the workers who perform the labor and the "bourgeoisie" who possess the capital. Marx asserted that the goal of history is the creation a classless society, a goal which must be brought about through revolution. He asserted that the whole process of history has been based on the struggle between various classes on the basis of economic factors. Marx believed that he had corrected the Hegelian idea of dialectical philosophy by considering the dialectical process to be purely material. He thereby developed what is now so well-known as dialectical materialism which was the philosophical foundation of Communism and still remains so for those who follow the Communist ideology or are philosophical Marxists. Although he showed great care and compassion towards the poor, Marx was virulently anti-religious and atheistic and believed that religion, which he called "the opium of the people" was one of the main elements that caused the subjugation of one class and one group of people by another and was therefore the source of injustice in society.

Henri Bergson (1859-1941 A.D.)

The French philosopher Bergson was another of the famous critics of Hegelianism who developed what is called process philosophy and was one of the first to develop evolutionism in a philosophical form. He spent most of his life in Paris where he studied. Originally a follower of the mechanistic philosophy, he changed his view and began to distinguish between time and duration as seen in his famous work *Time and Free Will: an Essay on the Immediate Data of Consciousness*. He defended free will against determinism which Hegelian philosophy and certain other systematic philosophies of the period had asserted. Bergson also set out to show the relationship between body and mind in his *Matter and Memory.* In 1900 he became a professor at College de France where he was immensely popular among Catholics and also in other philosophical circles. During these years he wrote his most famous book called *Creative Evolution* which shows the influence of biology and Darwinian evolution upon him. He believed that the mechanism of evolution is what he called *élan vital* or vital impulse which brings about the process of change and transformation in nature.

Bergson's last work, *The Two Sources of Morality and Religion*, discusses intelligence and intuition as the sources upon which both morality and religion are based. In this and other later works, Bergson drew closer to Catholicism and away from the *élan vital* concept. Because of his opposition to rationalism and ideological constructs of the thirteenth/nineteenth century and his emphasis upon intuition, Bergson attracted the attention of a number of Muslim thinkers of the late thirteenth/nineteenth and fourteenth/twentieth centuries and such figures as Muḥammad Iqbāl have spoken often about him.

Friedrich Nietzsche (1844-1900 A.D.)

One of the German philosophers of the thirteenth/nineteenth century who has exercised great influence upon the thought of the fourteenth/twentieth century, Nietzsche began his career with the study of philology at Basel. In 1872 he wrote *The Birth of Tragedy* about the dichotomy between what he called Apollonian and Dionysian modes of thought. This work has had many followers among fourteenth/twentieth century writers. In 1879, he retired from the university and began a period in which he wrote his most famous works including *Thus Spoke Zarathustra, Beyond Good and Evil*, and *On the Genealogy of Morals.*

Nietzsche was a very strong critic of contemporary culture and the Christianity of his time as he saw it practiced. He recognized the spiritual poverty around him and spoke of the "death of God." He believed that the only solution would be the coming of men who were beyond morality and the ordinary criteria of good and evil, who were what he called supermen.

Nietzsche wrote in a highly poetical style especially in *Thus Spoke*

Zarathustra and has exerted much influence in this century in both literary and philosophical circles. He had powerful intuitions while being at the same time possessed by an abnormal psychological condition so that he has been called by one contemporary traditional authority "an illuminated psychopath." Nevertheless, many consider him in fact to be one of the "prophets" of the thought patterns and the condition of human beings in the fourteenth/twentieth century, a singular thinker whose intuition allowed him to see the poverty of modern civilization and the spiritual degradation which modern man has suffered as a result of it. As far as the Islamic world is concerned, Nietzsche's influence can be seen in certain quarters especially in Muḥammad Iqbāl who refers to him often in his works as his main interlocutor from the West.

Edmond Husserl (1859-1938 A.D.)

Another major German philosophical figure, Husserl is the founder of what is called phenomenology, one of the most widespread forms of philosophy in the modern West. He sought to turn philosophy into a strict science by describing and analyzing consciousness and removing the opposition between empiricism and rationalism. Of Jewish background, Husserl turned to Catholic philosophy under the influence of Brentano and studied philosophy and mathematics together. Later in life, while in Vienna he converted to Lutheran Christianity and began to teach philosophy while turning his attention to the psychological basis of mathematics. These studies resulted in his *Logical Investigations* which Husserl began to describe as phenomenological.

Husserl considered phenomenology as a universal science based on the methodology which he called phenomenological reduction, that is, attention to uninterrupted basic experience which will lead to the essence of things and the function by which essences become conscious. In his *Ideas: General Introduction to Phenomenology*, which was never completed, he presented his program and the systematic outline of his method.

In later life, Husserl considered phenomenology as a renewer of the spiritual life. In his *First Philosophy* he claimed that phenomenology vindicates life and leads to the realization of man's ethical autonomy. His last work, *The Crisis of European Sciences and Transcendental Phenomenology*, speaks of the significance of phenomenology and independence of the mind amidst the confusion of the times. In fact, this work was written under the shadow of Hitler's Germany and marks one of the last free voices of philosophy at that time in that land. Husserl exercised great influence in Germany and later on in America and in England and to this day phenomenology, as interpreted by various later philosophers, remains a major philosophical school in the West.

Sigmund Freud (1856-1939 A.D.) and Psychoanalysis

Although not a philosopher, Freud, the Austrian physician and founder of psychoanalysis, is one of the most influential figures of this century in the West. Born into a Jewish family, Freud became attracted to philosophy early in life but decided later in favor of medicine in which he became distinguished in the field of neurology and the study of the nerve cell. Gradually, however, his interests turned to the psychological aspects of neurological studies and in the 1890's he began to develop his psychoanalytical theories, co-authoring *Studies in Hysteria* in 1895. In 1900 he produced his major psychoanalytical work, *The Interpretation of Dreams*, in which he pointed out what he considered to be the significance of the unconscious. Freud emphasized his views concerning the importance of repression, disguised wishes and the infantile origin of the contents of the unconscious dominated by sexual drives and hostility toward parents associated with what he defined as the Oedipus complex (that is, sexual desire toward the parent of the opposite sex and jealous hatred of the rival parent).

To propagate his theories Freud founded the Vienna Circle which was joined by such famous figures as Alfred Alder. At first, however, his views were criticized and his book *Three Essays on the Theory of Sexuality* strongly derided. Yet, Freud continued to practice, teach and write about psychoanalysis which he began to apply to other fields. In *Totem and Taboo* he sought to psychoanalyze the conditions of "primitive man," while in *The Future of an Illusion* he attacked religion virulently considering fear and hope as the basis of the belief in God and immortality. In *Moses and Monotheism* he went so far as to deny that Moses was Jewish, claiming that he was an Egyptian who had learned the doctrine of monotheism from Ikhnaton. This work turned believing Jews, many of whom had supported him earlier, against him.

In later life Freud devised a new theory of the mind based on the fundamental categories of life and death instincts and the division of the mind into the *id*, the *ego* and the *superego*. He considered the tension between the *ego* and the *superego* to be the origin of what is called conscience. Altogether he denied human moral responsibility and emphasized the effect of unconscious forces which determine human actions. He denied the immortality of the soul and reduced the Spirit to the psyche. He in fact originated a view of human nature which is among the most anti-religious known in the modern world and began the practice of psychoanalysis which has come to replace religion in the lives of many people. The psychoanalyst has become, along with the scientist, the new priest of the modern world while religious and spiritual realities have been reduced to psychological phenomena to be dealt with by means of the newly founded techniques of psychoanalysis.

It is true that other psychoanalysts turned away from Freud, the most important being Carl Gustav Jung who was much more interested in religious symbolism and myths than Freud. But Jung also relegated the archetypes to the "collective unconscious" of humanity and refused to distinguish clearly between the Spirit and the psyche. Therefore, he contributed further to the process of the psychologization of spiritual reality so characteristic of the modern world. In recent years the influence of Freud has begun to wane and many are now seeking to create a more humane psychology and psychoanalysis, some even turning to Eastern spiritual teachings. But the impact of the methods and ideas first practiced and asserted by Freud in destroying the religious meaning of life, reducing the grandeur of the human soul to unconscious complexes mostly of sexual origin and denying the reality of the Spirit by reducing it to psychic forces, continues to subsist in the modern world.

Alfred North Whitehead (1861-1947 A.D.)

One of the most significant philosophers of this century especially in America, Alfred North Whitehead, was of English origin and spent the first part of his life in England where he studied mathematics and philosophy. Later he taught in both Cambridge and London before migrating to America where he was to spend the last part of his life at Harvard University. Whitehead was first attracted to the Catholic Church which, however, he did not enter. In fact, while remaining very much interested in questions of religion throughout his life, he refused to join any organized religious institution. His early works were mostly on mathematics, and it was as a mathematician that he met his student Bertrand Russell and together they wrote the *Principia Mathematica* which took them until 1910. This major work of logic remains one of the basic texts of this century on the philosophy of mathematics and the relationship between mathematical and formal logic. Whitehead was also very much interested in the foundations of physics and wrote *Enquiry Concerning the Principles of Natural Knowledge* to that end followed by the non-mathematical treatment of physics in *The Concept of Nature.*

While in America, Whitehead wrote most of his metaphysical works beginning with *Science and the Modern World* in which he criticized scientific materialism and it was also there that he wrote his *Process and Reality* which is perhaps his most important work in which he developed the idea of process philosophy, a philosophy which sees the whole of reality as a series of becomings. His last major work *Adventures of Ideas* summarizes his views on God, humanity and the universe. Whitehead is known not only as the founder of process philosophy but also process theology, and these ideas have had notable influence in America mostly as a result of his famous student Charles Hartshorne, the American philosopher, who propagated Whitehead's teachings after the latter's death.

BERTRAND RUSSELL (1872-1970 A.D.)

Bertrand Russell, an early student of Whitehead, is one of the most well-known of the British philosophers and logicians of this century. At once an accomplished mathematician and philosopher, he was also an activist in the political realm especially during his later days. Much of his later fame in fact rests upon his political and social activities rather than the purely philosophical works for which he became known in his earlier years.

Early in life, Russell became a religious skeptic and remained so until his death. It was at Cambridge that, while studying philosophy, he became interested in the foundations of knowledge. Influenced first by idealists such as G.E. Moore, he turned more and more towards empiricism, positivism and materialism and remained a positivist the rest of his life. In *An Enquiry into the Meaning of Truth* and *Human Knowledge, Its Scope and Limits,* he sought to pair down and reduce to the simplest expression, the claims of human knowledge. In *The Principle of Mathematics,* he investigated the relation between philosophy and mathematics which culminated in the joint work, *Principia Mathematica,* with Whitehead. He exerted altogether an immense influence upon the analytical movement as well as on the study of logic in general in the fourteenth/twentieth century.

Russell also wrote a number of more popular works, such as *A*

History of Western Philosophy, Why I am not a Christian and *Autobiography* which made him more influential and famous than other philosophers in non-philosophical circles. He epitomizes the domination of positivistic philosophy which refuses to deal with any subject that cannot be logically, and for some operationally, defined and has a strong anti-metaphysical bias and opposition to religious and spiritual matters which have concerned so many philosophers over the ages. This type of philosophy has been dominant in most British and American universities during the past few decades. As a result, Russell has also influenced a number of Muslim writers and philosophers who have studied in England and America in contrast to the European continent, where existentialism and phenomenology have been more prevalent to this day.

Martin Heidegger (1889-1976 A.D.)

The German philosopher Martin Heidegger who was a student of Husserl, is without doubt the most significant German philosopher of this century following Husserl. He has remained a major force in Continental philosophy and his influence has spread to America during the last decades although Anglo-Saxon philosophy, both in England and America, remains mostly dominated by logical positivism. Heidegger was an acute critic of modern technology and technological society and the leading exponent of what has come to be known as existentialism. His early education attracted him to religion, the study of Catholic theology, medieval philosophy, in which he was influenced by Brentano, and also early Greek thought, which he studied in a series of important works. He was also influenced not only by his teacher Husserl but also Kierkegaard and Nietzsche.

Heidegger believed that the whole of Western philosophy took a wrong turn in its understanding of "being" from the time of Plato onwards and that this kind of philosophical activity has now come to an end with him. His most important work, *Being and Time*, influenced atheists such as Jean-Paul Sartre but also certain types of religious philosophers. His other important work, *What is Metaphysics*?, is the one in which Heidegger discusses the concept of "no-thing" or "nothing" and develops his own version of phenomenology which he believes to be the method to unveil man's ways of being and his way to Being.

JEAN-PAUL SARTRE (1905-1980 A.D.)

The most famous of the French existentialist philosophers, Sartre was at once a philosopher and an important man of letters. He studied in Paris where he lived and taught most of his life, a good part of it with Simone de Beauvoir, herself a noted philosopher and social critic. Sartre and de Beauvoir never married formally considering marriage to be a bourgeoie moral norm and a remnant of religion which both of them opposed.

Sartre's first work *Nausea* was a novel which was at once highly anti-social and fiercely individualistic, revealing some of his later existentialist ideas. He adopted the phenomenological method and applied it to several of his philosophical works of which the most famous is *Being and Nothingness*. In this work he opposes human consciousness as nothingness to being which is "thingness." Sartre was a defender of human dignity and freedom but also at the same time he considered all human endeavor to be useless. In later life, with *Existentialism and Humanism*, he began to equate freedom more with social responsibility and in his personal life he began to spend much of his time caring for the poor. He turned again in his later years to novels and especially plays such as *No Exit* which became famous. Politically he was an active leftist espousing Marxist causes although he turned against the Soviet Union after 1956. At that time he wrote *The Problem of Method* to revamp Marxism.

This combination of existentialism and Marxism, characteristic of Sartre, de Beauvoir and their followers had a deep impact upon French intellectual circles after the Second World War and through them upon a number of Muslims especially from North Africa who had spent their student days in France. In fact, the influence of Sartre in both literature and philosophy in modernist circles in the Islamic world is much greater than that of the German existentialist philosopher Heidegger who was, however, much more interested in questions of religion than was Sartre, who openly opposed religion as such and espoused strongly agnostic and in fact atheistic attitudes.

* * *

The various figures and schools of modern thought have followed upon the wake of one another starting with the rebellion of reason against both the intellect and revelation, leading to the development of critical philosophy trying to curtail the powers of reason and the rise of ideologies and system building in the thirteenth/nineteenth century, followed by the criticism of Hegelian and other types of systematic philosophy by existentialism. One can observe during this century the division of philosophy in the West into phenomenology and existentialism on the one hand, the latter based upon the anguish of individual existence and the like, and positivism based upon the use of logic closely related to experimental science and neglect of other problems and issues especially of a metaphysical nature on the other.

It is important to state here in conclusion that meanwhile also in the West, so strongly in the grip of highly anti-metaphysical and anti-religious philosophies, there began at the beginning of the century a restatement of perennial philosophy which is completely opposed to modern European philosophy that it considers as a deviation from the perennial heritage of humanity as far as philosophy and wisdom are concerned. This "school" is identified most of all with the French metaphysician René Guénon, the half Sri Lankan, half English metaphysician and art historian, Ananda K. Coomaraswamy, and the German metaphysician and gnostic Frithjof Schuon. There are, however, also a number of other eminent figures representing this perspective including Titus Burckhardt, Huston Smith, Martin Lings, Marco Pallis and others who during the century have tried to revive the perennial wisdom of various traditions and traditional knowledge lying at the heart of the authentic religions and standing opposed to the whole enterprise of modern philosophy from the Renaissance onward. Much of the activity of this school has been, interestingly enough, related to Islam and has issued from the inner dimension of the Islamic revelation.

Today, perennial philosophy, in its diverse formulations, remains an important aspect of the general philosophical scene in the West especially with the gradual demise of modern philosophical schools swept away by what is now being called post-modernism which, through internal criticism and the destruction of all of the structures of meaning that had existed before, as asserted by Jacques Derrida and other proponents of deconstructionism, is in a sense bringing modern Western philosophy to an end. Not only Heidegger, but also certain contemporary American philosophers such as Richard Rorty and others, consider the philosophical enterprise, as known until now in the West, to have come to an end. It is precisely in this period of confusion, when philosophy as practiced in the last few centuries in the West can do so little to help the West and, in fact, the whole of modern humanity so much in need of spiritual guidance, that perennial philosophy is once again seen by many as an alternative philosophy able to fulfill the needs of human beings for the highest form of knowledge which is at the same time none other than that wisdom lying at the heart of various religions. One must note here that this perspective is especially emphasized in the Islamic tradition which considers Islam to be the *dīn al-ḥanīf*, that is, the primordial religion, containing wisdom which has been revealed by God in one form or another through the chain of prophets and expounded later on in more human language by the *ḥakīm*s, sages and philosophers of centuries past.

It is very important for Muslims who wish to know the West to realize the significance of the philosophical ideas which have come into being during the last few centuries in the modern world, ideas which are not derived from a supra-individual source as is the case of traditional philosophy. Rather, modern philosophies are usually borne of the attempts of individual philosophers who seek, through the use of reason or empirical data, to create an all encompassing system which is then soon faced with the criticism by another philosopher who destroys the older mental construct to replace it with another.

Nevertheless, the ideas which have issued forth from the various figures and schools of philosophy in the West during the past centuries must be known because of their great importance in the political, social, economic, ethical, aesthetic and other realms. They in fact have created for the most part and define to this day what constitutes modernism and the world view of the modern world. Many a person from the East, including Muslims, is not able to understand modern Western civilization precisely because he or she only looks at its surface aspects without paying attention to the philosophical ideas which underlie that world. At this particular juncture of human history critical understanding and study of the ideas and history of Western thought, (which is also to a great extent the history of modern thought) from the Islamic point of view is absolutely essential. Many Western historians have studied Islamic philosophy and Islamic intellectual history on the basis of their own philosophical assumptions, but very few Muslims have done the reverse, that is, study the West from the point of view of the Islamic tradition. Yet, it is this study which is essential in order for the Islamic intelligentsia to be able to have a deeper understanding of Western civilization and of modern thought which both directly and indirectly through science, technology, modern education as well as social, economic and political institutions are having such an impact upon the Islamic world today.

CHAPTER 10
MODERN SCIENCE AND TECHNOLOGY

The central role played by modern science and its application in the form of technology in the modern world is so great that it is absolutely essential for Muslims, young or old, to understand the nature of modern science not only superficially but also in depth. They must also study the relationship between modern science as theoretical structure, as a knowledge of the physical world, and its application to various domains ranging from medicine to industry or all that can be called technology in the current sense of this term. Many Muslim thinkers during the last century have written a great deal about modern science and the majority among them, while opposing various cultural, religious and social values of the West, have lauded Western science in an almost absolute fashion and identified it in their own mind with science as it was known in Islamic civilization. Most have in fact claimed that modern science is nothing but the continuation and further development of Islamic science in the context of the Western world.

There is no doubt that modern science, as it was created during the Renaissance and especially the eleventh/seventeenth century, would not have been possible without the translations which were made from

Arabic into Latin during the earlier centuries mostly in Spain and to some extent in Sicily and other parts of Italy. Without the medicine of Ibn Sīnā, the mathematics of Khayyām or the optics of Ibn al-Haytham, the corresponding sciences of medicine, mathematics and optics would not have developed as they did in the West. Yet, there is not only a continuity between the two sciences, but also a profound discontinuity between Western science and Islamic science. As we have seen earlier in this book, Islamic science is related profoundly to the Islamic world view. It is rooted deeply in knowledge based upon the unity of Allah or *al-tawḥīd* and a view of the universe in which Allah's Wisdom and Will rule and in which all things are interrelated reflecting unity on the cosmic level.

In contrast, Western science is based on considering the natural world as a reality which is separate from both Allah and the higher levels of being. At best, Allah is accepted as the creator of the world, as a mason who has built a house which now stands on its own. His intrusion into the running of the world and His continuous sustenance of it are not accepted in the modern scientific worldview. There are in fact very profound differences between the worldview of Western science and that of Islamic science. To consider Western science simply as a continuation of Islamic science is, therefore, to misunderstand completely both the epistemological foundations of the two sciences and the relationship that each has to the world of faith and revelation. It is also to misunderstand the metaphysical and philosophical backgrounds of the two sciences. Islamic science always relates lower levels of being to the higher and considers the physical world to be simply the lowest plane in the hierarchic reality of the universe reflecting Allah's Wisdom, while modern science considers the physical world to be an independent reality which can be studied and known in an ultimate sense without any reference to a higher level of reality.

It is not possible here to deal in depth with the relationship of Islamic science to Western science except to point out the major differences as far as their religious impact is concerned. And this is particularly important because a young Muslim brought up in a society in which he always hears about the praise of knowledge, which in Arabic is known as *al-'ilm*, is usually confronted with the situation in which this religious celebration of knowledge is simply transferred to modern science without an awareness of the differences in the presumptions, natures, methods and matrices of the two forms of knowledge.

The background of modern science, although based to some extent upon medieval European and through it Islamic science and even going back to the ancient Greek and Egyptian sciences, is philosophically radically different from all of these traditional sciences. Modern science was born through the Scientific Revolution in the eleventh/seventeenth century at a time when, as we saw earlier, European philosophy had itself rebelled against revelation and the religious world view. The background of modern science is a particular philosophical outlook which sees the parameters of the physical world, that is, space, time, matter, motion and energy to be realities that are independent of higher orders of being and cut off from the power of God, at least during the unfolding of the history of the cosmos. It views the physical world as being primarily the subject of mathematicization and quantification and, in a sense, absolutizes the mathematical study of nature relegating the non-quantifiable aspects of physical existence to irrelevance. It also sees the subject or "mind" which studies this world as being the individual consciousness of human beings identified with the power of reason and divorced from both revelation and intellection.

Without this particular philosophical background, the Newtonian Revolution in science would have never taken place nor would modern science become what it has in fact become. It is no doubt true that as a result of its remarkable success on the mathematical and physical plane modern science became the most accepted form of knowledge and philosophy gradually became a handmaid to it, but this science itself arose on the basis of a very particular philosophical background which is very different from that of Islam or, for that matter, Christianity itself. Modern science is based upon certain assumptions concerning the nature of physical reality including the logical character of the laws dominating over the physical world, the independence of physical reality from other orders of reality, the possibility of experimental treatment of the physical world, the quantification of the result of experimentation and observation and the possibility of prediction based upon mathematical study of the physical world.

This science is also related to a particular view of the origin of the universe although there have been differences of view among individual scientists on this matter. Some scientists were and still are deists believing in the creation of the world by Allah who henceforth has been cut off from His own creation, while others were and remain agnostics or materialists who did not and do not believe in the Divine Origin of the universe.

The scientific theories of the origin of the universe all shared and still share one point in common and that is that they are based solely on material and mathematically definable causes for the origins of the cosmos. The theological and philosophical aspects of the question involving the act of the Creator or some divine power in the genesis of the universe, although held by many individual scientists, is systematically excluded from science as the word has been defined in the West since the Scientific Revolution.

It was on the basis of the quantification of nature that eleventh/seventeenth century science began first with the study of the movement of the planets and then with the development of the laws of physics on the basis of that study. The new science was developed mostly by the few well-known figures of the Scientific Revolution, that is, Galileo, Kepler and Newton while Descartes, Leibnitz and few other mathematicians provided important mathematical tools for the carrying out of the new quantitative study of nature. The quantification of the science of nature meant that those aspects of nature which are qualitative would be considered as secondary and unimportant, as clearly stated by Galileo himself. It was he who claimed that in nature there are "primary qualities" by which he meant quantity and "secondary qualities" and the function of science is to study the primary qualities which could be mathematically defined and analyzed such as for example weight, length or velocity in contrast to, let us say, color or form which are pure qualities and which cannot be treated mathematically in the same way. Henceforth, it was meaningless from the scientific point of view to see the cosmos as a book containing Divine Wisdom and phenomena as signs of Allah (*āyāt Allāh*), although this is precisely how the cosmos presents itself to us if we only open our eyes to see and are not blinded by subjective distortions and the so-called scientific worldview which we cast upon the world of nature.

From this conception of science was born the new physics which remained as the mother of the sciences during all the centuries that followed and still constitutes today the foundation of the sciences of the physical world. During the last few centuries all of the other sciences have tried to emulate physics in trying to create a purely quantitative science which would be able to treat various phenomena mathematically and to be able to predict on the basis of mathematical laws which themselves are experimentally verifiable.

Certain sciences such as biology did not lend themselves to such a treatment very easily. One does not observe a fundamental change in biology parallel with that which occurred in the field of physics. Aristotelian biology remained the basis of biology as the various flora and fauna were studied and classified. In fact to this day in a certain sense biology has not seen its Newtonian Revolution. However, in the field of biology a new idea issued forth in the thirteenth/nineteenth century which is one of the most important and also religiously problematic of all scientific ideas although its origin is strictly speaking philosophical rather than scientific, this being the theory of evolution. One might say that this concept was "in the air" in the thirteenth/nineteenth century and was picked up by Charles Darwin and a number of other biologists and made the foundation for the sciences of life. Its central thesis is that higher forms of life have evolved over long spans of time from lower forms of life and that the hand of the Creator has been cut off from the genesis of various species and the historical development of the universe. Allah may have created the original "soup of molecules," as modern cosmologists refer to the original condition of the cosmos, but the appearance of the various species is solely the result of a gradual evolution from within that spacio-temporal material matrix which existed at the origin of the physical cosmos without the intrusion of any transcendent causes. Nor is there a purpose to evolution. Rather, it operates through conflict between various species and "survival of the fittest."

This idea, especially as it came to be applied to fields other than biology, was very instrumental in destroying the spiritual meaning and the sense of the sacredness of Allah's creation. In fact the notion of "evolution" helped to destroy the awareness of the continuous presence of Allah as the Creator and Sustainer of living forms as stated in sacred scriptures, including the Quran, according to which Allah is both the Living (al-Ḥayy) and the Giver of life (al-Muḥyī). The theory of evolution also had a very great effect in alienating science from religion and creating a world in which one could go about studying the wonders of creation without ever having a sense of wonder in the religious sense of that term. Moreover, this idea spread very rapidly from biology to other sciences and even to non-scientific realms so that nearly everyone in the modern world talks about practically everything in evolutionary terms.

The evolutionary thesis has also penetrated into the Islamic world through the writings of many of the modernists who picked up the idea either in its scientific or philosophical sense. They then tried to extend the meaning of certain verses of the Quran to include the idea of evolution, although the Quran, like other sacred scriptures, states clearly that the world and all creatures were created by Allah and that the origin of man is not some prehistoric animal but the divinely created primordial man who in the Islamic tradition is called Adam.

In the fourteenth/twentieth century, there has been a great deal of criticism of the theory of evolution not only from theologians and philosophers but also scientists. In the West and especially the Anglo-Saxon world, however, where Charles Darwin became a great hero, such criticisms have been usually ignored and rejected by the "establishment" whether they be academic or cultural. These criticisms have not been taken very seriously despite the fact that much biological evidence has been brought against the theory of evolution not only in its Darwinian form but even in its neo-Darwinian or new forms which have been proposed in the fourteenth/twentieth century. The reason for this refusal is that evolutionism is one of the pillars of the modern worldview. If evolutionism were to be rejected, the whole structure upon which the modern world is based would collapse and one would have to accept the incredible wisdom of the Creator in the creation of the multiplicity of life forms which we see on the surface of the earth and in the seas. This realization would also change the attitude that modern man has concerning the earlier periods of his own history, *vis-à-vis* other civilizations and also other forms of life. Consequently the theory of evolution continues to be taught in the West as a scientific fact rather than a theory and whoever opposes it is usually brushed off as a religious obscurantist.

Evolutionism combined with the philosophical foundations of modern science brought forth an idea which is already to be seen in more rudimentary form in the beginnings of modern science, this idea being scientific reductionism. The ideal of the eleventh/seventeenth century physicists was to be able to explain all physical reality in terms of the movement of atoms. This idea was extended by people like Descartes who saw the human body itself as nothing but a machine. Chemists tried to study chemical reaction in this light and reduce chemistry to a form of physics, and biologists tried to reduce their science to simply chemical reactions and then finally to the movement of physical particles. The idea of reductionism which is innate to modern science and which was only fortified by the theory of evolution could be described as the reduction of the spirit to the psyche, the psyche to biological activity, life to lifeless matter and lifeless matter to purely quantitative particles or bundles of energy whose movements can be measured and quantified.

Scientific reductionism is one of the most powerful forces in the modern world. There is first of all, the innate sense of inferiority that most other disciplines feel *vis-à-vis* modern science which they try to emulate to the extent that there is now a whole category of disciplines called the social sciences or human sciences each trying to emulate the methods of the physical sciences by becoming as quantitative and "exact" as possible. Then there is the philosophical urge to reduce always the higher to the lower, to refuse to grant to life a reality which is above and beyond the material components which form a particular living cell, nor to the psyche any reality beyond the biological activities of the body which has psychic life, nor to the spirit any reality beyond the activities of the psyche. Belief in Allah is reduced to psychological complexes, consciousness to biological activity and life to molecular motion. In order to understand the modern world one must understand the power of scientific reductionism which lurks nearly everywhere in one form or another although it has been rejected by many a great scientist.

In fact, one can say that scientific reductionism is one of the main components of what can be called scientism in contrast to science. Modern science can be conceived as a legitimate way of knowing certain aspects of the natural world, a way which is able to discover some of the characteristics of the natural or physical world but not all of that world. If its limited range of vision could be accepted, it could be integrated into a more general scheme or hierarchy of knowledge in which higher forms of knowledge would dominate over but not necessarily obliterate the knowledge of the quantitative aspect of nature gained by modern scientific methods.

Scientism, however, is a philosophy which extends modern science to a total ideology, a way of looking at all things, and it is this outlook which has become so dominant in the modern worldview. It is scientism which refuses to consider any view but the scientific as being of serious consideration as far as knowledge is concerned and which refuses to accept the possibility of any other mode of knowing, such as that received through revelation. It is the domination of scientism which has made the religious view of the universe appear as intellectually irrelevant, reducing religion to only a subjectivized ethics and matters of private conscience. It is scientism which has destroyed to a large extent the spiritual reality which man always saw around him and has removed from nature what one might call the aspect of "enchantment" to which the Quran refers so often, destroying the basic Islamic idea of the phenomena of nature as being signs of Allah, the *āyāt* which Allah manifests in His creation. It is impossible to understand the modern world without understanding the power of scientism despite the opposition to it by many scientists. It is, in fact, mostly certain modern philosophers and even theologians who have become ever more subservient to the scientistic worldview than scientists, and a number of scholars in the field of the humanities, psychology and the social sciences who are today the real "priests" of scientism more than the physicists themselves.

As a result of the domination of scientism, modern and even what some now call post-modern society looks upon scientists as earlier societies looked upon priests. In earlier societies the priests or the men of God were supposed to possess a knowledge which came from God, which was absolute and certain and upon which people relied, although they might not understand the essence or details of that knowledge. People trusted the priests and scholars of religion although they could not spend their lifetimes testing the validity of the knowledge which these people possessed. They went to them for the answers to ultimate questions and relied upon their answers for their salvation. Today, to a large extent these functions have been transferred to the shoulders of scientists as far as the general public is concerned, even if individual scientists refuse to identify themselves with such functions. Nowadays, the majority of people, not only in the Western world but wherever modernism has spread, consider scientists to possess the ultimate answer to matters not only purely scientific but even to what lies beyond the domain of science. That is why books come out about the views of famous physicists concerning God or the immortality of the soul and even if some physicists make childish statements outside of their own field of competence, their views are considered to be very important precisely because they are physicists. It is essential to understand the function whom the scientists fulfill in the modern world as the ultimate authorities to which both private citizens and governments turn in all societies dominated by modernism.

As far as governments are concerned, their support for science, which is one of the main features of the modern world, comes not from the love of pure knowledge but from the love of power and wealth. One of the characteristics of modern science, which distinguishes it so much from Islamic and other traditional sciences, is that this science from the beginning had for its end power and dominion over nature as stated so clearly by the English philosopher Francis Bacon. It was because of this fact that the British Government from the eleventh/seventeenth century onward began to support science on the basis of the advice of men like him. Today, governments hope that through modern science they will gain power over nature and, therefore, economic and military advantages which they will be able to use to their advantage. Hence the support which they give to science throughout the Western world with, of course, very notable results as far as the military and economic domains are concerned. Governmental support of those types of research which do not have immediate economic or military applications has, however, always been more problematic.

The relation of modern science to power has posed for a number of scientists the question of moral responsibility because it is the discoveries made by scientists, who are oftentimes themselves humble and ethical men, that has enabled those in power to create methods of mass destruction in the form of military arms all the way from smart bombs to the hydrogen bomb not to speak of countless ways of destroying the balance of the natural environment which now threatens the very fabric of life on earth. The question has risen in the modern world as to who is responsible for the calamitous situation facing humanity today. Until recently most scientists believed that their role was to seek knowledge and that they were not responsible for the use that would be made of their discoveries. This attitude was a result of the divorce between science and ethics which has characterized modern science from the moment of its inception down to our own days. The negative possibilities of the applications of the sciences has, however, become so great, and this includes not only war time applications but even so-called peace time uses in such areas as nuclear energy and genetic engineering, that a number of Western scientists have now openly come to accept the proposition that they are responsible for what they discover. They agree that they bear some responsibility for providing the knowledge which they leave in the hands of politicians or other groups driven by greed or even national interest which in both cases do not have the welfare of the whole of humanity in mind. Still, however, the question of responsibility for the discoveries of modern science has not been totally solved and remains one of the great dilemmas of the modern world.

It is also important to mention that the transformation in modern physics during this century especially in the field of quantum mechanics and relativity resulting in changes in the Newtonian mechanistic world view has turned a number of scientists to the study of certain philosophical questions which had been laid aside since the eleventh/seventeenth century. These developments have made many physicists and other scientists interested in certain religious and mystical philosophies and doctrines although some of the harmony between religion and modern science in the fourteenth/twentieth century mentioned by so many sources is rather superficial. There is no doubt, however, that there is much greater interest among a number of physicists and scientists in general in religion and theology today than there was during the three centuries preceding our own day and that many physicists today are more seriously interested in theology than are theologians, many of whom are trying to dilute theology so as not to offend the domineering scientific worldview.

***

It is important for young Muslims to realize that technology and science are not synonymous although they are often associated with each other in circles outside of the Western world and even within the West although in the more scholarly and academic circles a clear distinction is made between them. Historically, modern technology did not become closely allied to modern science until the middle of the twelfth/eighteenth and early thirteenth/nineteenth centuries. It was really with the rise of the Industrial Revolution and the invention of modern machines that the means of production in the West changed and a technology which was closely allied to a purely materialistic science begun in the eleventh/seventeenth century came upon the scene. The result of the application of this science was the creation of modern technology which provided tremendous power to modern man to dominate both over nature and other civilizations which did not possess the same technological means. It also brought great wealth and at the same time poverty, remarkable discoveries of medicine along with overpopulation, certain daily conveniences but also decomposition of the very fiber of society, the possibility of easier travel together with the catastrophic destruction of nature.

As a result of this combination of limited positive results combined with dangerous negative effects, from the beginning of the fourteenth/twentieth century a great deal of criticism began to be leveled against technology as it was used blindly in the West. This criticism came originally from poets, writers and certain philosophers, then extended to social critics and today finds a rather strong voice in the many scholars and scientists who see in the unlimited application of modern technology the possible destruction of the natural environment and even the termination of human life on earth. The pollution of the natural environment is not only the result of military applications of modern technology and the horrors of the wars in which this technology has been used during this century culminating with the nuclear bomb, but also with the so-called peaceful uses of this technology and the very great danger that the gradual destruction of the environment will pose for the future for mankind.

These days, strangely enough, there is much greater awareness of the limits and dangers of modern technology in the West itself than in the non-Western world. Many Muslims, like other Asians and Africans, look upon Western technology as a kind of magic wand with which they can overcome all of the problems and vicissitudes within their society and bring happiness to members of their community. This is to some extent natural because it was as a result of this technology that the West was able to dominate over other societies for such a long time and still today dominates them economically if not directly militarily and politically. However, one must understand that this historical fact cannot change at all the nature of this technology which dehumanizes men and women and converts them into extensions of the machine and which if not checked will end with destroying the very network of nature which has made human life in this world possible. Those who believe in Allah cannot but put the rights of nature and all of the creatures of Allah including animals and plants in their place and not destroy other creatures with the help of modern technology in the name of the absolute rights of man which are so central to the modern worldview.

Today in the West, there is a profound crisis both on the theoretical level, as far as science is concerned, and on the practical level, in the realm of technology in its many forms. The most important steps at this moment of human history for Muslims, who become often hypnotized by the power of modern science and technology, are to study the roots of both seriously, to understand the foundations upon which they are based, to evaluate them within the framework of the Islamic worldview and to apply these sciences solely on the basis of Islamic teachings. Without taking such steps the Islamic world will suffer the consequences of modern technology and the dehumanization of people even more than has the West, and Islamic society will suffer from the same problems of segmentation and alienation which one sees in the West, even if the presence of the religion of Islam might modify such destructive forces to some extent.

By adopting Western technology blindly the Islamic world will only join the modern world in the rapid destruction of the natural environment which is accelerating with such incredible rapidity around us today. The Islamic world has a special responsibility as the recipient of the Quranic revelation to act as the protector of Allah's creation, of the world of nature, and not to betray the function of *khilāfah* or vicegerency, which all Muslims possess by virtue of being human, on the pretext that they have to modernize and catch up with the West. In the present situation the problem is not for Islamic society or for that matter any other society to catch up but to be able to sustain itself in harmony with the natural environment without which the very act of "catching up" would be synonymous with the destruction of the Islamic community and by extension the human collectivity as a whole. The natural world cannot sustain modern civilization which must come to an end in its present form if human life is to continue on earth. To survive, Islamic society must chart its own course and under no condition imitate blindly a civilization whose technological power now threatens the whole chain of life on earth.

CHAPTER 11
POLITICAL, SOCIAL AND ECONOMIC LIFE OF THE MODERN WORLD

POLITICAL LIFE

In order to understand the political aspect of the modern world, one has to go beyond the very complicated patterns, actions and reactions and events which dominate the political scene today to try to reach the roots and the causes which underlie current political life. Nor in fact can one do any more than to turn to the underlying causes in a study such as the present work since the analysis of the vast complexities of political or for that matter economic or social life in the modern world would require separate voluminous books. In contrast to the Islamic world where, from the very beginning, both religious and political authority issued from the revelation itself and the Prophet was himself both the founder of the religion and of the first Islamic society and state, in Christianity the spiritual and temporal authorities were divided from the beginning. Christ in saying "give unto God what is God's and give unto Caesar what is Caesar's" declared the clear separation of temporal and spiritual authority. Of course, when Christianity became the religion of a whole civilization leading to the foundation of the Christian civilization of the Middle Ages, political institutions of the West also became Christianized. Consequently not only were the emperors and kings who ruled over that world deeply-rooted in the Christian tradition, but they relied upon the church for their authority and legitimacy.

For many centuries there existed in the traditional civilization of the West two authorities: spiritual authority based, as far as Western Christianity was concerned, on the institution of the papacy and the hierarchy which issued from it, and temporal authority vested in the Holy Roman Empire on the one hand and in local kings—especially those of France and England—who wielded a great deal of power, on the other. There was also a hierarchy between these two authorities in the sense that the spiritual authority was always considered to be higher than the temporal, and it was, in fact, the Pope who blessed and legitimized the rule of various kings and even emperors. Towards the end of the Middle Ages, however, an important event took place which had far reaching consequences and which had to do with the rebellion of the temporal authority against the papacy. A concrete incident which marks the commencement of this general tendency was the abducting of the popes and their imprisonment in France in the eighth/fourteenth century. Gradually, the temporal authority began to consider itself independent of the spiritual authority of the papacy resulting in a protracted struggle between the two which had a great deal to do with the downfall of the unified Christian civilization of the Middle Ages.

Slowly in the Renaissance a new power began to arise in the West. This power was none other than the new mercantile class or the so-called bourgeoisie which became powerful especially in the southern part of Europe in such countries as Italy. The rise of the bourgeoisie continued, combined with the weakening of the aristocracy, until finally with the French Revolution the aristocracy was decapitated, the monarchy destroyed in France and the bourgeoisie took the power into its own hands. Then during the thirteenth/nineteenth century, movements began in the name of the working class or the proletariat against the bourgeoisie which by now had become dominant over the political scene in Western Europe and also in the colonies in America although the institution of the monarchy did not by any means disappear, and the aristocracy survived even in France but no longer possessed its earlier power. The rise of the idea of the rule of the proletariat reached its peak with the

1917 Russian Revolution which was carried out in the name of the proletariat against the bourgeoisie.

When one looks upon the political history of the West during the last 600 years, one sees that there were during the Middle Ages four important powers or classes within Western society, namely, the spiritual or priestly class associated with the Church, the aristocracy associated with kings and the monarchy, the bourgeoisie and the proletariat. There occurred first of all the rebellion of the aristocracy against the priestly class, then that of the bourgeoisie against the aristocracy and finally the proletariat against the bourgeoisie. But interestingly enough, none of these revolutions totally obliterated the powers that they had replaced with the consequence that with the ascendance of the power of kings and the aristocracy, the power of the Church continued although diminished. Also with the triumph of the bourgeoisie, although the monarchy disappeared in France where the French Revolution was carried out, even within France the aristocracy survived while the monarchy continued in other countries such as England, Spain and Italy. Likewise, with the Russian Revolution, although the Czarist regime was destroyed in Russia and later Communism took over a good part of Europe, in many other parts the bourgeoisie continued and finally contrary to Marxist predictions prevailed over Communism.

During this long history another important event took place which is of the utmost importance for Muslims to understand. This event was the gradual transfer of ultimate political power from Allah to the people. Originally Christians, like Muslims, believed that all power including the political came from God and kings ruled by divine right and reflected the presence of God in society in the same way that God is the King of heaven. With the signing of the *Magna Carta* in England in the seventh/thirteenth century, certain rights were transferred to the people and that marked the beginning of the ever greater transfer of power from the Divine to the people or what the West conceived as transformation from theocracy to democracy which means literally in Greek the rule of the people. Of course, in this process of the secularization of political life, there is no doubt that there remained those who continued to believe in the origin of power as coming from God Himself, and even to this day in a country like America which carried out the democratic revolution much more radically than Europe, there are still those who believe that ultimately power must come from God. Yet, for all practical purposes gradually in the West power was taken from the divinely ordained institutions related to the Church and the monarchy and transferred to the people.

While this ever greater transfer of power to the people continued resulting in the establishment especially in the Anglo-Saxon world of democracy in the modern sense—first in England itself and then in colonies in America, particularly the United States and Canada, and also in other countries where the Anglo-Saxons had established colonies, such as Australia and New Zealand, and while democratic processes also began to spread in continental Europe—another tendency in European political life continued to manifest itself. This tendency remained strong until a few years ago and is very far from having disappeared completely even today. This other tendency is the movement toward strong central authority or dictatorship by means of the rule of a single person, a party or a small political elite over the community but outside of the old traditional institutions of the Church and the monarchy which had prevailed over Western civilization for a long time. This new type of central authority was usually connected with a single dominant figure such as Bismark in the thirteenth/nineteenth or Hitler and Stalin in the fourteenth/twentieth century. In fact, these two aspects of the political life of the West entangled and wrestled with each other for a long time resulting in major wars of which the First and Second World Wars are the most evident demonstrations. It was this polarization where one side ruled in the name of the dictatorship of the proletariat that dominated over the Cold War until the fall of the Soviet Union in 1989. It is important to remember, however, that even that aspect of modern political life which is based on a doctrinaire ideology basing itself either on race or nationalism of one kind or another is very far from being dead as the events in eastern Europe since the demise of Communism have shown so clearly.

It is also important to realize that democracy which is now hailed as being global and universal and the aspiration of all peoples does not by any means have the same meaning in every single culture. English and American democracy even now is very different from French or Italian or in fact Irish democracy. If democracy means the sharing of people in the government, then of course there are many forms of democracy not only that which is institutionally called democratic in the West but many other forms of government which have existed in many non-Western societies including the Islamic world. However, the institutionalization of democracy in the form of elections, parliaments, the division of power and everything else that is associated with the modern democratic state are far from being the same in all the different countries in the modern world which are called democratic.

In certain democratic countries in the West there is still some degree of hierarchy within society; nor is the principle of aristocracy totally dead. In some countries family relations and certain local cultural links are of great significance paralleling formal governmental institutions much more so than they are in certain other types of societies. For example, in two countries such as Italy and the United States the relationship between families and certain cultural bonds in the former play a very different role than they do in the democratic institutions and processes of the latter. Altogether Muslims must be careful not to view all political institutions and practices in the West in the same light. It is also important to note that although everyone now talks about the significance of democracy which has spread to many parts of the world, the meaning of democracy is not always the same. One must always pay attention to the context and the historical background from which democracy has risen. In certain societies, such as that of the Islamic world, there has always been the participation of the people in government through specifically Islamic channels which are not institutionally the same as what is considered to be democratic in the West today. Yet, these channels have definitely permitted the participation of people and various social groupings in the processes of political rules.

Often in the West one can observe a mixture of democracy with strong notions of nationalism, religious identity and even sometimes ethnic association to the extent that whenever any of these elements is threatened there are violent reactions within a society which claims to be democratic. This phenomenon can be clearly observed in the immigration of a large number of non-Europeans or even east Europeans into western European countries in recent years and the violent reactions against them in such countries as France, Germany and even to some extent Britain where there has been a longer democratic background.

Therefore, in order for the Muslim to understand Western democracy, it is important to understand the historical development of the various institutions which have brought about the differences between various types of democracy within America, Britain and continental Europe and the role of various cultural elements in the development and working of democracy in the West. It is also important to understand that for some time now the West has been using democracy combined with capitalism as a kind of ideology of its own to combat those who have been against it. It has crusaded for democracy in the same way that in the Middle Ages the Christians crusaded against Muslims with the aim of spreading Christianity in the Holy Land. This crusading spirit, although often attributed in the West to Islam through a misunderstanding of the idea of *jihād*, is a strong aspect of Western culture itself and even when that culture has become secularized, something of this crusading spirit has remained in the attempt to spread capitalism and democracy to other lands, whether the inhabitants of those lands like it or not and without consideration of how participation of the people in the political process differs in various cultural contexts. This ideological use of capitalism and democracy has been especially true of the United States during this century.

The idea of democracy as dominating over political life has been combined until very recently in the West with the idea of nationalism which became particularly strong in the thirteenth/seventeenth century. The nation became nearly absolute in the West, asking of its citizens complete allegiance and, in a sense, replaced religion itself, creating a "civil religion" in the place of or complementary to revealed religion. One cannot understand the political life of the modern world without grasping the modern idea of nation and nationalism which must not be confused with the older Islamic concept of nation or *waṭan*, although this latter term began to gain, during the last century, the European meaning of "nation" as a result of the spread of modern nationalism into the Islamic world. Paradoxically enough, while for the past few decades Europe is moving more towards some kind of unity and away from excessive nationalism, the force of nationalism in the modern Western sense continues to be a dominant one in the Islamic world.

Another very important factor to consider in understanding political life in the West is, of course, the role played by economic and material factors. There are many who claim, in fact, that economics is the underlying determining factor of political life while others believe that ideas, ideologies and other non-material factors play a more important role without denying the economic dimension. Needless to say, Marxist historians, not only those who lived within what was the Soviet Union but also the large number of those in Western universities who have Marxist leanings, interpret economic factors as being all important.

Here again, it is necessary from the Islamic point of view to strike a just balance, neither denying the importance of economic factors nor falling into the trap of an economic or materialistic determinism which *à la* Marxism sees all political manifestations as being rooted in economic factors. There is no doubt that the search for markets, the need for raw materials or cheap labor and other factors of this kind play a role in political considerations of all nations including the powerful democratic and capitalistic countries in the world, and there is no doubt that democracy itself has sought to create a world order in which it is dominant and through which in fact the economic goals of the powerful democratic nations are achieved. But at the same time one must not reduce Western political life simply to economic factors as many people have sought to do not only among Western Marxist but also among a good number of Muslims, especially those modernized Arab intellectuals who have been deeply influenced by Marxism.

Finally, in seeking to understand the very complicated political life of the modern world as it has manifested itself in the West, it is important to remember that as modernism has spread outside of the West, it has not always taken Western political institutions with it. A country like Japan has accepted democracy while adopting Western economic and technological ideas, but its democracy is very different from that of America. Not only does the emperor still survive, but there is also a hierarchical structure within Japanese society and a sense of respect for elders and traditions which is missing nearly completely in the American type of democracy. Other lands which have modernized to some degree, in fact, have not adopted Western political institutions at all and there is today throughout the non-Western world including the Islamic world a tension created between the adoption of modernism in economics and technological domains and the refusal to accept modern Western political institutions. This is part of the crisis and struggle going on within the Islamic world to try to establish and create its own institutions, whether they be political, economic, social or otherwise, which would be authentically Islamic while responding to the challenges that modernism pose for it.

Social Life

The major upheavals alluded to above have also left their profound mark upon social institutions. The rise of the power of the aristocracy, then the bourgeoisie followed by the proletariat and the revolutions which have been brought about as a result of these transformations, especially those of the twelfth/eighteenth, thirteenth/nineteenth and fourteenth/twentieth centuries, beginning with the American and French Revolutions and ending with the Russian Revolution of 1917, all have been combined with upheavals in the social structure of the modern world whose traditional social structure has been for the most part destroyed, but again, not completely. The stratified and hierarchic social institutions which were found in the Christian West for over a millennium came to an end although something of them survives to this day. As a result, society became more atomized and much greater mobility was created, while at the same time many of the social bonds which had kept society together were weakened and are now faced with the possibility of being completely severed. Already in the thirteenth/nineteenth century, the rise of the Industrial Revolution not only caused the depleting of much of the countryside whose labor force came to the big cities, but also brought about the weakening of family bonds and the exploitation of men, women and even children by the machine and the new industrial complex. It was in fact as a result of reaction against this exploitation that many of the social critics of the thirteenth/nineteenth century began to oppose the existing social and economic order as reflected not only in the Marxist critique of capitalism, but also in Western literature, for example in the novels of Charles Dickens from England where the Industrial Revolution was perhaps more cruel than anywhere else in Europe. The process of industrialization combined with rapid urbanization, migration into big cities, the rise of population and many other factors in the West lead gradually in the thirteenth/nineteenth and earlier fourteenth/twentieth centuries to the breakdown of many of the traditional social bonds in larger towns and to a lesser degree in rural areas leading gradually to the atomization and weakening of the family.

In the West, as in the Islamic world, the main unit of society has always been the family. Christianity sanctified the monogamous family consisting of the father, the wife and the children but in earlier times, often grandparents, aunts and uncles and other relatives lived together in what is called the extended family which had a function very similar to what one finds in the Islamic world today. Even now, in the southern countries of Europe such as Spain, Italy and Portugal and even in Ireland and areas of the rest of Europe which are not as highly industrialized as the urban centers of England, France and Germany, something still survives of the extended family. The same is true of the United States where in the smaller towns and the less industrial areas of the country something of the extended family continues to function. But gradually, as a result of the pressures of the Industrial Revolution and the transformations that it brought about, for most of Western society the family came to mean the atomized family, that is, the family consisting of the husband, wife and their children.

During the past two generations the atomized family has also begun to break up almost like the splitting of the atom. The rate of divorce, which for a long time was banned by the Catholic Church, has risen so sharply that today more than 50% of all marriages in the big urban centers of America and much of Europe lead to divorce and many children are brought up in single parent families. Moreover, there are now even those who attempt to break the traditional meaning of marriage as being between the opposite sexes and try to give a new meaning to marriage as being any bond between two human beings even of the same sex as long as they want to live together. Therefore, in this last phase of modernism to which, as already stated, some refer as post-modernism, even the meaning of the family as it has existed throughout the ages is under severe attack.

The major force behind the changes that occur so abruptly in the social order in the modern world, to the extent that by the time one comes to study the pattern it has already changed, is what is called individualism or the rights of the individual. Individualism is one of the most important philosophical elements that issued from the Renaissance idea of humanism. It became much more strengthened, especially in America and the rest of the so-called New World, where the social bonds were weaker and where the possibilities of expansion physically, materially and economically were greater than in Europe, becoming part and parcel of the character of much of American culture and gradually spreading back into Europe as well. Individualism considers the right of the individual to be supreme, that is, above the rights of God, in a certain sense, and even of society to the extent possible. But here again one can see a debate in the modern world between the rights of the individual and those of society, the Marxists and many other socialists considering society to be real and the individual nothing but a cog in the machine of society, whereas most democratic thinkers believe the individual to be more important.

The political and economic spectrum in the West is, in fact, based to a large extent on this factor, the socialists emphasizing the importance of the rights of society represented by the state and the laissez-faire capitalists those of the individual and the private sector. Paradoxically, the politically conservative right at the same time supports more social norms and moral values and the liberal left the rights of the individual to do as he or she will. In any case, the assertion of individualism has lead to very rapid changes from almost decade to decade in the recent period and it is very difficult for a young Muslim, or for that matter anyone coming from outside of the Western world, to understand how rapidly the patterns of Western society change and even how some of the deepest bonds, such as that of marriage, have their very meaning transformed within a single generation.

The question of the relationship between the sexes not only within marriage but outside of marriage is a very good example of this rapid social change. Christianity, in contrast to Islam, considers sexuality itself to be related to original sin and, in fact, for a long time Westerners criticized Muslims for being immoral because polygamy is permitted in Islamic Law. Promiscuity has now become so prevalent in the West, however, that many people instead of calling promiscuity "promiscuity" simply have tried to change the moral norms themselves and believe that any kind of sexual behavior that is followed by an adult is morally acceptable as long as it does not affect the lives of other people. For many modern Westerners there is no longer any Divine Norm or morality of Divine Origin which is accepted in this crucial question. But again, this attitude is not true for everyone and there are many people in both America and Europe who still believe in the Christian idea of marriage and of sexuality.

There is in fact a deep clash in these matters as seen in the current political debates in the United States over both the question of rights of women *vis-à-vis* men and the question of abortion which is related of course to the question of sexuality and marriage as well as of the sanctity of life. The question of abortion also brings out in itself the conflict between the views of an agnostic humanism which considers the individual to be the highest principle and therefore the complete master of his or, more often, her body and life, and the view of those who consider life to come from God and human beings to be instruments for the creation of a new life form over which, therefore, they do not have the power of announcing the verdict of death.

Another important element in the social life of the modern world, as far as both America and Western Europe are concerned, is the question of the relationship between races. Although modernism is very much rooted in the idea of individualism and the rights of the individual, there is also the element of race which has continued to play an important role in European and especially American history. It is difficult for Muslims, brought up in a world in which race plays really a secondary and minor role, without our wanting to deny that racism is totally absent there, to understand the central problem of racism as it exists in the West. In the thirteenth/nineteenth century when many European colonial powers invaded Africa on the pretext of stopping the Arab trade of Black slaves, no one bothered to ask the question what had happened to these slaves who had been taken to Arabia. If they had studied the situation more carefully, they would have seen that all of the Blacks who were taken to Arabia were completely absorbed within Islamic society, very different from what happened in America. In fact, there is not a single Islamic country that has a black ghetto like Harlem. The Blacks who were brought to Arabia, the Persian Gulf or other Muslim countries, like the Turks before them from Central Asia, were rapidly integrated into Islamic society, some becoming rulers. When one prays in a mosque in Morocco with Arabs, people with definitely Black African features and Berbers with blue eyes and light hair one does not have a feeling of praying with people of different races. The Islamic character of the "people" (*ummah*) dominates completely over their racial traits in contrast to what one experiences in the West.

Racism in the West has always been a difficult problem because of a character of the European civilization which goes back to the Greek and Roman periods. It is interesting that the word for barbarism simply comes from the Greek term for stranger or foreigner. Strangely enough, until recently racism was considered in Europe to be basically an American malady. Then after the Second World War, with the rise of the number of Blacks from Africa and the Caribbean in Great Britain, the migration of a large number of Turks into Germany and Moroccans and Algerians into France, racial problems began to appear which have become more and more serious up to our own day, revealing the fact that this problem is not confined to America. In any case although racism seems to be opposed to individualism, it remains a very important element in the social life of the West and continues to play a central role in the political and social life and especially in the upheavals which the West is undergoing today.

In studying the complex social patterns that one can observe in the modern West, we have mentioned an ever greater migration of people from the countryside to the city and the destruction of farm life, the growth of industrial and urban centers with their negative impact on the environment, a greater degree of individualism, atomization of the family, the loss of meaningful relationships resulting often times in isolation and nihilism and the rise of psychological imbalance, maladies so common in big cities today. Moreover, these processes are not simply confined to the West but are spreading to other parts of the world along with the spread of modernism. One might say that the whole trend in the social transformation of the last few decades which is itself the result of what has been going on for several centuries in the West, is the uprootedness of individuals, cut off not only from their religious traditions but also from their family and social traditions. The new situation offers often great challenges, inviting at least some individuals to seek to reach their full potential, but it also often confronts human beings with a sense of despair in a world in which extreme competition and constant struggle and strife combined with the eclipse of spirituality leave their deep psychological and social scars.

For the young Muslim unfamiliar with the modern world, it must not be forgotten, however, that these negative tendencies are not the only reality in the life of society in the West as some Muslim critics of the West have claimed. Rather, the influence of religion still continues upon certain social institutions and there are segments of society in both Europe and America comprised of many devout and religious people where social bonds are still strong and where Christian virtue such as charity is still very much present. This fact can be seen especially in cases where there is a crisis or catastrophe when members of the society come to the help of others. One needs to consider how many people in the past few years in the West have come to the help of the weak and the hungry in Africa, Asia and other places where natural or man-made tragedies have created colossal human suffering. Therefore, in judging the social institutions of the West, it is not sufficient to study only the element of chaos and uprootedness which are certainly present and which threaten the very existence of modern society. One must also consider the continuation, despite everything, of the influence of Christianity and Judaism and the survival of certain religious virtues inculcated for centuries within the souls and hearts of Westerners, virtues which continue to manifest themselves even if numerous individuals turn against their own institutional religion and their traditional backgrounds.

Economics

Economics, needless to say, has been important in every civilization if by economics we mean that part of man's activity which deals with the production of goods, the amassing of wealth, labor, work, trade and exchange of material objects, etc. But in Islam, as in other traditional civilizations, economics was never considered as a separate discipline or distinct domain of activity. That is why there is not even a word for economics in classical Arabic, the term *iqtiṣād* being a fairly recent translation of the modern term "economics" in Arabic and having a very different meaning in classical Arabic where it means primarily moderation and keeping to the golden mean as witnessed by the famous book *al-Iqtiṣād fi'l-i'tiqād* of al-Ghazzālī.

In the West, however, ever since the eleventh/seventeenth century the practical philosophers such as Bacon, Hobbes and Locke began to write about the significance of the amassing of wealth and the importance of economic activity. Economics became gradually both a scientific discipline and distinct activity of its own and in many areas it became divorced from ethics. It must not be forgotten, however, that classical capitalistic economics, which arose in the eleventh/seventeenth century and which was brought to the New World by the Puritans was related to a certain aspect of Protestant ethics which emphasized the virtue of hard work and the amassing of wealth in contrast to Catholic ethics. But very soon the religious roots of capitalist economics became more or less eclipsed and there arose, as a result of the excesses of this type of economics based only on the importance of the incentive to amass wealth, the reaction to capitalism by socialism which was espoused by Marx and many other socialist thinkers of the thirteenth/nineteenth and fourteenth/twentieth centuries. This latter group sought to distribute wealth to prevent social injustice and opposed the power of capital exercised by those who possessed it against the workers whose labor created capital. Socialist economics also did have its Christian supporters and many identified Christian charity, feeding the poor and helping the destitute with certain socialist ideals. This combining of Christian ideals and socialism is to be seen to this day in the Liberation Theology movement in South America. But by and large socialism, even more than capitalism, became rapidly secularized and in the form of Marxism became violently anti-religious. Traditional Christian economic theories as found, let us say, in St. Thomas Aquinas are not, in fact, very far away from Islamic economic theories and both differ completely from modern economic theories which have sought to repudiate both of them in theory as well as in practice.

In the modern world economics has become more or less divorced from ethics and it has become, as mentioned already, the driving force in many political and social decisions. One can say that, in a sense, the Marxist view of the central significance of economic factors in life is not totally false as far as the materialistically oriented modern civilization is concerned. It is important to mention here that among those in the West who have sought to relate economics to ethics, most consider ethics itself in a purely humanistic vein believing it to be created by man. In contrast, in Islam not only is economics never considered as independent from ethics, but ethics itself is never considered to be independent of religion. Therefore, it is really the *Sharī'ah* or the Divine Law within which what is called Islamic economics must function and find its meaning. A corresponding view cannot simply be found in the West today save among those Christians and Jews who still cling to their traditional religion but who comprise a minority voice rarely effective in realms of economic decision making.

The Question of Law

It is important, while discussing political, social and economic factors in the life of the modern world, to say a few words about the notion of law in the West because all of the factors discussed in this chapter are deeply connected with the concept of law. In democracies laws having to do with the economic, the social or, of course, political domains are passed by elected legislatures. In all of these cases law is considered to be an expediency based on current social exigencies and decided by the voice of the people. The legislators are chosen by the people and in turn formulate the laws. There does exist an invisible presence of Christian ethical concerns which determine the decisions of certain individuals, but these Christian teachings are not used directly as the foundation or basis of the law. Laws in the West were based originally on Roman law, as well as on common law, and are complemented by the views given by each generation of jurists, the courts and the various parliaments and congresses.

As we have already seen, the concept of law in Islam is very different. Law comes from Allah and human beings can only apply and extend it to different situations but the source of the law always remains the Divine Revelation. There is, therefore, a notable difference as far as confrontation with the social problems is concerned between the modern world and Islam. In the modern world laws are passed to accommodate existing situations whereas in Islam existing situations must be transformed to conform to Divine Law. There is consequently a radical difference in the understanding of the concept of law in the two worlds. Therefore, it is very important for Muslims to understand the meaning of law, its function in Western society and why and how it works and also why it faces such a profound crisis in the United States today where the very excess of legal practice and law suits threaten to stifle and even destroy a great deal of the activity of society and to stultify positive activities in many ways.

***

In conclusion it must be mentioned that one hardly needs to be a prophet to realize that there exists a profound crisis within the modern world in all domains especially the social and economic. Even after the demise of Communism, when many people think that the modern system as developed in the West has now become completely victorious, the crisis continues and in fact intensifies as one observes in the social domain where alienation, crime, use of drugs, and many other social ills threaten the very fabric of modern society and in the destruction of the environment where the very existence and everyday functioning of the modern world threatens the balance of the natural environment and the future of human life on earth.

As far as the Islamic point of view towards this crisis is concerned, everything must be judged according to principles and norms which Allah has created for human beings wherever they might live on this earth. There is today a danger of disarray and total disorder in modern society even amidst all the political power and economic wealth which it possesses. It is necessary for young Muslims to know in depth the causes of this crisis beyond the facade of worldly success and at the same time to avoid much of the shallow criticism of "Western decadence" which has become fashionable in the Islamic world during the last few decades. Much of this kind of criticism is unaware of the deeper roots of the crisis at hand and has not come to terms with the reality of the presence of other forces in the West itself which are rooted in religious and traditional values and which are themselves seeking to correct existing deviations and to prevent the terrible social disintegration which the modern West is facing.

It might be said that the modern world, as it originated in the West five centuries ago and has by now spread over much of the globe, is coming to an end and that what many people in the West now call the post-modern world has already begun. But that post-modernism is so far simply one more step in the further dissolution of the modern world. What will be established after that dissolution will depend on how the traditional forces within the contemporary world in the West, as well as the Islamic world, and other non-Western peoples of the globe will confront the great challenges and dangers which modernism as well as its contemporary continuation in so-called post-modernism have posed and continue to pose to an ever greater degree for the whole of the human species.

CHAPTER 12
MODERN EDUCATION—ITS HISTORY, THEORIES AND PHILOSOPHIES

For the great majority of young Muslims who come to the West the Western institution most often encountered and the one with which they have the most intimate experience is the educational one. This is also true to some extent of young Muslims who are studying in the modernized educational institutions within the Islamic world itself, institutions which are modeled upon Western ones and have been created since the thirteenth/nineteenth century in different countries of the Islamic world with the express aim of introducing modern learning to Muslims. It is, therefore, important to have a deeper understanding of the role and meaning of education and educational institutions in the modern West and also the historical roots of Western education.

As in the Islamic world, so also in the West before the period of secularization and modernization during the Renaissance and the eleventh/seventeenth century, education was related to religion and the educational institutions were either directly or indirectly controlled by the Church. There were furthermore separate educational institutions for the Jewish minority in Europe wherever there was a sufficiently large number of Jews. Schools in pre-modern Europe sought, therefore, to educate the young in the theological, philosophical, legal and ethical teachings of the Church or in the case of the Jews the Jewish religion and on the higher levels to prepare Christian students for priesthood and important ecclesiastical positions and Jewish students to become rabbis. This situation is very reminiscent of the Quranic schools, *madrasahs* and other religious institutions in the Islamic world attended by students from an early age. However, education was more widespread in the Islamic world than in the pre-modern West.

In the early Middle Ages Islamic educational institutions themselves began to have an influence, especially in the domain of higher learning, upon their Western counterparts through Spain, Sicily and France as well as Italy. In fact, the whole college system which gave rise to the modern Western universities had a close relationship to the Islamic *madrasah* system which survives to this day in the Islamic world. Such terms as the "chair" used in Western universities is, of course, the direct translation of the Arabic word *kursī* and there are many educational practices which have survived to this day in the older institutions of higher learning of medieval origin in the West such as Salamanca, Paris, Bologna, Oxford and Cambridge which bear deep resemblance to practices in the classical Islamic educational system. It is also important to remember that the Western educational institutions, especially the university, are not part and parcel of the modern world and that in their origin they, like the Church, belong to the pre-modern history of the West.

Very early in the development of modernism, however, educational institutions were for the most part, although not completely, captured by the forces of modernism and modern education became the most important means for furthering the value system of the modern world, for the spread of secularization and for the criticism of the religious worldview. Through educational institutions, not only the sciences but also ideas concerning the amassing of wealth, furthering economic ends and creating greater social mobility within society were disseminated, this being especially true in America and only more recently in Europe.

The process of secularization of education in the West took several centuries and it is far from being complete. As more and more institutions of learning which had originally been founded by various churches were secularized, new institutions were often created by the state which sought to preserve a separation between religious institutions and those created by the state or other secular bodies. In some countries such as the United States and France this separation between religious and secular education in state sponsored institutions has been rigorously maintained and the government seeks to make certain that schools funded by public money do not have any religious coloring to them. In other countries such as Great Britain and Germany such is not the case and governments do support religious education.

In any case, through the universalization of education in modern times, that is, the establishment of elementary and secondary schools to educate nearly all children as well as through the spread of university education to a larger number of students, secular education has extended its influence. At the same time, however, the religious bodies, whether Catholic or Protestant, have also succeeded in preserving their own educational system from the kindergarten and elementary schools through the university. Furthermore, in both America and Europe there continue to exist to this day traditional Jewish schools called Yeshivas which resemble in many ways the Islamic *madrasahs*. Therefore, if one looks upon the general picture of education in the West, one will see that while there has been a continuous secularization of the older institutions which were originally founded by churches of various kinds and the establishment of numerous secular institutions, one can also observe the continuation of religious education on both sides of the Atlantic despite the great differences of educational philosophy between these two types of educational institutions, namely, the religious and the secular.

As far as the goals achieved by the educational system established by various European states and later on in America are concerned, these have consisted of the propagation of national ideals and philosophies such as the new secularism, nationalism, utilitarianism, public welfare and have included, of course, economic goals spurned by the idea of material progress which in the thirteenth/nineteenth century became almost a religion of its own. The concept of education in the classical sense of training the mind and the soul has not disappeared, especially in older educational institutions and church sponsored schools, and wherever liberal arts education flourishes, but it has been seriously challenged by the new educational philosophy. Consequently, the universities especially, and through their influence secondary and primary schools, have become on the one hand a kind of "secular church" for the spread of secular ideas and the professors and teachers have come to occupy to some extent the role of the earlier priesthood wielding definite authority in their fields especially in the field of the sciences. Almost all of the important secular ideas which have shaken the foundations of religion in the modern world such as evolutionism, the idea of progress, doctrinaire socialism, psychoanalysis, etc. have had their origin in or been spread by modern educational institutions and have spread from there to other parts of society. On the other hand, however, precisely because the university attracts unto itself usually the most perceptive and intelligent members of society and the institution itself predates the rise of modernism, universities have continued to serve even in the modern world as a critic of that world. In fact, the most profound criticism of the very idols of modern thought such as progress and the like have also come from university circles so that the university has been at once a bulwark for the preservation and the spread of modern secular ideas and at the same time a critic of many of the ideas which are now tearing modern society apart.

It is necessary to emphasize the important role of educational institutions in the West, especially since the thirteenth/nineteenth century, in the indoctrination of the general population with various ideologies from nationalism to Marxism, from Communism to Western capitalism and democracy or other ideologies which have been dominant in the modern West. Here, precisely because of the survival of the earlier religious foundation of education and the survival of many educational institutions with a religious orientation, especially in America, there has been and continues to be a constant conflict and tension between secularist ideologies and religious ideas.

It is difficult for a Muslim student brought up even in the semi-traditional Islamic educational system, not to speak of the classical *madrasah*, to realize how the teaching of various branches of knowledge has become separated from religious values in modern education. There has come into being in fact a compartmentalization not only of the branches of knowledge separated one from the other with no cohesive unity in contrast to what one observes in the traditional image of the various branches of the tree of knowledge related to the trunk of the tree, but also a nearly total separation between knowledge and spiritual values. This is to be detected in almost all Western universities except those which are directly sponsored by Catholic, Protestant and also Jewish religious organizations in which the values of those particular religions are openly taught to the students. For the majority of students going to so-called state sponsored or secular institutions, in fact, the refusal to teach spiritual values has been considered as being essential for the separation of religion from the educational enterprise. By default, therefore, knowledge has become separated from both spirituality and morality.

As far as morality itself is concerned, precisely because of the gradual separation of the educational system from its religious background, the question has now arisen as to what kind of morality to teach if one were to consider morality at all. The ethical dimension of life has become relativized and sometimes even put aside precisely because the teachers, the state and the various institutions responsible have not been able to agree as to what ethical norms should be taught to the students. This has resulted in a grave crisis which is now beginning to manifest itself especially among the younger generation in the West as the older ethical norms which even the modern secular West inherited from Christianity gradually begin to wane and disappear.

Western education is therefore caught to a large extent in the throes of the tension between religion and secular humanism. The battle lines have been drawn in many domains and subjects ranging from evolutionism versus creationism, various theories of society, Eurocentrism versus multi-culturalism, the question of the meaning of life, the problem of the relationship between the various fields of knowledge and ethics and many other subjects fundamental to the philosophy and theory of education. There exists also tension between what certain people claim should be "objectivism" in educational upbringing and the presentation of a particular point of view and an already determined philosophy within which educational practice should take place. These tensions and conflicts have resulted in the gradual disappearance from the philosophies and theories of education of the concept of truth itself. Today, in most modern Western institutions of learning one speaks seriously about the truth only in the natural and mathematical sciences, whereas in the humanities, the social sciences and the like one rarely hears a teacher speak about the truth and most subjects are presented in a completely relativistic manner as if there were no such thing as the truth. As stated earlier in this book, many modern philosophers even deny the meaning or significance of the term "truth."

The compartmentalization of knowledge, which is one of the characteristics of the mental and intellectual scene of the modern world, is not only reflected in modern education but is also caused by it. A number of important Western thinkers have sought to overcome this excessive compartmentalization but they have not succeeded in doing so because there is no longer a worldview which would unite various disciplines. There is already the division between the natural and mathematical sciences on the one side and the social sciences and finally the humanities on the other, each with different perspectives and methods while in the case of many practitioners of these latter disciplines there is the attempt to emulate the natural sciences.

Something still remains of the earlier pre-modern idea of the liberal arts, the *artes liberales* of the medieval period, which shares a great deal in common with the classification of knowledge and the curriculum described by certain classical Muslim thinkers and authors. The liberal arts education, which is to be found in America and England, preserves something of the unity of perspective which characterized medieval European learning when European civilization was a religious and integrated civilization in many ways similar to the Islamic, especially in the educational field, but even this hallowed educational philosophy has now become to a large extent compromised by the great emphasis upon the natural sciences and the creation of what are called the social sciences which try to emulate as much as possible the methods of the quantitative sciences and apply them to society as such. The social sciences, moreover, seek to engulf the humanities. As a result, the humanities themselves are struggling hard to survive as humanities.

It is interesting to note here, as far as the young Muslim student is concerned, that most Muslims who come to study in Western institutions rarely take up the subject of the humanities seriously. Most of them study either the sciences, medicine or engineering and, therefore, the humanities seem somewhat irrelevant to them. In the Islamic world itself also there is a great crisis in the modern established universities precisely because the systems from the West have been transplanted into that world without a close integration between the humanities, which should be drawn totally from Islamic sources, the religious disciplines and the sciences which have been imported from the West.

In any case, whether in the West or elsewhere, modern educational institutions, which are the main repositories of knowledge and which consider themselves to be the main guardians of modern Western civilization, contain within themselves the seeds of profound conflicts as far as the philosophies and theories of education are concerned, these conflicts reflecting and emanating from the separation created at the dawn of the modern period between the domain of knowledge and the domain of the sacred as contained in religion. Many Western educational institutions still preserve something of their medieval past but there are also many innovations based on views of man as the purely earthly and non-religious being defined by twelfth/eighteenth and thirteenth/nineteenth century philosophers or as a single cog in the social machine as envisaged by positivist and Marxist theoreticians since the thirteenth/nineteenth century. These educational institutions, therefore, remain in a state of constant tension with religious institutions and even with the earlier humanism which sought to view human beings as a whole in need of the development of both their mental and spiritual aspects.

There is no doubt that modern Western education has exercised a profound impact upon the Islamic world. This impact has come through the very large number of Muslim students who are sent to the West and who are sometimes bewildered to see the conflicts between what they are taught in class and services held on Sundays, between certain students who are very religious and others who are totally opposed to religion, all of these being representative of the divorce between religious values and science in Western education. But the impact of Western education on the Islamic world is also felt through the presence of modern educational institutions within the Islamic world itself where today there is a great crisis resulting from their conflict with the traditional institutions of learning which have their own philosophy based upon the unity of knowledge, the servitude of man to God, the centrality of the Divine Revelation and all the other principles which characterize the Islamic worldview. This conflict is to be seen to a large extent also in secondary and primary schools in many of the larger cities in most Islamic countries where Western models have been copied in one form or another usually depending upon the accidents of history. A country colonized by Great Britain copied British models as is the case of Pakistan and Muslim India or Nigeria; if it had been colonized by France then French models were copied as we see in North Africa and if colonized by the Dutch then the Dutch model as can be seen in Indonesia. Moreover, American educational models have also been incorporated in many Muslim lands in the past few decades often superimposed upon the earlier European models.

Today, the understanding of modern Western education in both its history and theories is absolutely essential for the Muslim student not only in order to protect himself or herself when that person studies in the West, but also in order to understand the conflict within the Islamic world of two educational institutions and philosophies which produce graduates who belong to the same countries and speak the same language but have two very different worldviews. These worldviews are, furthermore, reflected on every level from the role of the teacher who in Islam is considered to have a very high position in society to the extent that there is a saying attributed to 'Alī that, "He who has taught me a single word, I will become his slave," to the role of the student within that institution, to the relationship between knowledge and ethics, between science and religion, the content of the curricula, the meaning and goal of education and all of the other fundamental elements which constitute education. In the Islamic world as in the West education has always been central because it is through education that the younger generation is trained to carry out and carry forward the ideals, norms and principles of a particular society.

Today, Western education is in a great crisis even in seeking successfully to achieve the distorted goals of the secularization of knowledge, material domination, cultivation of individualism and all of the other elements which the Islamic worldview rejects. This system is doubly dangerous for Muslims both because it is in a state of crisis within itself and also because even if it were not to be in conflict within itself, it would be in discord with the Islamic perspective and the values which Islam cherishes most dearly. It is therefore, very critical at a time when Muslims must learn various Western disciplines, including not only science and technology but other disciplines as well, in order to be able to provide their own answers and master their own destinies in a world in which they are faced with vast challenges, that they become fully cognizant of the meaning, role and function of education and educational institutions, including especially the philosophies which underlie them. In this way, they may become able to learn to the extent possible what they wish to learn of Western disciplines without becoming excessively contaminated in an unconscious way by forces which could distort their religious perspective, uproot them spiritually and intellectually, alienate them from their own traditional background and simply add another potent element contributing to disorder and chaos within Islamic society itself.

CHAPTER 13
ART IN THE MODERN WEST

For most Muslim students the history of Western art usually seems to be a farfetched field and few Muslim students come to acquaint themselves with Western art in the narrower sense of this term. The understanding of modern Western art and its history is, nevertheless, important because this art reflects on the one hand the deeper currents of Western culture and many of the crises which the modern West has faced and still faces and has on the other hand itself contributed to the series of elements, forms and forces which have created the modern cultural ambience. In fact, the role of Western art in the creation of that ambience is very central, and its understanding is, therefore, essential for anyone who wishes to grasp the deeper ethos and impulses of the life of the West.

Western art until the Renaissance bore many resemblances to Islamic art although it was iconic, that is, based on the painting of the icon whether it be of Christ or the Virgin in contrast to Islamic art which has always avoided an iconic sacred art. Nevertheless, Western art before the Renaissance, that is, traditional Western art, precisely because it was traditional art, was based on certain religious and divine principles. It not only drew its inspiration from revelation, but its techniques and methods were transmitted from generation to generation going back to an inspiration which issues from the divine and angelic worlds above the purely human. It was only with the Renaissance that Europe broke away from its traditional Christian civilization and this parting of ways manifested itself first of all in art before it appeared in the fields of philosophy, theology or the structure of society.

The Visual Arts

The art of the Renaissance, which is famous because of the appearance of several great geniuses such as Raphael, Michaelangelo and Leonardo Da Vinci, certainly reflects worldly beauty more than the beauty of the spiritual world and opened art to the purely human but at the expense of departure from the sacred and celestial art of the Middle Ages. In fact Renaissance art reflects more directly than any other aspect of Renaissance culture the new humanism which placed man rather than God at the center of the scheme of existence. Although religious themes continued to be treated, the art of the Renaissance was no longer the sacred or traditional art of the earlier centuries. Even the Vatican, the center of Catholicism to this day built on the older building which was destroyed during the Renaissance, displays not the heavenly beauty of the medieval cathedrals but the atmosphere of a palace which reflects the power of the world and the humanistic characteristics of the age in which it was built. Interestingly enough, it was from that time on that Western art became such an accurate index of changes in society both reflecting and contributing to rapid transformations with the consequence that periods and styles of art became all important. Before that time for centuries Romanesque and Gothic art had survived and actually do so to some extent to this very day, creating a permanent style of architecture similar to what one finds in Islamic architecture. The same can be seen in Latin lettering and calligraphy which, although not as important in Western art as in Islamic art, nevertheless display the continuity that one observes in Islamic styles of calligraphy.

In the field of painting, however, which is much more central to Western art than to Islamic art, each age began to have its own style and the permanent immutable archetypes which are reflected in traditional art were lost as far as the mainstream of Western art is concerned. The Renaissance styles of painting of both Italy and the North, which produced so many famous artists, gave way to what was called classicism and the attempt to emulate the classical style of antiquity based on the naturalistic proportions of the body and other objects leading to an excessive naturalism against which the romantic movement in the thirteenth/nineteenth century set in, trying to move away from the rationalistic and naturalistic tendencies of the classical period. It was during the Romantic period that new schools of art and ways of depicting figures, colors and light came to the fore in several different schools of which perhaps the most significant is impressionism associated with such famous French painters as Monet and Renoir with their sensitive treatment of color and light. But this style was in turn superseded by other styles such as post-impressionism, expressionism and cubism and the breakdown of the classical form in favor of an abstract art which has dominated the fourteenth/twentieth century to a large extent. The founder of this movement was perhaps more than anyone else Pablo Picasso.

In architecture, likewise, styles began to reflect the philosophical and cultural fashions of the day. The tenth/seventeenth and eleventh/eighteenth centuries reflected more the rationalistic and naturalistic tendencies of the time and also the attempt to emulate classical models of ancient Greece and Rome and the thirteenth/nineteenth century with the Romantic movement a return to the revival of Gothic art and also certain more romantic styles of architecture. This led in turn in this century to the rather "abstract" and functional architectural forms of the Bauhaus in Germany and other movements of the kind, finally to be supplanted by the post-modernism of the last few years.

It is interesting to note however, that despite all these changes which have gone on from one century to another, the older traditional forms of art survive especially in architecture as we see in the continuation here and there of the Gothic, Romanesque and also Nordic styles. These styles of architecture have survived to this very day and still in the fourteenth/twentieth century in certain cities in the West beautiful Gothic buildings such as the Washington Cathedral in Washington, D.C. which was just completed, are constructed not based on the passing styles of a particular period but emulating the traditional Gothic style which has had centuries long history and which goes back, like the Romanesque, to a supra-individual source of inspiration. Needless to say, however, this permanence of the traditional styles of architecture remains secondary in comparison to the ever changing styles which dominate the skyline and streets of most modern Western and to an ever greater degree non-Western modern cities.

The same fact can be observed although to a lesser extent in the pictorial arts. In this domain what has survived unchanged is the painting of the icon in strictly religious circles such as those associated with the Eastern Orthodox Church, whereas, in total contrast the mainstream of Western art has undergone rapid changes during the past few centuries and has not been able, as a consequence of ever changing cultural fashions, to preserve a style which would be widely accepted to several generations and over a long period of time. The traditional arts have also survived in the margin of the art scene, for example in the crafts which continue to be produced in such countries as Spain, Ireland and Mexico and even in the more industrialized countries of northern Europe or rural America. The West, however, began to divorce art from the crafts or the making of useful objects in the twelfth/eighteenth and thirteenth/nineteenth centuries when the Industrial Revolution took place bringing about the distinction between industrial products and so-called "fine arts." whereas, as already mentioned, in the Islamic world—as in fact in all traditional civilizations—there has never been a difference between the two, arts and crafts being ultimately the same thing.

All traditional art has for its goal the making of objects which are to be used and not simply the creation of luxury. The reason for art was never what is called art for art's sake by certain theoreticians of art in the West since the thirteenth/nineteenth century who could find no better excuse for the existence of modern art. The traditional perspective shared by Islam does not mean utilitarianism in the ordinary sense of the term because it takes into consideration man's spiritual needs as well as his physical ones. It is only in modernized circles in the Islamic world that such terms as fine arts or *beaux-arts* in French have become translated into Arabic, Persian and other Islamic languages and used for painting, sculpture and the like. Muslims who accept such concepts do not always realize that this divorce of art from the crafts represents the divorce of art from life in the modern world and the surrender of the art of making the objects which surround man and affect his soul most deeply to the machine.

One of the most striking elements which Muslim students detect when they come to the West is that there are great museums in which objects of art are preserved and which are very impressive in themselves. At a moment when so much of humanity's artistic heritage is being destroyed, museums are of course precious, but at the same time their existence means that what is kept in them is separated from the rest of society and from the daily activity of human beings for whom art is no longer integrated into everyday life. Traditional societies which produced so many beautiful objects of art, that are kept in museums today, never possessed museums themselves because art was never divorced from life. Art was life and life was art; and as has been stated by one of the great theoreticians of Oriental art, Ananda Coomaraswamy, in traditional societies the artist was not a special kind of man but every man was a special kind of artist. In fact, the major distinction between the role of art in modern Western society and its role in traditional Islamic or for that matter other traditional societies, is precisely the divorce between life and art or what one makes and what one does in one society and their unity in the other.

Western pictorial art is both the most direct indication of the deeper impulses of change within the souls of Western man and an indication of the phases of Occidental culture and in itself it has contributed a great deal to Western man's own self image. There has existed a kind of concordant action between an art which human beings have experienced and with which they have identified and the ever greater humanization of the spiritual or inner reality of human beings which was in turn reflected upon the canvas. This process, beginning in the Renaissance and culminating with the naturalism of the twelfth/eighteenth and thirteenth/nineteenth centuries, led finally to the breakup of forms and the beginning of abstract art in the fourteenth/twentieth century, an event which coincides in fact with the breakup of forms in other domains of Western culture. This breakup of forms did not mean in most cases an opening of these forms to heavenly influences but most often to a dissolution from below and descent to the lower strata of the human psyche.

It is important to note that much of modern Western art is based on individualism, subjectivism and psychological impulses of the individual painter rather than the Divine Norm which would transcend the individual artist, whereas, of course, Islamic art as all traditional art, has seen the source of art to be above and beyond the individual. Moreover, in contrast to Western art, especially in the modern period, which is so psychological, Islamic art has always tried to transcend the psychological domain and to relate art to the reflection, in an objective mode, of the spiritual realm which lies beyond the merely psychological and subjective dimensions of human existence.

Music

Beside the visual art of painting and sculpture which complements it and which like painting has played an important role in modern humanistic man's definition of himself, one of the most important arts in the West, whose significance is again difficult for most Muslims to grasp, is music. In the traditional Islamic world, as we have seen earlier in this book, music is either related to the chanting of verses of the Quran, although this is not technically called music, or poems in praise of Allah, the Prophet and religious themes or to certain social functions such as the military going into battle, peasants singing during the harvest or weddings and the like. On another level one can observe the presence of the interiorizing music associated with Sufism. But music for diverse social functions as it is prevalent everywhere in the West, did not exist in classical Islamic civilization.

In the West, on the contrary, although music started as a purely religious art, it spread rapidly outside of the religious realm to create many forms of what is called secular music including classical Western music which has no equivalent exactly in the music of Islamic people although Muslims also possess their own long and rich classical musical tradition. In the Islamic world, however, the classical traditions of music remain more for private circles, for those trained spiritually to hear this music in an inward sense, whereas classical music in the West became much more of a public affair.

Western classical music is one of the richest and most important art forms in the Western world. In the Renaissance this music continued to be closely allied to medieval music and most of its inspiration came from Christianity and the Church, especially from the Gregorian Chant which was the most pure form of church music. However, gradually the courts began also to become patrons of music and during the Renaissance one begins to see the introduction of instrumentation in addition to the human voice even in religious music and the development of what is called secular music and the rudiments of the opera. However, as the other forms of Western art became more and more humanistic and worldly, some of the deepest religious and theological impulses of Western man took refuge in music and this remained true especially up to the twelfth/eighteenth century. Perhaps the greatest of all composers of the West, Johann Sebastian Bach, who lived in the twelfth/eighteenth century, produced music which is of a much more religious and spiritual nature than what was being produced in the architecture, poetry or literature of his day. In many ways Bach is to Western music what Dante, who lived some 450 years before him, is to Western literature.

After the twelfth/eighteenth century, however, music also gradually became more worldly and with the rise especially of the Romantic movement subjective, psychological and emotional elements became strongly present in it. But even at that time some of the great composers like Mozart, who was the last of the major classical composers before the rise of Romanticism, as well as Beethoven, Brahms and some of the other great Romantic composers nevertheless did create pieces which still reflect something of the cosmic and spiritual quality of music. It was only in the fourteenth/twentieth century that classical music, like the pictorial arts, experienced a dissolution of forms "from below" as one sees in the twelve-tone music associated with Schönberg, minimalism and many other schools of contemporary classical music which often sound strange even to the ear of trained Western listeners. In any case, classical Western music is one of the richest aspects of the art of the West with many diverse developments which make it a unique musical tradition and for that very reason it has been deeply appreciated on a wide scale by non-Western cultures throughout the world although much of this music, in fact, is not conducive to interiorization or the remembrance of God.

There exists in the West, in addition to classical music which has had a very important social function providing music for the more educated and trained strata of Western society, both folk and popular music. What is called folk music in the West, although partly modernized in certain countries with its instruments changing in the thirteenth/nineteenth century, nevertheless represents a type of music not completely dissimilar to the folk music of the Islamic world especially if one turns to such Western countries such as Ireland and Spain where older folk musical traditions have been preserved. Folk music has a quality which does not come from the Industrial Revolution and the age of the machine or the humanism and naturalism of post-medieval civilization. Often times its composers have been anonymous and it has an aspect of simplicity of expression and at times passive spiritual quality which must not be confused with the specifically modern products of European civilization.

In contrast to folk music what is called popular music, some of which in fact has its roots in folk music, has come to the fore especially during the last century as a direct expression of modern ideas and sentiments and in fact has had an important role to play in both reflecting the state of each generation of Western society and contributing to the psychological state of that generation. One can see the power of popular music in the types of music that have developed among the young during the last few decades with wild rhythms, played very loudly and with frenzy. As examples, one can cite rock, heavy metal and similar kinds of music which appeal to the lowest animal instincts and attract tens of thousands of young people to concerts which often result in riots and social disorder. To say the least, these kinds of music do not issue from submission to God nor lead the soul to submission, nor are most of its star performers, who have become among the cultural heroes of the current scene, models of spiritual discipline or moral probity.

And yet these kinds of music have found a large attraction among the youth in the rest of the world including some Islamic countries. These kinds of music both reflects the rebellion of the youth against the norms of the society in which they have been born and also to a large extent contribute to the sense of "freedom" from order although this freedom is often nothing other than the freedom of the lower impulses of the soul and the psyche from any higher principle rather than freedom in its spiritual and religious sense. But even here there is a deeper significance to the rise of these types of popular music. Such kinds of music mark to a large extent the coming to an end of the cultural world which was associated with modernism since the Renaissance. It is, in a sense, a way of destroying that rationalism and the cerebral treatment of all things with which so much of European culture has been associated since Descartes and an attempt to rediscover the significance of the body as a reality in addition to the mind. That is why also it is usually played so loudly trying to penetrate the body almost with its physical presence. Whether it succeeds in bringing down the walls of the citadel of cerebral activity and rationalism without substituting more inferior elements of the lower psyche in its place is, to say the least, open to question.

In any case, the different categories of music in the West whether they be classical, folk or popular music of different types and also forms of music in between such as jazz, which has an African folk origin but developed in America primarily among African-Americans and which also has developed a certain element of popular rather than folk character, these musical forms represent a rather vast spectrum which is difficult for most Muslims to understand especially when they first come to the West. Nevertheless, it is important to grasp their meaning in order to understand what is going on in the Western world and what forces and cultural factors are at play in the creation of such sounds which in many cases appear to be so strange for a person coming from what remains of traditional Islamic society.

LITERATURE

It is impossible in a short chapter to deal with all facets of modern Western art even in a summary fashion and, therefore, only a few can be treated. This chapter will have to conclude with the brief discussion of the third important category of art which cannot be passed over in silence and that is literature. Of course, every civilization has its own literature and the West is no exception. It has also produced great literature not only in Latin which was the classical language of the West but even during the Middle Ages and certainly later in many of the local vernacular languages. It is also interesting to note that the early literary works in European vernacular languages had to do with religion and traditional Christian civilization as did the *Divine Comedy* of Dante in Italian, which is perhaps the greatest work of Western literature, the *Sermons* of Meister Eckhart in German or Chaucer's *Canterbury Tales* in English. Like the other fields of art, however, with the Renaissance there was a sudden rise of what one could call secular literature. Of course, in the Middle Ages also there had been many love poems composed in different languages by the troubadours. There is also the later love poetry of the High Middle Ages which, like troubadour poetry, has common roots with the Islamic poetry of Spain (the word troubadours itself having an Arabic origin) but this type of literature is not technically speaking secular because courtly and troubadour love poetry also possess a level of meaning related to the love of God. There exists in fact a profound relation between the mystical poetry of Christianity and this kind of love poetry. But it was in the Renaissance that secular literature, properly speaking, began to be composed both in the form of poetry and prose leading gradually to the development of a new literary form called the novel.

The novel in the modern sense of the term is a form that did not exist in classical Islamic literature although short prose works which could be called short philosophical novels were written in both Arabic and Persian but with very different aims from the modern novel. As mentioned before, the central form of literature in Islam continued to be poetry whether it was of the epic or lyrical kind. In contrast, in the West the novel became gradually the central vehicle for the expression of literature, much more important than poetry which began to decline especially in the areas dominated by the major European languages. Although English, which is the most widespread of European languages, did continue to produce great poets as did to some extent German, nevertheless the role of poetry as a whole in Western civilization has gradually diminished to this day to the extent that today except perhaps in the Spanish-speaking world, there is no Western country in which the poet plays as great a role as he still does in the Islamic world or as he did in the earlier centuries of European history.

The novel gradually became a mirror to reflect society and the actions of human beings and from the late thirteenth/nineteenth and early fourteenth/twentieth centuries to penetrate more and more into the psychological realm within the consciousness of the individual. The novel became a mirror of life itself and as longer novels began to be written especially in the thirteenth/nineteenth century, the novel became a world of its own in a sense independent of the created world outside. It is true that a number of the great novelists of the thirteenth/nineteenth century such as the Russians Tolstoy and Dostoievski or the French Victor Hugo were men who had a religious vision and who believed in God, but gradually the very experience of reading the novel in a sense became a substitute for sacred and religious art and life. Literature, especially in the form of the novel, began to create an ambience to compensate many readers for the loss of God in Western society while at the same time the novel continued to be a profound critic of what was going on in European and American societies. Some of the European writers such as Charles Dickens in England, Emile Zola in France or John Steinbeck in America had an important role to play in pointing to some of the injustices and evils of the society of their time but by and large the novel moved literature away from the religious role it had played in earlier Western society and still plays in what remains of the traditional Islamic world.

It is interesting to note, however, that with the advent of modernism in the Islamic world, the novel has begun to influence Muslim writers and one has today eminent Arab, Persian, Turkish and other Muslim writers who are novelists and the novel has now become an accepted literary form within the Islamic world. But it is important to understand that this form of literature which is so central to the understanding of the Western ethos of the last two centuries is, in fact, a fairly new form and came into being as a result of the secularization of culture and of literature itself. It is also important to mention that while this process of secularization of literature was taking place even before the development of the novel, great writers were appearing in the West, such giants as Cervantes, the greatest of Spanish writers, Shakespeare, the foremost writer of the English language, and Goethe, perhaps the most outstanding poet of Germany. Such men used literature not only as means of depicting the human condition but also as a way of pointing to truths and realities beyond the purely earthly. They were all observers in one way or another of the frailty of human life and the imperfection of the human condition but they also pointed to a spiritual reality beyond the merely human.

It is not possible for a Muslim to understand the West fully without knowing at least something about such figures and also the role of literature and especially the novel in the modern West. Again like painting, literature in the form of the novel and to a lesser extent poetry has been a mirror for each age reflecting some of the deepest cultural impulses of each generation. The great novelists have also tried to be teachers and have spoken of certain values and ethical norms which they have tried to present in their works and which through their works have become inculcated to some extent in the society around them. Some, like the Russian novelist Solzhenitsyn, depicted in the starkest terms for both the Communist world and the West the barrenness of human life without a spiritual dimension and even contributed to the downfall of Communism.

Altogether, however, as the very process of modernization has accelerated, the impact of the men and women of letters has by and large decreased especially in the last few decades with the predominant influence of the visual media of television and the cinema. Today, people read less and the central role played by the written medium in the West from the time of the spread of the art of printing to the fourteenth/twentieth century is now waning to some extent. Nevertheless, literature continues to be, along with the visual arts and music, one of the most important of the arts in the Western world and even many of the languages in the West which are not associated with countries of great military or economic power continue to produce great men of letters, this being especially true of the Spanish-speaking world and of Ireland. The Irish have produced some of the greatest poets and novelists of the English language although Ireland is a small country and the Spanish-speaking countries continue to produce some of the outstanding poets and writers in the Western world. That is not to say, of course, that America and England or Germany, France or Italy do not continue to produce important writers.

Literature remains very much alive although older texts are now attacked like works in so many other fields by nihilism and "dissolved" by the deconstructionism which have become philosophically fashionable in the last few years. Despite everything, literature continues to survive and is one of the means whereby the more sensitive souls of Western society, especially those who have been given the art of writing and the keen eye with which to observe the crisis in which the modern world is immersed, continue to play a role as critics of the modern world. At the same time modern literature also continues to fulfill its share in the destruction of the sacred and substitution of a subjective world for one in which God's presence is ubiquitous. It is necessary to remain aware of both of these roles of literature in modern Western society. It is also important to remember that the first profound criticism of modern society which was read widely in the English-speaking world came from the poets, especially T.S. Eliot, and that the most scathing criticism of the Communist world which became known to the West and influenced to a large extent the views of many people towards what was going on in that world came from the pen of Solzhenitsyn. There are, furthermore, many other figures including some of the French and English Christian novelists and poets such as W.H. Auden, F. Mauriac and C.S. Lewis who have been at the vanguard of bringing out and making known publicly the flaws and contradictions, the spiritual poverty and the depth of chaos which modern society faces. At the same time such writers in contrast to many other literary figures have tried to hold up before men and women at least some of the spiritual values which alone can allow humans to be truly human, values which have been recounted in countless forms over the centuries in so many of the traditional masterpieces of Western literature going back to the origin of European civilization.

CHAPTER 14
THE MODERN LIFESTYLE

The impact of the modern world upon young Muslims, whether they happen to live within the Islamic world or have come to the West to study, comes most of all through what can be called the modern lifestyle. Much more than modern philosophies and theologies or ideologies, the modern lifestyle, which needless to say reflects a particular philosophy on its own level, affects the Muslim youth directly and immediately with an impact which can be seen in almost all major urban centers of the Islamic world as well as among many Muslims studying or living in the West. This infatuation of the young with the modern lifestyle, which has its origin more in America than Europe, is in fact not limited to the Islamic world. Rather, it is a worldwide phenomenon and reflects the attraction of many of the youth, on whatever continent they happen to be living today, for what appears to be complete individualistic freedom from tradition and principles which have been handed down over numerous generations.

Today, one sees an intense attraction among the young throughout the world for so-called pop music whether it be rock, heavy metal or other forms and for the wearing of such typically modern dress as blue jeans which reflect the idea of freedom from constraint and of mobility and of the individual declaration of independence from social norms.

There is also attraction for fast cars and forms of entertainment which involve speed and daring as seen in Western-made movies and other forms of mass entertainment. Most of the youth are traveling fast without knowing where to go. This fascination or even mesmerization with the everyday modern lifestyle emanating from the West, which is worldwide, is shared by large numbers of young Muslims especially those bombarded by television and other forms of mass media transmitting the cultural values of the modern or so-called post-modern world.

It would take us too far afield in this brief survey to point out the profound social, psychological, philosophical and religious reasons for the manifestation of such phenomena in today's world. It is, however, important for young Muslims to realize that these phenomena are related to deeper causes some of which have been outlined in this book, and are not spiritually neutral. Moreover, the new style of living does not accord even with the patterns of life in Western society as it existed during the last few centuries and demonstrates the disintegration of that society. The rapid falling apart of Western society as it has existed until now can be seen in the fact that only a generation ago many of these patterns of modern life or lifestyle were totally absent. For example, till a generation ago the family, held fairly steadfast in the West although sexual relations were much more free and less controlled than in traditional societies. Nevertheless, much more of Christian ethical values survived and were prevalent than what one finds today. It is especially during the last few decades with the generation that grew up after the Second World War that the sense of the meaninglessness of life and nihilism set in along with distrust of the older generation, opposition to the many hypocrisies which the youth saw in the generation of their parents, the breakup of the family the loss of the traditional roles of men and women and their relation with each other and the loss of authority of any kind not only ethical and spiritual but even social and to some extent political. These phenomena first appeared in what came to be known as the counterculture and have now manifested themselves more fully in what many people simply call post-modernism. In any case, the new lifestyle represents a radical departure from the norms of the modern world as they have existed until now and are at the same time its logical unfolding. Whereas modernism marks a solidification from the spiritual point of view, this new phase marks the dissolution which follows upon the wake of solidification.

Of course, one of the most important characteristics of the new lifestyle is rebellion against what the youth consider to be tradition, not tradition in the sense that we have discussed in this book as the sacred which comes from Heaven, but as customs and habits and all that has been transmitted to them from older generations. Perhaps no generation in recent memory has tried to turn away from the legacy of its parents and ancestors more than the present generation of Western youth. This has created what is called the generation gap which has not existed until now in this way in the Islamic world. Many young Muslims are surprised when they come to the West and hear people always talking about the generation gap, teenage rebellion, the crisis of youth against their parents and other phenomena of this kind which, although present to some extent in the modernized segments of the Islamic world, cannot be seen anywhere to such an extensive degree in that world.

It is important to understand the significance of this revolt against the older generation, the generation gap and the chasm which separates many youth especially in big cities in the West from their parents. To this must be added the fact that to an even greater extent many children are brought up in a home in which one of the parents is absent and the other parent, not being able to fulfill the authority of both parents, often times relinquishes that responsibility which parents had in traditional families to transmit ethical values and provide a structure for the life of the youth. Therefore, many young people have to make up their own life as they go along.

Another consequence of this transformation is the radical revolution in sexual relations. The Christian norm is, of course, still present in certain circles. There are still many people in the West who follow Christianity but to an ever greater extent especially in big cities not only sexuality outside of marriage but also infidelity within marriage, as well as various forms of homosexuality, have become more and more prevalent during the last generation. Traditional sexual ethics have, in fact, become ever more questioned by not only agnostics but even by some who still claim to accept religion. It is only the fear in the last decade of such dreaded diseases as AIDS that has to some extent, but not completely, put a limit on uncontrolled sexual practices which have come to dominate over the life of the youth with numerous consequences such as ever-increasing teenage pregnancy.

The discovery of the body and instantaneous bodily gratification has another aspect which is in general much more wholesome although not without its own problems, and that is the emphasis upon physical training and sports. Of course, sports have existed in all cultures in one form or another. One need only recall horse and camel racing and falconry among Arabs, polo among the Persians and archery among nearly all the traditional Muslim peoples especially the Persians and the Turks. Today, however, sports have become like a religion in the modern West. While the participation in sports plays a central role in the building of the body and even character and is one of the positive aspects of modern Western life, its commercialization and over-emphasis have brought its significance out of proportion and made it into almost a substitute for certain types of religious activity.

In the Islamic world the assembly of very large crowds in a public function has almost always been in relation to religion as one can see in the *ḥajj* or in the Muḥarram ceremonies in the Shi'ite world. Today, however, there are vast sport spectacles which have by and large replaced traditional religious functions and represent the secularization of what the West inherited from its Christian past and also from ancient Greece and Rome, as can be seen in the case of the Olympics. Furthermore, with the ever greater commercialization of sports even the secularized conception of sportsmanship as cultivated in amateur sports is becoming ever more eclipsed by commercial considerations. There are now sports heroes who make more of a salary in one year than the greatest Western scientist or scholar will do in his or her lifetime. The sports champion along with heroes of pop art and especially pop music, constitutes the new cultural hero in a society given to the worship of the body and the senses.

There is a strain in the current lifestyle which concerns the attempt to live in the present moment indifferent to one's history and the past and immersed in instantaneous sensuous gratification and glorification of the body. The worship of sports heroes and the continuous quest for record breaking and the domination over nature represents one dimension of this concern with the body, while a much more destructive aspect of the same tendency is found in the use of drugs including of course alcohol, free sexual relations and the like, all of which reflect the attempt of the soul to immerse itself completely in immediate bodily and sensuous gratification. Sports, of course, require discipline and hard work and have a positive aspect to them but the glorification of sports and near worship of sports heroes is related to the excessive importance given to the body. Furthermore, the role given to sports is far from being unrelated to the desire for sensuous gratification which manifests itself so destructively at the antipode of the care for the body in that other aspect of the modern lifestyle connected to drug abuse and uncontrolled sexuality. In both cases there is also a nostalgia for the re-discovery of the sacred as manifested in the body, the regaining of the vision of a reality which disappeared from the horizon of the modern West several centuries ago.

There is another important factor to consider when seeking to understand the rebellious character of the modern lifestyle. This factor involves the loss of faith by the youth in the earlier ethical norms of Western society and their rebellion against many of the contradictions which they detect in the mores and ethical behavior of their parents who remain faithful to the value system which created the modern world. These contradictions include the presence of various forms of injustice in society, such as racism, against which the young now react strongly and also the destruction of the environment and the of hatred of nature which has dominated over industrial society in the West for the last two centuries with deeper roots going back to earlier centuries when the sacred view of nature became lost in Western civilization. Many young people are sensitive to the importance of living in harmony with the natural world and their rebellion is not against an established and harmonious order. Rather, it is at least in some cases, if not in all, an attempt to destroy an already ailing "order" and to regain a balance with the world around them, both with the world of nature and with other ethnic and racial groups which have been segregated in Western society until recently.

The modern lifestyle is also characterized to a large extent by an earnest search for meaning. It is the loss of the meaning of life for many of the young that leads them either down the road of immediate sensual gratification through sexuality or the use of drugs and in some cases to violence and crime or to the quest for new philosophies, cultures and even religions. This phenomenon of the search for the re-discovery of the meaning of life has had both a positive and a negative aspect. Its positive aspect is that many spiritually sensitive and intellectually alert young people in the West have become, for the first time, open to the spiritual message of other cultures and religions and there is much more receptivity to other spiritual worlds among them than there was among thirteenth/nineteenth century British or French colonizers of the Islamic world or of the other cultures of Asia, Africa and the Americas.

As for its negative aspect, it is that much of this openness turns to shallow emulation of often times non-authentic forms of Eastern religions and cultures to the detriment of what still remains of the authentic Christian and Jewish traditions in the West and also the sudden appearance upon the scene of what are called new religions. These new religions are often elements of the more spiritual and esoteric dimensions of authentic religions cut off from the formal dimensions of those religions and presented independently by themselves. In other cases, they are simply psychological interpretations of traditional teachings by clever and sometimes deceitful figures who are able to attract the young to themselves. In any case, the new religions depart from the great traditional religions of humanity in many fundamental ways. They are usually against opposition and resistance to the forces of the modern world and, in fact, in many ways complement those forces. If the modern world marks opposition to tradition and religion as traditionally understood, these new forces represent in many instances the setting up of a counter-tradition and counter-religion and the dissolution of the traditional worldview. Therefore, in a sense they go hand in hand with the nihilism, relativism and deconstructionalism which can be seen in so many fields, especially in the philosophical and literary domains as already mentioned in this book.

One of the basic features of the modern lifestyle is, of course, the impact of the mass media. One cannot over-emphasize the significance of the role of the media upon the creation of the worldview of the youth and, in fact, almost everyone else in modern society today. It is the mass media which creates cultural heroes and which tailors people's views of the political and social scene and even of reality itself. In fact, as has been said by one of the most famous students of the meaning of the mass media, Marshall McLuhan, the media gradually becomes the message.

The tremendous power of the media is combined with the impact of ever greater change, the kaleidoscopic effect of which is all pervasive. The presentation of change to the viewers and listeners of the various media is at the very heart of the functional role of the media in the modern world. As the decades pass by, not only does change continue but it becomes ever more accelerated aided by the all pervasive role of the media. This rapidity of change can be seen in fashions of dress, outward manners of living and even modern art, all of which change practically every few years and in the case of dress fashions every year. Decades become themselves the criteria for periodization of various artistic styles to which one refers as the style of the 60s, the 70s, the 80s, etc. Moreover, fashions concern not only dress but even modes of thought and of art so that any concept of the permanent and the abiding is brushed aside especially in that illusory manner in which the media present the world to people.

It seems that the aim of the modern life-style is to exhaust with the help of the media all the possibilities which exist within the present human order. Most of the sources of this change in manners of dressing or acting or various forms of music or other arts come from the lower psychic domains but there are occasionally also openings to the higher world, and so one is confronted on the one hand with the spectacle of the dissolution of the modern world and on the other hand glimmers of light here and there and the remanifestation of the truth as it has been lived and presented by tradition over the centuries.

A young Muslim cannot understand the modern world and cannot continue to live as a Muslim in the modern world without understanding, in depth, not only the various aspects of the modern lifestyle in its ever changing kaleidoscopic nature, but also the impact that this lifestyle has, often unconsciously, upon Muslims who may not be fully prepared to respond to the challenges which it poses for themselves as individuals and most of all for them as Muslims who have dedicated themselves to Allah and have surrendered themselves to the Divine Will. Needless to say, it is this Will which has the last say because Allah's Will is always triumphant. But in our contemporary world the very presence of this lifestyle poses a challenge of the utmost importance, complementing the philosophical, scientific and theological challenges of modernism, and, in fact, presents a more powerful current against which the Muslim youth, whether they are in the Islamic world or studying in the West, must learn to swim and presents challenges for which Muslims of different ages, whether parents or the younger generation, must learn to provide authentic Islamic answers.

Part III
Epilogue—Responding to Modern Challenges

Chapter 15
The Young Muslim and the Islamic Response to the Modern World

Needless to say the young Muslim encountering modern civilization may respond to it in many ways based on his background, education, family upbringing, psychological and emotional makeup and intellectual capabilities. Here, in this final section of this book, our aim is not to outline what all of these responses might be, but what an Islamic response on behalf of the young Muslim who wishes to remain within the boundaries of the Islamic universe could be to challenges posed by modernism as outlined in the earlier part of this book. This response falls into several different categories and so we shall treat it in four parts, the first dealing with the religious, spiritual and intellectual, the second with the social, economic and political, the third with the artistic and the fourth with the lifestyle associated with the modern world.

1. The heart of an Islamic response to the modern world consists, of course, in the religious, spiritual and intellectual aspects of human life. It is these aspects which determine how a human being acts and how he

views the world about him. Starting with religion itself, the most important response that can come, the most important step that must be taken by a young Muslim is first of all to preserve the strength of his or her faith and not to lose confidence in the validity and the truth of the Islamic revelation. The modern world corrodes and seeks to destroy all that is sacred and religious in its midst, and is especially opposed to Islam as a religion which has refused to abandon its sacred view of life and the Divine Law which encompasses every human activity. Most Western orientalists have been attacking Islam for nearly two centuries and have been trying to teach Muslims how to understand their own religion with the excuse that since their civilization makes better syringes, they can also understand better what the Quran is saying or is not saying, whether the Quran is the Word of Allah or an amalgamation of the sayings of earlier prophets as claimed by so many Islamicists.

Muslims must first of all provide an Islamic response to the challenge posed by the modern world to religion as such and then to the Islamic revelation in particular. Here the task is, of course, not one that should be placed on the shoulders of a young Muslim who might not know his own tradition well but is the responsibility of mature scholars of the Islamic world who must provide the intellectual defense of the religion and its spiritual aspects from which younger Muslims can benefit and learn. Fortunately, many such expositions have been made in the past few decades and what the young Muslim needs to do is to acquaint himself with such writings and through them with what lies at the heart of his own religion. With their aid he will be able to ward off criticisms that are often made against Islam ranging from denial of the authenticity of the Quran and attack against many aspects of the life of the Prophet or many elements of Islamic ethics to slanted views of later chapters in the history of Islam.

There must be an Islamic response to each of the criticisms that have been leveled against the religion and, as has already been mentioned, one must draw from authentic Islamic teachings in order to provide necessary answers for such a task. In order to achieve this very important task, it is essential to present Islam in a contemporary language which can be understood by those who have not had long years of training in the traditional Islamic sciences even if their mother tongue happens to be still Arabic, Persian, Turkish or one of the other Islamic languages. The presentation of Islam in a contemporary language, which fortunately, again, has been carried out to some extent already and with which we have ourselves dealt in the first part of this book and elsewhere, needs to be carried out further and meanwhile young Muslims must learn what is at the heart of their religion and what it is that has enabled Islam to preserve a way of life and of salvation for humanity even after some fourteen hundred years. They must not only learn the criticisms which have been leveled against Islam from many quarters, especially from the West during the last few centuries, but also the inner dimensions of their own religion which has provided the answers to the deepest philosophical and existential questions facing the *ummah*.

The response to challenges to Islam must also be based on the most universal and all encompassing teachings of Islam avoiding narrow sectarianism and opposition within the Islamic world itself, leaving sectarian and theological or juridical disputes to jurists or theologians and religious scholars who have had the necessary training to carry out such debates. Of course, even in their case, the day has come for them to be able to adopt the larger view of Islamic orthodoxy based on the two *shahādahs* and the universality of the teachings which have emanated from the Quran and the *Ḥadīth* of the Prophet and to avoid sectarian infighting.

But whatever the case may be for older religious scholars of the Islamic world, for the young what is most important is to cling to the universal message of Islam in its teachings concerning Allah, human beings, the world of nature, man's final end and revelation and to follow the *Sharī'ah* and other spiritual and ethical teachings of the religion. So there must be on the one hand the putting aside of sectarian bickering and on the other hand the presentation of the truth of Islam in a contemporary language which then the young must not only learn but be able to master enough to ward off the criticisms that are made against them. It is our hope that this book itself will be aid in the achievement of this task.

Another important responsibility of the Islamic intelligensia is to study Christianity, Judaism and other religions from the Islamic point of view. During the last two centuries the Islamic world has been witness to the appearance of a whole army of Western scholars, some outstanding scholars without predetermined prejudices and some even sympathetic to the Islamic cause but many with preconceived notions and often bitter opposition to Islam, who have studied Islam and have deformed it precisely because of the distorted point of view from which they have begun. Yet, there have not been many studies of the other religions seriously from an Islamic point of view in a contemporary language in the same way that our ancestors studied other religions a thousand years ago. Where such contemporary studies, although still limited in number, have already begun, they have borne some fruit. It is important for the young to acquaint themselves with such studies and to continue to pursue this line of study and to be able to have a perspective on Christianity, Judaism and other religions not simply based on the opposition of some narrow minded people but on the universality of the Quranic understanding of religion. Even a cursory study of the Quran reveals that it reasserts over and over the universality of religion and the fact that religion has been sent to all humanity.

The young must also be aware of the magnanimity of Muslims during most of history towards religious minorities living in their midst. Moreover, in the study of other religions, Muslims, especially the young who go to the West, must be aware of the distinction between the forces of modernism which are opposed to all religion including what remains of traditional Christianity and Judaism in the West and those religions which, if understood well, can become allies with Islam against the forces of materialism and secularism that are seeking to destroy or at best privatize all religions and banish them from the public realm.

It is also of the utmost importance that young Muslims come to learn more about their own intellectual tradition embracing all the different Islamic disciplines from jurisprudence and the principles of jurisprudence to theology, philosophy and the spiritual sciences of Sufism not to speak of the basic disciplines of Quranic commentary and *Ḥadīth*. It is, of course, impossible for a young Muslim to master all these subjects, but it is not impossible for him or her to have a rudimentary knowledge of this intellectual tradition so as not to feel a sense of inferiority *vis-à-vis* the main thrust of the challenge of the West which is most of all in the domain of knowledge and therefore is intellectual, if not in the authentic sense of the term at least in the sense of the rational and that which deals with the fruits of the activity of the mind. It is again hoped that this book will provide some assistance in the acquiring of such a knowledge.

Also the young Muslim must learn enough of his own intellectual tradition to be able to draw from it responses to such modern and "post-modern" challenges as nihilism, agnostic or atheistic existentialism, materialistic Marxism, psychologization of the spiritual world and of spiritual reality as we see in so many different schools of psychology, as well as the challenges posed by modern science and now, of course, the environmental crisis which threatens human existence itself. Furthermore, it is necessary to actualize the Islamic response to such challenges in such a manner that the young Muslim will be able to apply his or her knowledge to concrete situations of private and social life as they present themselves often in unforeseen ways. Only too often when a young Muslim comes to the West, even if he comes from a devout family and has been able to learn the rites of his religion and certain verses of the Quran and is pious, he has nevertheless not been taught his own intellectual tradition so as to be able to draw from it in the new situations which he faces from every quarter within the modern world. This holds true not only for those living in the West, but even for the young who live within the modernized circles in the Islamic world.

It can then be said that the only way to provide an Islamic answer to the modern world on behalf of the young Muslim is to be able first of all to defend the religion of Islam from distorted interpretations from the outside by relying upon what is most authentic and central to the religion and avoiding the pitfalls of sectarian opposition which in other circumstances was perfectly understandable but which today only diminishes the spiritual and intellectual energies of the Islamic community, especially when confronted with the modern world. Secondly, the young Muslim must be able to draw from the Islamic intellectual tradition to provide responses to the challenges posed by various philosophical and scientific theories and practices emanating from the modern world. Finally, it is most important for the young Muslim to be able to distinguish between modernism and what remains of the authentic religious traditions of the West which have a great deal more in common with Islam than secularism which, although it grew in the West, is not at all related in its roots to the religious and sacred perspectives of the other monotheistic religions which are, in fact, sisters of Islam and also members of the Abrahamic family of religions.

2. When one turns to the social, economic and political domains of life, the most important point to note first of all is that most young Muslims are not able to distinguish between the authentic Islamic teachings which have been incorporated to a large extent into the social structures of the part of the Islamic world in which they have grown up and

local customs and habits which also surround their life. It often happens that when they meet other Muslims from other parts of the world, there is at first much discussion as to which one of them is practicing or following authentic Islamic norms whereas, in fact, they all are but with different social and cultural contexts within which the teachings of Islam have manifested themselves historically. Many of the attacks which have been made by modernists in the West against Islamic social institutions are, in fact, attacks against all non-modern traditional institutions which they identify specifically with Islam but which are also shared by non-Muslims living within Islamic societies and elsewhere.

An example of the question at hand is the covering of the hair of women. This is, of course, an Islamic practice, but it is also a social practice which is to be seen among Christians and Jews of the East as well as Muslims. It is important to be able to make the distinction in this particular case and state clearly that this practice is based both on the *Sunnah* of Islam and on social practice whereas certain other aspects of the social relation between the sexes are not explicitly stated in either the Quran or the *Ḥadīth* but were social practices incorporated not only by Muslims but also by members of other religions such as Christianity which existed in the societies of Western Asia and North Africa before the advent of the modern period.

Islamic social institutions within the Islamic world must be evaluated by young Muslims Islamically and not on the basis of modern criticism against them because most of these modern criticisms are based on certain assumptions concerning human nature and the final end of human beings which are both false in reality and opposed explicitly to the teachings of Islam. The modernist attacks made against the traditional family structure, relation between the sexes, the rapport between various generations and the like in the Islamic world must not be accepted passively and with a sense of inferiority by young Muslims as if they were established truths or scientifically established criteria of judgment. On the contrary, every few decades fashions and criteria for judgment that emanate from the West change. In fact, such criticisms must be viewed as issuing from a worldview which is totally alien to that of Islam, from a society which itself is in the process of rapid change and in danger of dissolution.

A perfect case in point is that of the role of women in Islamic society. Almost every Westerner who wants to attack Islam first of all attacks the role of women in Islamic society. But the role of women in the West was itself very different a hundred years ago, in the last decade of the thirteenth/nineteenth century, from what it is in the last decade of this century; and what guarantee does the Islamic world have that in the last decade of the next century the West will not have a completely different view? Each time it is on the basis of the current fashions that are prevalent in the West that Islamic society, as well as other non-Western societies, are judged by Western critics. Therefore, such critics must not be taken that seriously. Of course, their views must be understood, but they should not be considered to possess infallible criteria of the worth or the lack thereof of Islamic social institutions with the result that a young Muslim would feel a sense of the weakening of his social and family bonds as a result of such criticisms.

The same can be said of Islamic ethics. In the modern world, despite the fact that ethical values have become so weakened in society and that there is such a blatant disregard for ethical norms on behalf of so many of those who hold real power in their hands at the present moment, continuous criticism is being made against various aspect of Islamic ethics. These criticisms must be understood by the young Muslims as coming from another and moreover false view of man and of his society based on individualism, humanism, rationalism, the divorce of man from the sacred, rebellion against authority, the loss of the sense of transcendence, the atomization of the family and the quantification of life and the reduction of society to simply the quantitative sum of atomized individuals to which we have alluded earlier in this book. Naturally the young Muslim must oppose bigotry or injustice within his own society as anywhere else that he happens to live, whether it is in the West or some other part of the world, but the criteria for such judgments must be based on Islamic ethics itself and not on what happens to be fashionable in the modern world, precisely because what happens to be fashionable today will fall out of fashion very rapidly tomorrow. As a matter of fact, every few decades there is a new goal of certain types of agnostic or atheistic moralists in the modern world who need what would appear to be a "moral cause" in order to survive in a world in which they have forgotten God, but a "moral cause" which has no objective criteria based on revelation and the Divine Law but which is based on purely human constructs that, therefore, change with the rapidity of change in human beings immersed in the whirlpool of rapid transformation bordering on chaos.

In the field of economics it is important for the young Muslim to remember the virtues of relating economics to ethics which Islamic civilization has always done and the great dangers which appear when the two are divorced from each other and when economics becomes a "science" almost independent of human beings, dealing only with quantity without any regard for the qualitative aspects of life. In this domain, the revival of Islamic economics which has been going on to some extent for the last two decades must at least become well known to the young Muslim and at the same time the shortcomings resulting from not applying the Islamic economic norms within various parts of the Islamic world must also become known. Not everything that is practiced in the Islamic world is Islamic especially in the economic domain where, as a result of international conditions and the experience of the last few centuries many practices are no longer based on the teachings of the *Sharī'ah* It is important, on the one hand, to avoid identifying everything that is going on in the economic domain in the Islamic world with Islam and, on the other hand, to abstain from criticizing everything that goes on in the Islamic world on the basis of Western economic theories and in the name of a false idealism which cannot, in fact, exist and which is against human nature. What must be done is to know the *Sharī'ite* teachings concerning the relationship between economic activities and ethics and apply those as criteria to economic activity wherever it happens to be.

Perhaps the most difficult realm in the practical aspect of life with which the young Muslim is faced is politics. Within the Islamic world, again as the direct result of the destruction of most of the traditional Islamic political institutions and the penetration of various powerful forces such as nationalism and certain institutions of government from the West which are not congruent with the teachings of the *Sharī'ah* there exists a great deal of tension throughout much of the Islamic world in the political realm, and there does not always exist the freedom to discuss this question openly in many Muslim countries. Therefore, when the young Muslim comes to the West, on the one hand, he feels the sense of freedom of being able to discuss political issues and, on the other hand, he is often attacked by Westerners who criticize the lack of democracy in Islamic countries and oppose much of what is going on in the Islamic world politically. At the same time, behind the scenes all kinds of manipulations are carried out by certain "democratic" governments so as to maximize the political and economic interest of powerful Western nations in the Islamic world without regard for the demands of spreading democratic ideology.

This complex field is one in which one cannot provide a simple guideline as to how to respond, especially since young Muslims hail from countries with very different political situations and in most places Islamic political institutions and practices are not followed. The most important point here is, once again, to learn what the traditional teachings of Islam concerning political rule have been and again not to be over idealistic and unrealistic as has happened so often where what is half good has been destroyed with the hope of creating a perfect solution but instead ending up with replacing what existed with something much less perfect and much less open to the influences of traditional Islamic values. There are certainly advantages on a certain level to the political institutions in the West based on the idea of democracy, advantages which do not exist in many parts of the Islamic world where political confrontation and tensions are so great that they affect negatively all facets of social life and people do not have the freedoms envisaged for them by the *Sharīʿah* and traditional Islamic institutions.

Still, young Muslims should never simply submit to the idea that democracy, as crystallized in Western political institutions, is simply the ideal norm of government everywhere, especially in the form that it has taken in the West. They must realize that popular participation in the government always existed in the Islamic world before the modern period but through other means than simply casting of votes in a box and that the Islamic world must be given its own space and freedom of choice to be able to develop its own political institutions in conformity with the principles of Islam and the structures of Islamic society, an opportunity which, in fact, is not provided for Muslim countries at the present moment often because of the actions of those very nations which criticize political practices in those countries.

3. Coming to the artistic realm, in the general sense of the term, unfortunately many young Muslims, while even living in the Islamic world which has now lost much of its traditional civilization, do not have a first hand knowledge and experience of the great beauty and significance of traditional Islamic art save perhaps for a few monuments of Islamic architecture which, thank God, still survive in many parts of the

Islamic world. The first step for young Muslims is to acquaint themselves with their own artistic tradition which is based on a certain hierarchy of values and a philosophy of art very different from that which one finds in the West.

As stated already in this book, in Islam the supreme arts are calligraphy and architecture followed by the arts of dress and the making of the objects which surround the human being in his and her everyday life, such as carpets and the like and which, therefore, determine the immediate ambience for human beings. Parallel to these arts, there are of course the non-plastic arts of poetry which is central to Islamic culture and, music and chanting of various kinds, of which by far the most important is the psalmody of the Quran, the central sacred art of Islam. The important point to note here, first of all, is that young Muslims should understand how rich the artistic traditions of Islam are and should not remain without a response when they hear the criticism of modern critics that Islam has not produced any significant plastic art or music as if every civilization has to produce the same kinds of art with the same hierarchy of significance.

The young Muslim, who is aware of his or her artistic heritage and its significance, can always retort back in such cases and say that if Islam has not created sculpture or given the same significance to painting as has the West, the West in turn has not produced to the same extent, the depth and grandeur of mystical poetry based on the love and knowledge of Allah which adorns the literature of almost all Islamic peoples. Besides, except for sculpture which is banned by Islamic Law, as it is also in Judaism, and in the perspective of the aniconic art of Islam which forbids the making or painting or divine images, Islam has produced the highest form of art in practically every category of art conceivable. Even in painting which is not so central to Islam, the Persian miniatures followed by Indian and Turkish ones are among the great masterpieces of world art.

The young Muslim, especially coming to the West, must remain aware of the influence which modern art exercises upon the soul. He cannot provide a response by changing that art, but he can be careful about the forms of art with which he surrounds himself. It is always possible for him to surround himself in the space of his personal life with objects of Islamic art which bring the *barakah* of the revelation to him, to listen to the chanting of the Quran, as well as to classical works of poetry or music, and to create, at least on the smaller scale, an ambience in which the sacred and traditional arts of Islam resonate and provide around him both support and the reminiscence of the spiritual reality of Islam. A small piece of traditional Islamic calligraphy or design in a room in which he lives makes a great deal of difference as far as creating an Islamic ambience is concerned in comparison with his putting in his room a piece of modern or naturalistic painting from the thirteenth/eighteenth century from the West which belongs to a very different world-view. The same holds true of poetry, music and all the different sonoral arts which penetrate the soul through the ear and have a great deal of intimacy with man's inner being. The young Muslim should do his utmost to preserve his familiarity with his own artistic world both visually and sonorally without, of course, closing himself off from acquaintance with Western art which comprises a part of his education and which a young Muslim, who tries to understand the Western world, must come to know well.

The criticism which must be answered by the young Muslim in the domain of art is often based on the assertion, made especially by certain shallow Western art critics, that Islamic painting is not alive or naturalistic, although this latter criticism has been made less in recent years now that Western art itself has ceased to be naturalistic. There is also the criticism that Islamic art, in contrast to Greek art is not able to emulate movement in the body of the figures that it depicts or recapture three dimensional space and other criticism of this kind. Such criticisms are in reality meaningless and irrelevant if one were only to understand the meaning of Islamic art, but nevertheless they are often made.

Another type of criticism that is made is that Islamic art has been static and has not changed significantly over the centuries, as if change itself is a great virtue. Young Muslims must reverse the argument and face their critics by pointing to the significance of an art which, precisely because it does not change constantly, speaks over the ages much more eloquently even to the uneducated masses than does the ever changing art of the Western world, even if one were to leave the content of the two arts in question aside. One wonders whether a beautiful piece of calligraphy done in the permanent *naskhī* style speaks more to the simple person walking in the bazaar of Cairo or some surrealistic or some other kind of modern painting by a New York or Paris painter to the person walking in the streets of those cities. We think the answer is quite clear and the young Muslim has a very strong argument in presenting to his critics the significance of an art which, being of a traditional order, is able to present the highest truths beyond the changing fashions of time and touch the hearts and minds of various levels of Islamic society in a way that cuts across the idiosyncrasies and transient accidents of each age in a manner that could never be even imagined in the case of modern art.

4. Finally, coming to the question of lifestyle, it must be granted that it is very difficult for a young person, whether he be Muslim or from another religion, to resist the very powerful appeal which the modern lifestyle has for the young because this lifestyle appeals precisely to the passionate and rebellious element in the soul, to which it is much easier to surrender oneself to than the higher elements of the self the submission to which requires discipline and which involves ultimately surrender to Allah. Let us not forget that the first duty of every Muslim is to live according to the Will of Allah as concretely expressed in the Islamic tradition and there is no situation in which he cannot do so. Moreover, in doing so he not only renders the greatest service to Islam but also renders the utmost service to his own soul as an immortal being and also to humanity. It must not be forgotten that one of the most important functions of Islam, from the spiritual point of view in this dark age of humanity, is to continue to bear witness to the overwhelming reality of Allah and submission to His Will.

The first step to take, therefore, is to resist many of the aspects of what is called the modern lifestyle in order to remain a serious Muslim. Here, of course, the problem is very different for the young Muslim who comes from the Islamic world itself to study in the West or in other parts of the modern world, such as Japan, and the Muslim who is born in a Muslim family living in the West and who has never encountered traditional Islamic culture. The pull of modern life upon these two types of young Muslims, as well as for the youth within modernized sectors of the Islamic world itself, is not the same, but in all these cases there are difficult challenges involving different aspects of life, all the way from the manner in which one dresses, the way one uses language and the way one eats to the type of music that one hears and the kind of entertainment that one enjoys.

It is is this realm that the young Muslim faces the most powerful part of the wave of modernism which seeks to inundate the Islamic world, and it is precisely here that only the grace that emanates from the sacred rites and a well trained mind and a soul immersed in faith will be able to withstand the pressures to conform to such a lifestyle, especially for those Muslims brought up in the West but also for those who come from the Islamic world itself at a still fairly young age. Of course, the greatest pressure to conform to the new modern lifestyle is exerted during teenage years and the early twenties, but nevertheless it does not disappear even for people somewhat older. It is most important, therefore, to understand the significance and effect of all the aspects of what is called the modern lifestyle. Also if one has to adopt certain of them, one must seek on the basis of this acquired awareness to moderate them whenever possible and to avoid what can be avoided, substituting for them other forms of living and acting which are based on the surrender of man's will to Allah. One must shun acts based on the rebellion of the individual against both Allah and what remains of the traditional values of society, a rebellion which so much of the way of living of the young reflects, as can be seen in the current violence, use of drugs, uncontrolled sexual activity and the like.

***

One could go on endlessly to talk about this crucial problem of the response of the young Muslim to the modern world. Unfortunately, this book has already become longer than originally planned and there is no space left to pursue this important subject any further. What needs to be remembered in conclusion is that Islam is a living reality while the modern world is, also for the moment and despite its falling apart from within, still a powerful force to be reckoned with in the arena of history. Muslims, therefore, whether they are among the youth or of the older generation, have no possibility of surviving as Muslims, individually or as members of a great civilization and the *ummah* of the Prophet, without being able to respond to the challenges which the modern world poses for them. They must understand the modern world in depth and intelligently and respond to its challenges not simply emotionally but on the basis of authentic knowledge of that world by relying upon knowledge of the Islamic tradition in its fullness.

At the heart of this enterprise lies the preservation of *īmān*, that is, faith in Allah, His omnipotence, omniscience and love for those who submit themselves to Him, as well as faith in His Word, the Noble Quran and the teachings which emanate through His final Prophet. It must never be forgotten that the Quran and *Ḥadīth*, the twin sources of the Islamic tradition, provide all the guidance of which Muslims young and old are in need, now or in the future, to the end of history. It is for each generation to continue to have faith in their teachings and to apply them to the situations in which they find themselves according to the Will of Allah with the certitude that there is no human condition, "no world," to which the teachings of Islam do not apply, whatever may appear to the contrary. The voice of the Truth is always the final word for it comes from Allah, one of Whose Names is the Truth (al-Ḥaqq), and to paraphrase the well-known dictum of the Noble Quran, when the Truth comes, falsehood shall fade away.

wa'l-ḥamdu li 'Llāh wa bihi nasta'īn

General Index

A

U

V

W

Waḥīd, 18
waḥy, 83
wajh, 26
Washington Cathedral, 219; D. C., 219
Wāṣil ibn 'Aṭā', 71
West Africa, 47, 67, 121
Western African languages, 108; art, 143; Asia, 244; Church, 137; education, 215, 216; Europe, 141, 194, 202; ideas, 60; people, 79; science, 101, 128, 182; society, 34; technology, 128; thought, 22; world, 33, 47
What is Metaphysics?, 176
Whitehead, Alfred North, 174, 175
Why I am not a Christian, 176
Word of Allāh, 10, 11, 105, 110, 112, 115, 137, 240
Word of God, 9, 66, 69, 70
Word, 21
World as Will and Idea, The, 168

Y, Z

Ya Sīn, 18
Yathrib, 17
yawm al-qiyāmah, 42
Yemen, 47, 74, 111, 114
Yesewiyyah Order, 107
Yeshivas, 211
Yunus Emre, 107
Yūnus, Ibn, see Ibn Yūnus
Ẓāhirī, 47
zakāh, 8, 49
Zamakhsharī, Maḥmūd ibn Aḥmad, 11
Zayd, 9
Zaydī, 47
Zayn al-'Ābidīn al-Sajjād, 105
Zaytūniyyah, 73
Zia Gökalp, 121
zīj, 91
Zīj-i shahriyār, 88
zījes, 101
Zola, Emile, 226
zoology, 96
Zoroastrian (s), 53, 63, 70
Zoroastrianism, 5, 67
Zosimus, 87
Zunūzī, Mullā 'Alī, 83, 167